Women's Equality in America

Recent Titles in Contemporary Debates

Political Control of America's Courts: Examining the Facts
Helena Silverstein

America's National Debt: Examining the Facts
Thomas Arndt

Vaccination: Examining the Facts
Lisa Rosner

Women's Equality in America

Examining the Facts

Nancy Hendricks

BLOOMSBURY ACADEMIC
NEW YORK • LONDON • OXFORD • NEW DELHI • SYDNEY

BLOOMSBURY ACADEMIC
Bloomsbury Publishing Inc
1385 Broadway, New York, NY 10018, USA
50 Bedford Square, London, WC1B 3DP, UK
29 Earlsfort Terrace, Dublin 2, Ireland

BLOOMSBURY, BLOOMSBURY ACADEMIC and the Diana logo are trademarks of
Bloomsbury Publishing Plc

First published in the United States of America 2024

A catalog record for this book is available from the Library of Congress.

ISBN: HB: 978-1-4408-7946-3
ePDF: 978-1-4408-7947-0
eBook: 979-8-2161-8378-5

Series: Contemporary Debates

Typeset by Newgen KnowledgeWorks Pvt. Ltd., Chennai, India
Printed and bound in Great Britain

To find out more about our authors and books visit www.bloomsbury.com
and sign up for our newsletters.

Contents

How to Use This Book

Women's Equality in America: Examining the Facts is part of Bloomsbury Academic's Contemporary Debates reference series. Each title in this series, which is intended for use by high school and undergraduate students as well as members of the general public, examines the veracity of controversial claims or beliefs surrounding a major political/cultural issue in the United States. The purpose of this series is to give readers a clear and unbiased understanding of current issues by informing them about falsehoods, half-truths, and misconceptions—and confirming the factual validity of other assertions—that have gained traction in America's political and cultural discourse. Ultimately, this series has been crafted to give readers the tools for a fuller understanding of controversial issues, policies, and laws that occupy center stage in American life and politics.

Each volume in this series identifies thirty to forty questions swirling about the larger topic under discussion. These questions are examined in individualized entries, which are in turn arranged in broad subject chapters that cover certain aspects of the issue being examined—for example, history of concern about the issue, potential economic or social impact, or findings of latest scholarly research.

Each chapter features four to ten individual entries. Each entry begins by stating an important and/or well-known **Question** about the issue being studied. The entry then provides a concise and fact-based one- or two-paragraph **Answer** to the featured question, followed by a more comprehensive, detailed explanation of **The Facts**. This latter portion of each entry uses quantifiable, evidence-based information from respected sources to fully address each question and provide readers with the information they need to be informed citizens. Importantly, entries will also acknowledge instances in which conflicting or incomplete data exists or legal judgments are contradictory. Finally, each entry concludes with a **Further Reading** section, providing users with information on other important and/or influential resources.

The ultimate purpose of every book in the *Contemporary Debates* series is to reject "false equivalence," in which demonstrably false beliefs or statements are given the same exposure and credence as the facts; to puncture myths that diminish our understanding of important policies and positions; to provide needed context for misleading statements and claims; and to confirm the factual accuracy of other assertions. In other words, volumes in this series are crafted to clear the air surrounding some of the most contentious and misunderstood issues of our time—not just add another layer of obfuscation and uncertainty to the debate.

Introduction

With only a few exceptions, such as the society of the Haudenosaunee (Iroquois Confederacy) in North America, the concept of women's equality appears to be a relatively recent development in world history. Advocates of women's rights have often faced legal, religious, and social restrictions that delineated clearly defined roles for both genders. During the early years of the women's equality movement in America, the issues included gaining the same opportunities for education and employment as males, along with legalizing property ownership for females. In addition, some early equal rights advocates also sought suffrage for women at the ballot box.

Opposing Voices

Those who have opposed the women's equality movement over the centuries have often argued that traditional gender roles were assigned by God, with women naturally suited to cooking, housework, and raising children, while men assumed a place in the outside world. Opponents of women's equality often frame attempts to alter those roles as tantamount to defying the will of God.

Some opponents also assert that the concept of feminism, which is closely associated with the women's equality movement, poses dangers to family and societal stability and prosperity. Some of the most strident critics even claim that feminist women want to take control of all aspects of society, pushing men aside. Proponents of women's equality ridicule such fears as the unfortunate product of distortions and lies about gender equity. They also frequently argue that males are also harmed by traditional gender roles and that all Americans, not just girls and women, would benefit from greater gender equity.

First and Second Waves

Many observers cite the passage of the 19th Amendment in 1920, granting American women the right to vote, as a watershed event for women's equality. It marked what is generally recognized to be the culmination of the period known as the "first wave" of the women's equality movement, which focused much of its efforts on winning female suffrage. However, the 19th Amendment had its limitations. Even after it passed into law, it took several more decades for many nonwhite women in America to secure the vote.

During the 1970s, the "second wave" of the movement coalesced in the United States around a proposed constitutional amendment called the Equal Rights Amendment (ERA). Although the ERA narrowly failed to gain passage due to conservative political opposition, women did secure a number of legal and social advances during this period. This so-called "women's liberation movement" elicited strong conservative opposition to the goals of the second wave, whether through such organizations as STOP ERA or in the form of provocative media personalities denouncing women's rights advocates as unattractive man-hating "feminazis."

Third and Fourth Waves

The "third wave" in the women's equality movement arrived in the early 1990s.

Third-wave issues such as curbing sexual harassment in the workplace, earning equal pay for doing the same job as men, and alleviating violence against women came to the forefront via the newly emerging social media of the day.

Many identify the early 2000s as the starting point for the "fourth wave," which is often characterized by the #MeToo movement, spotlighting allegations of sexually predatory behavior by powerful men.

During this time, however, a growing men's rights movement also gained strength, championing a viewpoint that males had become "guilty until proven innocent" for alleged misconduct toward women. Men's rights advocates also alleged that women enjoyed unfair legal advantages in such areas as divorce and child custody and that today's men were often unfairly passed over for college admission, jobs, and promotions in favor of women due to reverse gender discrimination.

Intersectionality

With the rise of social media in the 2000s, the term "intersectionality" became better known to both women's rights advocates and opponents. It had originally been coined in 1989 as a legal term to describe the ways in which characteristics such as class, race, and gender intersect and overlap, resulting in varying degrees of both advantages and oppression for an individual. One commonly cited example of intersectionality is the experience of Black women in America, which differs in fundamental ways from the experiences of Black men and white women.

Intersectionality is of particular relevance because of the racial discrimination that shadowed the women's equality movement from its beginnings. Most white suffrage leaders and organizations focused their efforts on securing the franchise for white women only, leaving African American women behind. Similarly, the second wave of the feminist movement, which took place a half-century later, also was dominated by white women and their concerns.

Supporters of the third and fourth waves claim that the inherent racism of their predecessors was mitigated by their own general policy of inclusiveness in contemporary times. However, new debates have arisen regarding the extent to which women's rights activists can and should support equal rights for LGBTQ and trans individuals and communities.

The Fall of *Roe v. Wade*

One of the most contentious issues surrounding the women's equality movement is abortion rights. In 1973, the US Supreme Court issued a ruling known as *Roe v. Wade*, which found that women had a constitutional right to have the medical procedure known as an abortion to terminate a pregnancy. The milestone ruling essentially legalized the practice in the United States until 2022, when a conservative-majority Supreme Court overturned *Roe v. Wade* and returned abortion laws to the purview of individual states.

After its enactment in 1973, *Roe* proved to be one of the most divisive matters on all sides of the women's equality movement. Many Americans strongly supported it as a cornerstone of women's rights. But other Americans, including some women who support gender equality, remained opposed to abortion, citing moral convictions or religious beliefs. With the overturning of *Roe* in 2022, many of the clashes over abortion rights have shifted to the state level.

Measuring Progress

Some people believe that American women have achieved equality with men. They cite women having the right to vote, gaining admission to higher education, and being able to pursue a wide range of employment opportunities.

Examples of entities such as the Equal Employment Opportunity Commission (EEOC) and the passage of Title IX of the Higher Education Act are seen by many as evidence that women have made substantial gains toward equality. They cite greater numbers of women who are business executives and government officials, and point to examples of strong female characters as part of popular culture in movies and on television.

However, women's rights advocates claim that the work is far from over in these areas. They point to polls and studies that consistently find, for example, that women still make less than men for comparable work, that they carry out the majority of child care and housekeeping tasks, and that they are at high risk of being sexually harassed and assaulted in their lifetimes.

Apart from reproductive rights issues, there were some results of the 2022 midterm elections that might have astonished those in attendance at Seneca Falls in 1848. "Glass ceilings" were broken in races for state governor across the country, with a dozen women winning that office in 2022—a new record—as they joined other sitting women governors. In addition, Los Angeles, California, the nation's second-largest city, elected its first female mayor.

Following the 2022 election, twenty-five women were serving in the US Senate, almost reaching the record number of women serving simultaneously, which was set in 2020 when twenty-six women had seats due to special appointments.

Regarding the 2022 race for the US House of Representatives, Vermonters voted in favor of a female congressional candidate, producing a landmark. With Vermont having been the final state to do so, all fifty states have elected a woman at one time or another to represent them in the nation's capital.

Since the early 1800s, issues surrounding women's rights in America have provoked heated and heartfelt debates. With the reversal of *Roe v. Wade* in 2022—and the likelihood of other pivotal Supreme Court decisions on gender equality issues—these contentious debates are expected to continue into the foreseeable future.

1

The Early Women's Equality Movement in America

The Seneca Falls Convention of 1848 is often heralded as the birthplace of the women's rights movement in America. The conference was held in the upstate New York town of Seneca Falls over two days, July 19 and 20, 1848, for the express purpose of discussing "the social, civil, and religious condition and rights of woman."

At the end of the conference, some attendees signed what was titled the *Declaration of Sentiments*, which included resolutions regarding issues such as women's rights to education, employment, and property as well as being allowed an equal role in religion and in the family. After some debate, a resolution favoring women's right to vote, or female "suffrage," was eventually included in the *Declaration of Sentiments*. However, seeking women's suffrage was not popular among all conference attendees, some of whom opposed it as too radical a step.

The Seneca Falls Convention was soon followed by other conferences on women's equality, including the Rochester Women's Rights Convention in Rochester, New York, two weeks later. In 1850, the first in an annual series of national women's rights conferences began in Worcester, Massachusetts, underscoring increased calls for women's equality in America as the decades passed.

Q1: Did Support for Women's Equality in America Exist Before the 1848 Seneca Falls Convention?

Answer: Yes, but such expressions of support were largely limited to individuals such as future First Lady Abigail Adams, who urged her husband John, a founding father and the nation's second president, to "remember the ladies" in constructing a new government for the United States.

However, the prevailing viewpoint among men during the early days of the independent United States was that a woman's job was to influence her husband morally and raise sons and daughters in accordance with traditional understandings of gender roles. Most men saw it as their natural responsibility and obligation to represent their wives, mothers, and daughters in political affairs and legal matters, including the enactment of laws that affected women.

The Facts: America's Declaration of Independence, written in 1776, proclaims, "We hold these truths to be self-evident, that all men are created equal, that they are endowed by their Creator with certain unalienable rights, that among these are life, liberty and the pursuit of happiness." Neither the Declaration of Independence nor the US Constitution (created in 1787) addressed women's equality. The reference to "all men" being created equal did not signify "all humanity," nor was it all-inclusive. Women, white men who did not own land, most free Blacks, enslaved people regardless of gender, Native Americans, and other non-whites were all walled off from the rights that white men with property enjoyed.

Women in the new nation were still prohibited from voting in elections, nor could they serve on juries. A woman had little opportunity for education or employment, nor did she have much in the way of property rights.

Even after the colonies won the War of Independence against the British, the status of women in the newly created United States remained founded on the Blackstone interpretation of British common law. English jurist William Blackstone (1723–1780) wrote *Commentaries on the Laws of England*, which was published in 1765 and became the most influential interpretation of English law for decades.

As in the colonial era, the legal codes according to Blackstone maintained that in the eyes of the law, a woman did not exist as a person during marriage, being consolidated into the person of her husband. After the Revolution, "coverture" laws still applied, so that women were still "covered" by males and thus were the property of men, just as they had been before American independence.

One woman, Abigail Smith Adams (1744–1818), broached this issue with her husband, John Adams (1735–1826), after he was selected to help draft the Declaration of Independence in 1776. Abigail Adams had managed their Massachusetts farm and protected their children in a war zone for long periods of time during the Revolution while her husband attended to affairs of the Continental Congress in Philadelphia. In her famous letter of March 31, 1776, she urged her husband and other Continental Congress members to recognize the capabilities of women and grant them greater agency over their own lives:

In the new Code of Laws which I suppose it will be necessary for you to make, I desire you would Remember the Ladies, and be more generous and favorable to them than your ancestors. Do not put such unlimited power into the hands of the husbands. Remember all men would be tyrants if they could. If particular care and attention is not paid to the ladies we are determined to foment a rebellion, and will not hold ourselves bound by any laws in which we have no voice, or representation. (Adams, Abigail, n.d.)

In her "Remember the Ladies" letter, Abigail Adams may have attempted to lighten the tone with humor, stating that if the condition of women was not improved under the new laws being created, females might "foment a rebellion" of their own just as men had done in fighting for their liberty in the Revolution. While the reference to women's rebellion might have been playful, her point was a serious and timely one. By stating that women should not have to be bound by laws in which they have no voice, she echoed the same grievance that the American patriots used against England: "No Taxation Without Representation."

John responded to Abigail's letter with an attempt at humor of his own: "As to your extraordinary code of laws, I cannot but laugh. ... Depend upon it, we [males] know better than to repeal our masculine systems" (Adams, John, n.d.). Like most men of his time, John Adams did not share his wife's views on women's rights, despite her comparison to the Revolutionary era adage regarding taxation without representation. As seen in his response, the call for women's rights was so extraordinary that he could not even take the matter seriously.

Therefore, despite the ideals of freedom and equality espoused by leaders of the new nation, women made little progress after the Revolution from their status in colonial days. Even in the tightly structured Puritan colonies of New England, some colonial women had to take on men's work while their husbands were away at sea or otherwise engaged. But in areas such as education, employment, and legal matters, "19th century women appear to have gone backward from those pioneer days despite the narrowness of colonial theology" (C. Johnson, 2017, 50).

While the theocracy of the New England colonies had indeed been restrictive for women, such as forbidding them to speak in church, there were some avenues that were open to females in colonial days that were closed off after the Revolution. In the hardscrabble early days, many women toiled beside their husbands and were expected to do so. Beyond manual labor, many colonial New England women "worked alongside their husbands (and by themselves after their husband's death) as doctors and lawyers" (C. Johnson, 2017, 50). But after the Revolution, society became more conservative. The all-male leaders of the new nation who determined policies in such areas as education and employment tended to exclude women.

Soon after the United States created its new government, it found itself embroiled in yet another conflict with Britain, the War of 1812. Afterward, with confidence gained from America's victory in that war, some citizens began seeking reforms that would expand the nation's promise of freedom and equality. The 1830s and 1840s brought about a spirit of social activism among many Americans. Some believed it was morally required of them by their Christian faith to do so, especially in opposing slavery.

During that time, a few reformers suggested that women were equal to men in both abilities and intellect. Some changes were notable mostly for their symbolism, such as when revivalist preacher Charles Grandison Finney (1792–1875) granted women permission to pray aloud in mixed-gender religious services at Rochester, New York, in 1831. In June 1848, a month before the Seneca Falls Convention, women's suffrage was included as part of the platform of the Liberty Party, a short-lived political group that called for the abolishment of slavery in America as well as the promotion of other forms of freedom for disenfranchised people. In 1848, many of its members joined forces with the Free Soil Party, which was led by Henry Stanton (1805–1887), husband of women's rights advocate Elizabeth Cady Stanton (1815–1902). However, the Free Soil Party's major focus was on combating slavery rather than seeking women's rights.

In the mid-1800s, the women's equality movement often became linked to antislavery causes. Both movements based their arguments on the American ideals of freedom and equality. In 1832, writer and abolitionist William Lloyd Garrison (1805–1879) organized antislavery groups in which women were allowed full participation. However, other abolitionists frowned on women's involvement in these political affairs, and some dissenters splintered off to form their own male-only antislavery groups that excluded women from membership.

Some women of this era become prominent abolitionist voices—and a few explicitly linked their antislavery efforts to the quest for women's equality. In the 1830s, for example, sisters Sarah Grimké (1792–1873) and Angelina Grimké (1805–1879) of South Carolina published antislavery essays as well as speaking to mixed-gender abolitionist groups at a time when many Americans still thought it unladylike for a woman to speak in public.

Ernestine Rose (1810–1892) of New York began speaking to groups across the country in the mid-1830s advocating female suffrage. With Susan B. Anthony

(1820–1906) and Elizabeth Cady Stanton, Rose became a founder of the National Women's Suffrage Association. A Jewish woman who had been raised in Poland, Ernestine Rose was unique among the early equal rights advocates—both for her religion and for her fellow immigrants. She addressed state legislatures and other gatherings on antislavery, temperance, and women's rights, which was especially remarkable as she was not only a woman but also a "foreigner," which was often code for being Jewish. Nonetheless, the power of her speeches led to her being called "Queen of the Platform" ("Ernestine Louise Potowski Rose," 2022).

In 1839, Margaret Fuller (1810–1850) began hosting small discussion groups in Boston for women to consider issues facing their gender. In 1843, she wrote a magazine article called "The Great Lawsuit. Man 'versus' Men. Woman 'versus' Women." It was expanded and published in 1845 as the book *Woman in the Nineteenth Century*, arguing for women's access to education, employment, and politics. Although she is generally a little-known figure today, Fuller was one of the most important proponents of women's rights in the United States during her own time. She is credited with being the first American female war correspondent, covering revolutions in Europe. Fuller not only wrote about her beliefs but also acted upon them, making her life "a series of undertakings to live up to her own ideal of transcending the then-customary gender differentiations" (Howe, 2021).

A French philosopher named Charles Fourier coined the word "féministe" in 1837. The associated concept of "féminisme" is not known to have been documented in the United States until 1890, with its first dictionary appearance in 1895. The words, later anglicized into "feminist" and "feminism," were used to describe individuals and philosophies focused on equality of the genders, especially in the worlds of education and the workplace. Dismissed by traditionalists in America, Fourier believed that "the essence of women's emancipation lay in eradicating their legal and economic subordination to men" (Offen, 1988).

During the mid-1800s, women's rights in the United States became increasingly intertwined with the abolition of slavery due to the work of social reformers active in both spheres. In addition, supporters of the temperance movement often found common ground with abolitionists and women's rights advocates in what they saw as a general quest to improve society.

In 1840, the World Anti-Slavery Convention was held in London, England. American abolitionists Lucretia Mott (1793–1880) and Elizabeth Cady Stanton traveled there with their husbands. At the London conference, however, women were forced to sit in the gallery and were not permitted either to speak or to vote. Quickly establishing a friendship, Mott and Stanton decided to organize a woman's rights convention in America that would be distinct from abolitionist issues and causes.

Soon after their return to the United States, Elizabeth Cady Stanton gave her first recorded public speech, a temperance lecture she delivered to about a hundred women in 1841 at Seneca Falls, New York. The town of Seneca Falls was a center of progressive reform fostered by the many Quaker families who lived there. Although Stanton's 1841 speech concerned the issue of alcohol, she wrote to a friend,

> I have made my debut in public. I made a Temperance speech at Seneca Falls, & was so eloquent in my appeals as to affect not only my audience but myself to tears … I infused into my speech a Homeopathic dose of woman's rights, as I take good care to do in many private conversations. I intend to "keep it before the people." ("Letter from Elizabeth Cady Stanton to Elizabeth J. Neall, 1841," n.d.)

In 1847, Lucy Stone (1818–1893) gave her first public speech on women's rights. At a time when females were discouraged from making speeches as well as speaking during religious services, she spoke out openly for women's equality at her brother's church in Gardner, Massachusetts. Her oratory was so effective that she recruited future women's rights icon Susan B. Anthony to the cause of gender equality.

Mott and Stanton met several times through the 1840s to discuss their plan to organize a woman's rights convention. If they succeeded in their goal, such a gathering would be the first known woman's rights conference in America.

Further Reading

Adams, Abigail. n.d. "Letter from Abigail Adams to John Adams, 31 March–5 April 1776." *Massachusetts Historical Society*. Retrieved from https://www.masshist.org/digitaladams/archive/doc?id=L17760331aa.

Adams, John. n.d. "Letter from John Adams to Abigail Adams, 14 April 1776." *Massachusetts Historical Society*. Retrieved from https://www.masshist.org/digitaladams/archive/doc?id=L17760414ja.

DuBois, Ellen & Dumenil, Lynn. 2012. *Through Women's Eyes, Volume 1: To 1900: An American History with Documents*. New York: Bedford/St. Martin's.

"Ernestine Louise Potowski Rose." 2022. *National Women's Hall of Fame*. Retrieved from https://www.womenofthehall.org/inductee/ernestine-louise-potowski-rose/.

Howe, Daniel. 2021. "Margaret Fuller." *Stanford Encyclopedia of Philosophy*. Retrieved from https://plato.stanford.edu/entries/fuller-margaret//.

Johnson, Claudia Durst. 2017. *Daily Life in Colonial New England*. Santa Barbara, CA: Greenwood.

Johnson, Reinhard. 2021. *The Liberty Party, 1840–1848: Antislavery Third-Party Politics in the United States*. Baton Rouge: Louisiana State University Press.

"Letter from Elizabeth Cady Stanton to Elizabeth J. Neall, 1841." n.d. *Digital History Reader*. Retrieved from https://www.dhr.history.vt.edu/modules/us/mod04_women/evidence_detail_15.html.

"Liberty Party." n.d. *Ohio History Central*. Retrieved from https://ohiohistorycentral.org/w/Liberty_Party.

Offen, Karen. 1988. "On the French Origin of the Words Feminism and Feminist." *Feminist Issues*, 45. Retrieved from https://www.researchgate.net/publication/238363178_On_the_French_origin_of_the_words_feminism_and_feminist.

Q2: Did the Seneca Falls Convention Launch the Women's Equality Movement in America?

Answer: Some scholars qualify designations of the Seneca Falls Convention of 1848 as the beginning of the women's equality movement in America since advocates for women's rights had raised their voices and urged reform well before the mid-nineteenth century. However, the Seneca Falls Convention remains a watershed event of the early movement toward women's equality. The conference is especially noteworthy for its *Declaration of Sentiments*, even if only symbolically. When that document was published nationwide, it was an important factor in publicizing the concept of women's rights in America, even though it was scorned by many for its inclusion of women's suffrage. Although the Seneca Falls Convention did not include African American women or women from lower socioeconomic classes, it is still considered a landmark in the history of women's rights in the United States.

The Facts: Lucretia Mott and Elizabeth Cady Stanton met in 1840 at the World Anti-Slavery Convention in London, England, where women in attendance were not allowed to speak, or even be seated among the delegates with their husbands. Afterward, Mott and Stanton decided to organize a woman's rights convention in America—the nation's first known gathering of its kind.

In 1848, while Mott was visiting the Stanton home at Seneca Falls, New York, they made plans to organize a woman's rights conference. At that time, the

Seneca Falls area was home to a large number of Quakers, a progressive religious group supportive of gender equality and social reform in America.

Seneca Falls was chosen as the site for the event. On flyers and in newspaper ads, the gathering was advertised as "a convention to discuss the social, civil, and religious condition and rights of woman." News of the event quickly spread, frequently through word of mouth.

Although the Seneca Falls conference was largely coordinated by Quakers, the venue was the town's Wesleyan Chapel, a Methodist house of worship, since it was large enough to hold several hundred people. Spanning July 19–20, 1848, the first day had been announced as being exclusively for women. However, about forty men arrived anyway, expecting to attend. The males were not turned away, but as was customary for women in most public and religious settings, the men were asked to remain silent that day. On the second day of the conference, males were allowed full participation in the proceedings.

The agenda at the Seneca Falls Convention included lectures and discussions about women and their inferior social, economic, educational, and political status in America. The meeting featured well-known advocates for women's equality, including powerful speakers such as Mott and Stanton. An especially commanding speaker was famed abolitionist Frederick Douglass (ca. 1817–1895), the only African American to attend the conference.

None of those three major figures at the Seneca Falls Convention—Douglass, Mott, and Stanton—would live to see the day in 1920 when American women attained the right to vote. However, Douglass was able to celebrate the passage of the 15th Amendment to the Constitution in 1870, granting the vote to Black males.

On the first day of the conference, Elizabeth Cady Stanton made a speech outlining the purpose of the meeting. Using the kind of language that had inspired the American Revolution, she stated that the Seneca Falls gathering was to protest a form of government that existed without the consent of the governed; in this case, the female half of the population, who were barred from voting. She also described man-made laws that forced women to pay taxes without representation. In addition, she denounced the legal system that gave a husband the arbitrary right to take his wife's inherited property and earnings to do with as he pleased and to permanently separate her from her children if she tried to leave. Stanton called such laws "a shame and a disgrace to a Christian republic in the nineteenth century" ("Today in History—The Seneca Falls Convention," n.d.).

A major component of the Seneca Falls conference was the creation of what was called the *Declaration of Sentiments*, a document that was submitted for attendees to sign. Based on America's Declaration of Independence, the *Declaration of Sentiments* called for women's equality with men in such areas as education and employment. An additional demand—women's right to vote—proved to be the most controversial resolution. It was the only clause in the declaration that was not unanimously adopted. A large portion of the prominence attributed to the Seneca Falls Convention stemmed from the *Declaration of Sentiments* because it was printed in publications around the country. Despite often being received with scorn, it helped to publicize the Seneca Falls gathering nationwide as well as the women's equality movement in general.

The Seneca Falls Convention of 1848 was the first known organized gathering of people who advocated women's equality in America. In the book *History of Woman Suffrage*, a multivolume work published between 1881 and 1922 with Elizabeth Cady Stanton as one of the authors, the Seneca Falls Convention is given pride of place as the beginning of the American women's equality movement. Stanton and Susan B. Anthony felt there was a need to reinforce the women's equality movement by highlighting its beginnings. They commissioned the *History of Woman Suffrage* series of books and held anniversary events to commemorate the Seneca Falls conference in order to keep women's suffrage in the public eye, starting with the 25th anniversary celebration in 1873. Each anniversary event placed a greater spotlight on Seneca Falls as the original keystone of women's rights.

The Seneca Falls Convention of 1848 paved the way for a cascade of other such gatherings espousing women's equality. One was the Rochester Women's Rights Convention in Rochester, New York, which met a few weeks after Seneca Falls in 1848. Another, the Worcester National Women's Rights Convention, which was held in 1850 at Worcester, Massachusetts, is described by some historians as the beginning of the national women's rights movement.

The Worcester event in 1850 was followed by the second national women's rights convention in 1851, also in Worcester. This series of women's rights conferences became annual events that were held in various venues, including Cincinnati, Cleveland, Philadelphia, and New York City.

One woman who is documented as having attended the Seneca Falls Convention in 1848 also lived to see women win the right to vote in 1920. Charlotte Woodward (1830–1924) was a teenager when she saw a flyer for the Seneca Falls gathering. She traveled to the conference in a farm wagon with a few friends, and her name appears as one of the attendees who signed the *Declaration of Sentiments*.

On Election Day, November 2, 1920, American women were allowed to vote for the first time. Woodward, "aged 91, bedridden and unable to vote herself, was aware of the occasion, but sad to miss casting her own ballot" (Eschner, 2017).

Further Reading

DuBois, Ellen & Dumenil, Lynn. 2012. *Through Women's Eyes, Volume 1: To 1900: An American History with Documents*. New York: Bedford/St. Martin's.

Eschner, Kat. 2017. "Only One Woman Who Was at the Seneca Falls Women's Rights Convention Lived to See Women Win the Vote." *Smithsonian*, July 19. Retrieved from https://www.smithsonianmag.com/smart-news/only-one-woman-who-was-seneca-falls-lived-see-women-win-vote-180964044/.

Lange, Allison. 2015. "The Call for Suffrage at the Seneca Falls Meeting." *National Women's History Museum*. Retrieved from http://www.crusadeforthevote.org/seneca-falls-meeting.

McMillen, Sally. 2008. *Seneca Falls and the Origins of the Women's Rights Movement*. New York: Oxford University Press.

NCC Staff. 2021. "On This Day, the Seneca Falls Convention Begins." *National Constitution Center*. Retrieved from https://constitutioncenter.org/blog/on-this-day-the-seneca-falls-convention-begins.

"Participants of the First Women's Rights Convention." 2015. *Women's Rights National Historic Park New York, National Park Service*. Retrieved from https://www.nps.gov/wori/learn/historyculture/participants-of-the-first-womens-rights-convention.htm.

Tetrault, Lisa. 2017. *The Myth of Seneca Falls: Memory and the Women's Suffrage Movement, 1848–1898*. Chapel Hill: University of North Carolina Press.

"Today in History—The Seneca Falls Convention." n.d. *Library of Congress*. Retrieved from https://www.loc.gov/item/today-in-history/july-19.

Wellman, Judith. 2015. "Charlotte Woodward." *Women's Rights National Historical Park New York, National Park Service*. Retrieved from https://www.nps.gov/wori/learn/historyculture/charlotte-woodward.htm.

Wellman, Judith. 2004. *The Road to Seneca Falls: Elizabeth Cady Stanton and the First Woman's Rights Convention*. Kindle edition.

Wellman, Judith. 2019. "The Seneca Falls Convention: Setting the National Stage for Women's Suffrage." *Gilder Lehrman Institute of American History*. Retrieved from https://ap.gilderlehrman.org/history-by-era/first-age-reform/essays/seneca-falls-convention-setting-national-stage-for-women%E2%80%99s-su.

Q3: Was Women's Suffrage a Popular Demand at the Seneca Falls Convention?

Answer: Female suffrage, or the right of a woman to vote in elections, was a highly contentious issue among women's rights advocates in general, including those at the Seneca Falls Convention. A proposed resolution in the conference's *Declaration of Sentiments* sparked heated debate and was almost barred from the document. Two-thirds of the participants at Seneca Falls refused to sign the document after the clause demanding women's suffrage was included. As some of these non-supporters feared, the suffrage resolution within the *Declaration of Sentiments* became a lightning rod for criticism and derision after the document was published.

The Facts: Elizabeth Cady Stanton is credited with drafting the *Declaration of Sentiments*, which called for women's equality with males. It was modeled on America's Declaration of Independence, with its core statement modified at Seneca Falls as follows: *"We hold these truths to be self-evident: that all men **and women** are created equal."*

Its title was patterned on the American Anti-Slavery Society's own *Declaration of Sentiments* that was created in Philadelphia at the abolitionist group's formation in 1833. The Seneca Falls *Declaration of Sentiments* made reference to the principles of equality as put forth in America's Declaration of Independence but noted that those principles, as adopted by the Founding Fathers, applied only to males.

Among its provisions, the *Declaration of Sentiments* put forth resolutions calling for women's equality in education, employment, religion, and the family as well as the right to own property. It also called for the legal status of women to allow them to be recognized as human beings, not defined—as they were under the practice of coverture—as entities that ceased to exist upon marriage, becoming the property of males.

After discussion, the ratification of the *Declaration of Sentiments* was put forward for debate followed by a vote. Some of the resolutions were groundbreaking, such as one asserting that men should be held to the same moral standards as women, a notion reflected in the contemporary concept of the "double standard."

However, the resolution that caused the greatest degree of dissension was one that called for women's suffrage. Some attendees asserted it was not appropriate to make female suffrage a part of the *Declaration of Sentiments*, preferring that the document address only the legal, religious, and social rights of women, not political ones. Some attendees completely opposed the entire concept that women should vote. Others feared that including the radical idea of female suffrage in the *Declaration of Sentiments* would cause its less controversial resolutions to lose support. Some felt the inclusion of a female suffrage demand would damage the women's equality movement as a whole by making them a laughingstock.

Avid abolitionist Henry Stanton, husband of Elizabeth Cady Stanton, attended the Seneca Falls Convention with his wife. However, he warned her against including women's suffrage as part of the *Declaration of Sentiments,* stating that it would make a mockery of the proceedings. Even Lucretia Mott herself, who had helped plan the Seneca Falls Convention, opposed the suffrage resolution for fear of making those who advocated women's rights at the conference look ridiculous.

In rebuttal, Elizabeth Stanton argued that by having the vote, women could gain more equitable civil rights by being part of the electoral process that affected future legislation, including laws that impacted women.

Frederick Douglass spoke in favor of women's suffrage, stating that the world would be a better place if women, as half of the intellectual and moral power of the human race, were allowed to participate in its governance. Douglass later claimed that his life's greatest satisfaction was to be at Seneca Falls, which he called "the manger in which [the] organized suffrage movement was born" (Schrad, 2021).

In the years that followed, Douglass would become a symbol of suffrage for both women and African Americans. Although he did not acknowledge the nomination or actively campaign, Frederick Douglass was named to be the vice presidential candidate alongside Victoria Woodhull (1838–1927) on what was called the Equal Rights Party ticket in the election of 1872. Woodhull's presidential campaign is usually seen by historians as largely symbolic. Many African Americans as well as all women, including Woodhull herself, were unable to cast a ballot in 1872. The Equal Rights Party ticket of Woodhull and Douglass received only a few popular votes in its favor and no electoral votes, but it remains a symbolic moment in history.

At Seneca Falls, the suffrage resolution eventually passed and was included in the *Declaration of Sentiments*, which was signed by one hundred people: sixty-eight women and thirty-two men. With about three hundred in attendance at the conference, the hundred names of those who signed represented only a third of those who were assembled at Seneca Falls. It is not known how many of the two-thirds who did *not* sign the Declaration refrained from doing so because of the suffrage issue.

As some feared, the suffrage clause was used as a weapon by critics of the Seneca Falls Convention. "Convention attendees were mocked and harassed and the Declaration was called ludicrous" (Blakemore, 2016). Jibes that came from newspapers after the conference often centered on women's right to vote, focusing on what one of the virtually all-male journalists called the most shocking unnaturalness "ever recorded in the history of womanity [*sic*]," continuing in the same vein, "Where would be our dinner? Where our domestic firesides and [mending] the holes in our stockings?" ("Oneida Whig," n.d.). Some opponents even attacked the conference and the *Declaration of Sentiments* on religious grounds, condemning both for advancing the "unnatural" idea that women were equal to men. Such beliefs, they charged, contradicted the word of God.

Regardless of the mockery, both the Seneca Falls Convention itself and its *Declaration of Sentiments* were foundational to the effort to attain civil rights for women. Some historians state that the ideals expressed in the *Declaration of Sentiments*—that men and women are created equal, with both deserving a voice and a vote—spoke powerfully to many Americans. It made the *Declaration of Sentiments* "the single most important factor in spreading news of the women's rights movement around the country in 1848 and into the future" (Wellman, 2019). When national women's rights conventions began taking place annually in the 1850s, the issue of female suffrage was a fundamental element in aiming toward the objective of women's equality.

Further Reading

Blakemore, Erin. 2016. "Five Things to Know about the Declaration of Sentiments." *Smithsonian*, June 8. Retrieved from https://www.smithsonianmag.com/smart-news/five-things-know-about-declaration-sentiments-180959352/.

Lange, Allison. 2015. "The Call for Suffrage at the Seneca Falls Meeting." *National Women's History Museum*. Retrieved from http://www.crusadeforthevote.org/seneca-falls-meeting.

McMillen, Sally. 2008. *Seneca Falls and the Origins of the Women's Rights Movement*. New York: Oxford University Press.

"Oneida Whig (Utica, N.Y.) 1834–1853." n.d. *Library of Congress*. Retrieved from https://www.loc.gov/exhibits/treasures/images/vc006199.jpg.

Schrad, Mark. 2021. "The Forgotten History of Black Prohibitionism." *Politico*, February 6. Retrieved from https://www.politico.com/news/magazine/2021/02/06/forgotten-black-history-prohibition-temperance-movement-461215.

Wellman, Judith. 2019. "The Seneca Falls Convention: Setting the National Stage for Women's Suffrage." *Gilder Lehrman Institute of American History*. Retrieved from https://ap.gilderlehrman.org/history-by-era/first-age-reform/essays/seneca-falls-convention-setting-national-stage-for-women%E2%80%99s-su.

Q4: Did the Women's Equality Movement Spring from Abolitionism?

Answer: Some historians feel that the women's equality movement in America emerged, at least in part, from antislavery groups. However, others believe the quest for women's rights predated widespread calls for abolition. In any case, the evolving schism regarding racial matters as they pertained to the women's suffrage movement led to a splintering of women's rights groups, with some consciously choosing to separate their cause from the abolitionist crusade.

The Facts: When America was founded, it declared that principles of equality and freedom were foundational to its existence. In the early United States, however, only white land-owning males were permitted to vote, hold elective office, or work in professions such as the legal and medical fields. Women were forbidden from pursuing most forms of education, speaking in public, or voicing their beliefs in church. Meanwhile, the practice of slavery was deeply entrenched across much of the American South.

A number of reform-minded efforts emerged in the United States in the 1830s to combat the evils of slavery. At some antislavery gatherings, both men and women were in attendance. However, the groups were led by males, who were the only ones permitted to be heard; women were barred from leadership roles or even from speaking. Generally drawing disapproval from abolitionist groups, females who voiced their opinions publicly on antislavery issues were usually also ridiculed by the press.

Despite these barriers, a number of women continued to be active in the antislavery cause. Many were affiliated with the Quakers, a religious group that had a tradition of progressivism. The belief among Quakers that all men and women were equal in the eyes of God was generally considered radical and occasionally led to their persecution. Nonetheless, a number of Quakers supported equality for women along with the abolition of slavery.

One Quaker woman, Lucretia Mott, was an abolitionist who was also an instrumental part of the women's equality movement in America. In 1833, she and newspaper editor William Lloyd Garrison were among those who founded the American Anti-Slavery Society. Women comprised a large portion of its general membership, although some, frustrated by restrictions on their gender, formed separate, female branches of the antislavery organization on the local level.

One of those, called the Philadelphia Female Anti-Slavery Society, was founded by Lucretia Mott in 1833. This group, which promoted gender and racial equality, was radical not only for opening leadership roles to females, but also for its inclusion of African American women.

Generally, members of abolitionist groups sought to shape public opinion through lecturing, writing newspaper articles, and hosting fundraising events. Reflecting methods from Revolutionary-era America in which patriots refused to buy products made in Britain, Lucretia Mott helped organize a boycott in Pennsylvania of products made by slave labor.

Starting in the late 1830s, however, several prominent abolitionist groups became riven with internal conflict. The American Anti-Slavery Society, for example, split into three groups, in part because of differences over whether women should be eligible for leadership roles.

Named for William Lloyd Garrison, one group was generally known as Garrisonian abolitionists and were also supporters of women's rights. These individuals tended to stay in the American Anti-Slavery Society.

A second group formed, calling themselves the American and Foreign Anti-Slavery Society. This organization restricted its membership only to males, although females could be part of women's auxiliaries.

A third segment joined a political group, the Liberty Party, which at first limited women solely to fundraising rather than participation. Eventually, the party's reform-minded platform led them to support women's rights, although by the mid-1800s, the Liberty Party had effectively disbanded.

Through whatever roles women were allowed to play in these antislavery associations, they gained valuable experience in organizational skills, effective writing, and the opportunity to lead and lecture, even if solely in women-only groups. Still, many grew frustrated at the appearance of hypocrisy in the discrimination they faced in organizations that called for human rights but denied them to women.

Through the 1800s, an evangelical spirit among some religious groups, grounded in scripture, developed a quest for the abolition of slavery. As antislavery sentiments intensified, some reform-minded groups eventually included women's rights among their causes.

Some historians state that with many people actively supporting both causes, the women's rights movement was the offspring of the abolition movement. They point to those who organized the Seneca Falls Women's Rights Convention in 1848 who were also active in the antislavery movement, including Lucretia Mott and Elizabeth Cady Stanton. At the Seneca Falls conference, famed abolitionist Frederick Douglass, a former slave, delivered a powerful address supporting women's rights.

Antislavery efforts and the women's rights movement both promoted the fulfillment of America's promise of liberty and equality for American citizens regardless of race or gender. However, some observers noted a racially based strain that developed between the two causes, with much of the women's equality movement attention focused on white women.

This was underscored in a powerful oration in 1851 by an abolitionist and former slave named Sojourner Truth (1797–1883), an address that has become known as her "Ain't I a Woman" speech. In what is said to be her first documented instance of public speaking, she delivered remarks at the national women's rights convention that was held in Akron, Ohio, in 1851. As a female, she argued that she should be included in the fight for women's rights regardless of her skin color: "I could work as much [as a man] … and bear the lash as well! And ain't I a woman? I have borne thirteen children, and seen most all sold off to slavery, and when I cried out with my mother's grief, none but Jesus heard me! And ain't I a woman?" Accusations of racism in the women's equality movement have continued for decades and is currently debated as part of the concept known as intersectionality. Some observers recall an incident in 1921, when a statue of suffragists was donated to the US Capitol building in honor of women having earned the right to vote. Susan B. Anthony, Lucretia Mott, and Elizabeth Cady Stanton were depicted in the statue, but African American women were not even invited to the unveiling celebration. Mary Ovington, a white woman who was cofounder of the National Association for the Advancement of Colored People (NAACP), took note, stating that "the omission will be keenly felt by thousands of people throughout the country" (Faulkner, 2011, 216).

The racial aspect in women's rights continued to be debated in the mid-1800s, but it did not dim the commitment of many Americans to abolition as well as women's equality. Although national women's rights conventions were suspended during the Civil War (1861–5) for patriotic reasons, in 1864, the National Woman's Loyal League, led by Susan B. Anthony and Elizabeth Cady

Stanton, gathered almost a half-million signatures on a petition to end slavery immediately. Although females could not vote, this petition was a tool used by women's groups to support what ultimately became the 13th Amendment in 1865, outlawing slavery in the United States.

In working for the antislavery petition of 1864, some women such as Angelina Grimké recognized the restricted status of females. However, Grimké argued that even though slavery was said to be a political issue and therefore off limits to women, it should not be left to men exclusively, as if women had nothing to do with it: "Are we aliens because we are women?" she asked. "Have women no country … no partnership in a nation's guilt and shame?" (Lerner, 2004, 8).

The 15th Amendment was proposed in 1869, giving African American males the right to vote in the United States. A number of abolitionists who were also women's suffrage advocates such as Elizabeth Cady Stanton fought to include women in the expansion of voting rights through that amendment, but were terribly disappointed to find that they had failed.

In the constitutional abolishment of human bondage in the United States, many antislavery groups disbanded. Some people who had supported both abolition and women's rights lost touch with each other. Although new women's rights groups were formed, the broken connections weakened the unified power of the women's equality movement.

Before the groups split, the fusion of abolition and women's equality manifested itself not only into the pursuit of female suffrage, but also in other areas of women's equality, such as the ordination of women in religious groups. In 1853, Antoinette Brown Blackwell of the Congregational Church became the first woman to be ordained in the United States. However, female ordination was the rare exception rather than the norm. The resistance to women's roles in religion was a factor in the publication of *The Woman's Bible*, written by Elizabeth Cady Stanton and others, which was released in several parts between 1895 and 1898.

A number of reform-minded women turned to other causes, some of which had religious underpinnings. In the latter part of the 1800s, such women as suffragist Susan B. Anthony also became involved in temperance societies to curtail the use of alcohol in America.

Further Reading

"Abolition and Women's Rights." 2020. *Harvard University*. Retrieved from https://hwpi. harvard.edu/files/pluralism/files/abolition_and_womens_rights_0.pdf.

"The African American Odyssey: A Quest for Full Citizenship." n.d. *Library of Congress*. Retrieved from https://www.loc.gov/exhibits/african-american-odyssey/abolit ion.html.

"Antislavery Connection." 2015. *Women's Rights National Historical Park* New York, *National Park Service*. Retrieved from https://www.nps.gov/wori/learn/historycult ure/antislavery-connection.htm.

Drinan, Susan. n.d. "Artifact: 'Free Labor' Pinafore." *Encyclopedia of Greater Philadelphia*. Retrieved from https://philadelphiaencyclopedia.org/archive/artif act-free-labor-pinafore/.

Faulkner, Carol. 2011. *Lucretia Mott's Heresy: Abolition and Women's Rights in Nineteenth-Century America*. Philadelphia: University of Pennsylvania Press.

Lange, Allison. 2015. "Women's Rights Movement Emerges from the Abolitionist Movement." *National Women's History Museum*. Retrieved from http://www.crusad eforthevote.org/abolition.

Lerner, Gerda. 2004. *The Grimké Sisters from South Carolina: Pioneers for Women's Rights and Abolition*. Chapel Hill: University of North Carolina Press.

"The Quaker Influence." 2020. *Women's Rights National Historic Park* New York, National Park Service. Retrieved from https://www.nps.gov/wori/learn/historycult ure/quaker-influence.htm.

Wickenden, Dorothy. 2021. *The Agitators: Three Friends Who Fought for Abolition and Women's Rights*. New York: Scribner.

Q5: Was the Temperance Issue a Factor in the Early Women's Equality Movement?

Answer: The temperance movement in America, which at first only promoted moderation in consuming alcohol before eventually aiming to completely ban its manufacture and sale in the United States, was a keystone of the reform-minded spirit of the 1800s. Although temperance has often been portrayed as a woman's cause that led to what many believe was the failed experiment of Prohibition, both males and females were involved in temperance societies. In later years, as the temperance movement took on a political stance, men assumed a more dominant role. However, despite being put aside, as in abolitionist societies, many female suffragists in the 1800s and early 1900s learned useful skills in the temperance movement that were later applied to the advancement of women's equality.

The Facts: During the colonial era and the early days of the independent United States, the prevailing wisdom was that even though women did not have legal rights or political power, females did have a specific role to play. According to this viewpoint, which was popular among American men, a woman's job was to gently influence her husband morally and to raise virtuous sons and daughters. While men engaged with the wider world, a woman's domain was said to be solely within the family.

Because of that established ethos, many women, seeing their families being damaged through alcohol abuse, presumed that they, as wives and mothers, were responsible for correcting the situation. This proved to be a challenge due to the economic, legal, and sociopolitical realities of early America.

Much of the social and political life of males in early America centered on the consumption of alcohol, as men "met in taverns to drink while they heard speeches or considered matters of public importance" (Johnson, 2017, 265–6). Alcohol consumption was a common element of many men's lives in early America, providing a source of relaxation and socialization for males while women stayed home.

There was also an underlying rationale for regularly indulging in alcohol in early America, either at taverns or drinking "home brew" around the family hearth. Water was considered polluted, which it often was. Commodities such as tea and coffee were expensive and not always available.

Taverns, on the other hand, were well stocked with alcoholic beverages such as ale, rum, and wine. At home, hard cider was often brewed, becoming the everyday beverage of choice for many. Far from being condemned by the church, alcohol was "freely imbibed not only by ordinary citizens but by the clergy and religious magistrates" (Johnson, 2017, 265–6).

However, not all people had the same level of tolerance for alcohol, and it was possible for drinkers to overindulge. Some went home intoxicated, becoming abusive to the women and children in the family. In New England, although even the clergy freely consumed alcohol, public drunkenness was not tolerated. "The punishments were occasionally limited to fines, but often involved being placed in the stocks and/or beaten severely" (Johnson, 2017, 266). Often, if the man was in the stocks or beaten to the point that he could not work, the family could not eat.

Therefore, both directly and indirectly, women and children were affected by male drinking habits. Many women became drawn to the temperance movement because it represented the only weapon they had at their disposal to fight alcohol abuse. Temperance was widely regarded as a uniquely female concern because of the role that women traditionally played in preserving the morality and order of the family home—and the threat that alcohol allegedly posed to that very same morality and order.

Formal temperance groups began to be organized in America amid a spirit of social reform in the early 1800s. One of the earliest, the American Temperance Society, also known as the American Society for the Promotion of Temperance, was established in 1826. More such organizations began springing up in the reform-minded era of the 1830s.

Many of these early temperance societies did not completely condemn the moderate consumption of beer, wine, or cider. Instead, they took aim at distilled spirits. Hard liquor was not only felt to be more harmful in terms of abuse and addiction, but also seen to generate a windfall of profit for a few manufacturers at the expense of the many who were its victims.

Some temperance groups at the time welcomed drinkers who would take a pledge to abstain from hard liquor, although beer and wine were often acceptable to these organizations. The term "teetotaler" has been traced back to those individuals who marked a pledge sheet during this era emphasizing their promise to avoid *all* alcohol, including beer and wine. A person who marked "T–Total" on his or her pledge card was vowing to totally abstain from all alcohol. As one scholar noted, "Being a T-Totaler was a distinct identity" (Diamond, 2019).

As with abolitionism, the issue of women's suffrage intersected with the temperance movement. Women who would go on to become prominent in the women's equality movement, such as Susan B. Anthony and Elizabeth Cady Stanton, were also active in temperance causes.

Some women saw the battle against alcohol abuse as a kind of holy war, underscoring their belief that they had been assigned by God to be the protectors of their family against vice and temptation. However, this led to some internal conflict. Most women were interested only in alleviating alcohol abuse in order to protect their families, not to gain the vote or seek gender equality. Many female temperance societies arose under the patronage of Christian denominations, a religious framework where there was little appetite for altering traditional gender roles.

Even in the progressive era of the mid-1800s, many Americans viewed most social activism as no place for women, except in the sphere of temperance because it affected the family. Ironically, a number of women who went on to campaign for the vote were able to argue effectively for enfranchisement under the umbrella of temperance societies. Temperance was a tangible problem to be addressed for the safety of their homes rather than fighting for the contentious, vague issue of women's voting rights.

The increasing urbanization of America that came with the rise of the industrial revolution in the late 1800s brought more people relocating from the countryside to the cities. On the one hand, in the burgeoning urban areas, there were plentiful saloons virtually on every block, offering the lure of alcohol. To attract hungry workers, some offered a "free lunch" with the purchase of at least one alcoholic beverage.

On the other hand, cities were locales where temperance groups could recruit larger numbers of potential members to fight against alcohol. Meetings and rallies could be arranged more easily in cities than was possible in the less-populated rural landscape that had predominated in America's past. Thus, the temperance movement grew during the 1870s and 1880s.

The general image of temperance societies during this era is often portrayed as members being upper- and middle-class white women who had the time, the means, and the evangelical fervor to champion such a cause. However, the importance of other groups in the temperance movement and its intersection with women's equality has often been overlooked. In fact, a number of the nation's "most vocal prohibitionists weren't privileged white evangelicals, but its most marginalized and disenfranchised communities: Native Americans and African Americans ... [Minority temperance advocates] "worked hand-in-glove with other freedom movements—abolitionism and suffragism—that fought against the entrenched system of domination and subordination" (Schrad, 2021).

The primary target of African American and Native American temperance advocates was the booming liquor industry. They felt that purveyors of distilled spirits addicted untold numbers of customers in order to build the distillers' own private wealth. Women in African American and Native American temperance groups saw the damage wrought by this practice of addiction-for-profit, which they felt was immoral in any population but especially in impoverished communities such as their own.

There was also a racial aspect to America's early alcohol industries, as "the brewers, distillers and saloonkeepers who were making money hand over fist tended to be well-to-do whites" (Schrad, 2021). Their customers cut across all demographic lines, but those who paid the highest price for addiction were marginalized minority communities, where women "had no vote, no legal standing, no political or economic power, and thus no recourse in opposing their systemic alcohol-subordination" (Schrad, 2021).

Since many temperance organizations generally denied membership to African Americans, a number of independent Black "temperance lodges" sprang up, primarily in the cities of the northeast. "The first Black temperance society [began] in Pittsburgh in 1834, calling for 'total abstinence' in order to gain 'the esteem of all wise and virtuous men'" (Schrad, 2021). This, many felt, would allow African Americans to elevate themselves in the eyes of whites.

One of the most powerful voices at the intersection of temperance, abolitionism, and women's rights was Frederick Douglass. He had been one of the few males and the only African American to attend the Seneca Falls conference in 1848. Calling himself a "proud woman's rights man," he stated that "all great reforms go together" (Schrad, 2021).

Douglass often gave credit to the African American women who were active in the temperance and suffrage movements, such as writer Frances Ellen Watkins Harper (1825–1911). Dealing with issues of race, temperance, and the role of women, Harper's 1892 novel, *Iola Leroy or Shadows Uplifted*, was among the first published by an African American woman.

Harper belonged to one of the most well-known temperance groups, the Woman's Christian Temperance Union (WCTU). At a national convention in Cleveland, Ohio, in 1874, it proclaimed its mission to protect American families, especially its youth, by combating the influence of alcohol.

Although its chapters were generally segregated, many Black women joined the WCTU. Frances Harper became a leader in the organization, directing what was called the "Department of Work Among the Colored People" (Frances Willard House Museum staff, n.d.). Through her temperance work, Harper became a powerful speaker and writer on the subject of suffrage for Black women, whom she saw as struggling under the double burden of both racism and sexism.

Through the late 1800s, the Woman's Christian Temperance Union gained strength. Under its president, Frances Willard (1839–1898), it grew into one of the largest women's religious-based organizations of the nineteenth century. Willard also supported female suffrage and women's equality, which she said was based on God's law. She was a dynamic speaker who used the argument of women being the protector of the home to gain adherents among average women who did not necessarily support female suffrage or the women's rights movement in general.

As the temperance movement took on a larger political footing, men assumed a more dominant role. While a few temperance groups were not entirely opposed to some degree of moderation in drinking habits, the Anti-Saloon League, founded in 1893, had a different goal: the total prohibition of all alcohol in the United States.

By 1895, the Anti-Saloon League was overshadowing the Woman's Christian Temperance Union. Under the leadership of Wayne Wheeler (1869–1927) and other men, the Anti-Saloon League lobbied politicians using pressure politics, public demonstrations, and powerful public relations tactics in their pursuit of totally prohibiting alcohol.

With Wheeler at the helm, the Anti-Saloon League became the most powerful alcohol-related lobby in America, surpassing women's groups such as the WCTU. Called the "mightiest pressure group in the nation's history" (Okrent, 2010, 2), the Anti-Saloon League aimed for a complete ban on alcohol. In 1919, the Anti-Saloon League won its own constitutional amendment prohibiting the manufacture and sale of alcohol in the United States. Despite the triumph of the male-dominated Anti-Saloon League, historians note that "perhaps no other social movement in American history is as synonymous with women as temperance, and none is as vilified" (Schrad, 2019).

Even though the Woman's Christian Temperance Union was ultimately surpassed by the Anti-Saloon League in national influence, there was a collateral benefit to potential supporters of women's equality through their involvement with the temperance movement. Emulating the skills of the WCTU's Frances Willard, women gained confidence and experience in areas such as leadership, politics, publicity, organizational techniques, recordkeeping, and speechmaking. In addition, the WCTU "provided the suffrage movement with a grassroots constituency" (Osborne, 2019).

Further Reading

"Abolition, Women's Rights, and Temperance Movements." 2016. *Women's Rights National Historical Park* New York, National Park Service. Retrieved from https://www.nps.gov/wori/learn/historyculture/abolition-womens-rights-and-temperance-movements.htm.

Bordin, Ruth Birgitta Anderson. 1981. *Woman and Temperance: The Quest for Power and Liberty, 1873–1900*. Philadelphia, PA: Temple University Press.

Diamond, Anna. 2019. "Where Does the Word 'Teetotaler' Come From?" *Smithsonian*, October. Retrieved from https://www.smithsonianmag.com/smithsonian-institution/where-does-word-teetotaler-come-from-180973091/.

Frances Willard House Museum staff. n.d. "Frances Harper and Black Women in the WCTU." *Frances Willard House Museum and Archives at the Center for Women's History and Leadership*. Retrieved from https://scalar.usc.edu/works/willard-and-wells/black-women-and-the-wctu.

Johnson, Claudia Durst. 2017. *Daily Life in Colonial New England*. Santa Barbara, CA: Greenwood.

Lappas, Thomas. 2020. *In League against King Alcohol: Native American Women and the Woman's Christian Temperance Union, 1874–1933.* Norman: University of Oklahoma Press.

Lewis, Michael & Hamm, Richard. 2020. *Prohibition's Greatest Myths: The Distilled Truth about America's Anti-Alcohol Crusade.* Baton Rouge: Louisiana State University Press. Kindle edition.

Okrent, Daniel. 2010. *Last Call: The Rise and Fall of Prohibition.* New York: Scribner.

Osborne, Lori. 2019. "Temperance and Suffrage: Connected Movements." *Suffrage 2020 Illinois.* Retrieved from https://suffrage2020illinois.org/2019/05/28/temperance-and-suffrage-connected-movements/.

Schrad, Mark. 2019. "Why Do We Blame Women for Prohibition?" *Politico*, January 13. Retrieved from https://www.politico.com/magazine/story/2019/01/13/prohibit ion-women-blame-history-223972/#:~:text=One%20hundred%20years%20ago%20t his,largely%20blamed%20women%20for%20that.

Schrad, Mark. 2021. "The Forgotten History of Black Prohibitionism." *Politico*, February 6. Retrieved from https://www.politico.com/news/magazine/2021/02/06/forgot ten-black-history-prohibition-temperance-movement-461215.

Sklar, Kathryn Kish. n.d. "Temperance and Suffrage." *Not for Ourselves Alone.* Retrieved from https://www.pbs.org/kenburns/not-for-ourselves-alone/temperance-suffrage/.

2

The First Two Waves of the Women's Equality Movement in America

It has become customary to describe the women's equality movement in terms of distinct "waves," or periods in which there were surges in female activism, although historians say that the quest for women's equality was continuous and did not unfold in a simplistic series of waves. Still others argue that assigning distinct "waves" to the women's equality movement places too much emphasis on single issues, such as suffrage in the first wave and the Equal Rights Amendment (ERA) in the second, when the battle for women's equality has historically been fought on a wide range of socioeconomic fronts.

Those criticisms notwithstanding, most scholars generally date the so-called second wave, with its call for "women's liberation," to have originated in 1963, when a bestselling book called *The Feminine Mystique* by Betty Friedan (1921–2006) was published. The second wave encompassed the call for the ERA to be added to the Constitution.

The wave faded in the 1980s after the amendment narrowly failed to gain ratification at the state level. Nonetheless, the second wave was a cultural watershed crafted and led by women "who, though often divided, still significantly influenced economics, theology, political activism [and] electoral success" across America (Maxwell & Shields, 2018).

Q6: Was the First Wave of Feminism Only About Gaining the Vote for Women?

Answer: It is inaccurate to state that the first wave of American feminism was solely about women's suffrage, since there were other issues at stake, including equal opportunities for females in education, employment, and property rights. Some activists felt those matters were more important than the right to vote and that seeking suffrage would be seen as ridiculous, decreasing chances of attaining the other goals. Conversely, others felt that if women gained the vote, all other rights would follow.

The Facts: Many sources mark the beginning of the first wave as the Seneca Falls Convention of 1848, and it ended with women being granted the right to vote in 1920. In doing so, the women's suffrage issue becomes paramount. While it is not synonymous with the suffrage issue, the first wave of the women's rights movement can be said to mark the "first sustained political movement dedicated to achieving political equality for women" (Grady, 2018).

The act of including the call for women's right to vote in the *Declaration of Sentiments* at Seneca Falls was significant because the document was published nationwide. It stimulated many people to begin thinking about the female suffrage issue—both for and against—more seriously than in the past.

Women seeking voting rights, or suffrage, began to be called "suffragettes." According to scholars, they did not label themselves in that way. Instead, "it was coined by their opponents. … It was intended to be divisive, and it was also intended to be derogatory" (Debuk, 2015).

Adding the suffix "ette" tends to transform a word into a smaller version of the original, such as "kitchenette." The "ette" suffix often also implies that something is "slight, trivial, of lesser value" (Debuk, 2015). The word suggested that supporters of suffrage were of little consequence. Modern linguists consider the word "suffragette" to sound more lightweight than "suffragist," which was the term that women's rights advocates preferred.

In fact, even the phrase "women's rights" spurred some discord. In the early days of the first wave, the cause was referred to as the "*woman* movement" or "*woman's* rights," utilizing the singular form of the word. The organizers of the event at Seneca Falls termed the gathering as a "Woman's Rights Convention." Some scholars have stated that to contemporary ears, the singular sounds awkward and grammatically incorrect. However, the "nineteenth century women's consistent usage of the singular *woman* symbolized, in a word, the unity of the female sex. It proposed that all women have one cause, one movement" (Cott, 1987).

While the diminutive "suffragette" continued to be invoked, especially by the press, to describe those who fought for voting rights, the plural terminology of "women's" rights became standardized over time.

Many attendees at Seneca Falls believed that by including female suffrage in the *Declaration of Sentiments*, their overall cause would be damaged since the idea of granting women voting rights was such a radical idea. As many predicted, the demand for female suffrage provoked more hostility than any other clause after the *Declaration of Sentiments* was published nationwide.

Nonetheless, as advocates for women's equality pressed forward after Seneca Falls, it was the suffrage issue that came to be most firmly identified with the first wave. Winning the right to vote was a concrete objective and one that activists recognized as essential to having greater say over their own lives. Many suffragists became enthusiastic about supporting a sweeping piece of federal legislation: a constitutional amendment granting American women the right to vote. This became a goal for subsequent generations of "suffrage sisters" as well, even as they "faced public disdain, humiliation, rotten eggs, violent opposition, and prison … for their simple rights as citizens" (Weiss, 2019, 7).

In 1869, the 15th Amendment was proposed, stating that the right to vote could not be denied on the grounds of race, color, or previous condition of servitude, with no mention of gender. After the Civil War ended in 1865, some women believed universal suffrage would be implemented in the United States, granting *all* citizens the right to vote. However, they were "very severely disappointed and angered when they're told that's not going to happen" (Pruitt, 2021). It was at this juncture that women's rights advocates began to differ on the strategies they employed in their pursuit of female suffrage.

In 1869, the National Woman Suffrage Association (NWSA) was founded by Elizabeth Cady Stanton and Susan B. Anthony. As an organization, NWSA was not known for being all-inclusive, discouraging African Americans from joining. Although Anthony and Stanton had been staunch abolitionists, their stance on excluding Black people from NWSA opened them to charges of racism. They rationalized that promoting female suffrage would be more successful among the white male lawmakers in Congress if there was not a specific demand for the right to vote to be guaranteed for Black women.

That same year, another group emerged led by abolitionist Lucy Stone, African American suffragist Frances Ellen Watkins Harper, and Sojourner Truth, famed for her "Ain't I a Woman" speech. That organization, the American Woman Suffrage Association (AWSA), supported universal suffrage, which would specifically include the right to vote for African American women. AWSA members felt that winning support from individual state legislatures would be the key to ratification of a women's suffrage amendment and worked on a state-by-state level, using traditional methods such as circulating petitions, making speeches, and lobbying lawmakers.

NWSA, on the other hand, aimed toward gaining women's suffrage by any means necessary, including tactics that kept them in the public eye through the news media by utilizing acts that were considered aggressive and "unladylike." These included boisterous rallies, picketing, and hunger strikes. Along with a female suffrage amendment, NWSA supported the kinds of ideals for women's equality that were seen as more radical shifts in society, such as females being considered the equivalent of males in all forms of employment, including professions such as medicine and law.

At first the larger group was AWSA, which was viewed by many as the more conservative and less confrontational of the two organizations. However, eventually some AWSA supporters began to feel that their traditional strategies were having no effect. The group's inclination toward graciousness in their "ladylike" approach to lawmakers began to attract derision among AWSA members. They felt it was ineffective in advancing women's cause "while waiting for men to do them the honor of giving them the vote" (Weiss, 2019, 14). They saw a lack of response to their graciousness from male politicians who would "unpack all the old chestnuts: women were too emotional, too high-strung for the rough-and-tumble of political life, too inclined to hair-pulling spats" (Weiss, 2019, 24).

Members of the other group, NWSA, also felt *their* patience being strained by the inaction of government officials toward enfranchising women. NWSA stepped up its efforts in "unladylike" behavior in order to garner maximum attention to their cause.

One of the most striking of such actions took place on July 4, 1876, when America was celebrating its 100th birthday. Risking arrest, members of NWSA disrupted the nation's signature event, the centennial celebration at Independence Hall in Philadelphia. Gaining access to the speaker's platform among some of the country's leading politicians, Susan B. Anthony thrust a copy of what was called the *Declaration of Rights of the Women of the United States* at the astonished men who had just finished reading the nation's Declaration of Independence. The NWSA women then quickly left the building, distributing copies of the document to the crowd that gathered outside. The *Declaration of Rights of Women* was less restrained than the Seneca Falls *Declaration of Sentiments* had been. Instead of simply airing grievances, the 1876 document included "Articles of Impeachment" against the nation's leaders for their alleged offenses.

Through efforts by Susan B. Anthony and Elizabeth Cady Stanton that spotlighted the group's "unladylike" disruptive acts, NWSA began attracting more members. AWSA membership declined to the point that its cofounder Lucy Stone approached NWSA about merging the two organizations. Negotiations ultimately led to the merger of the two organizations as the National American Woman Suffrage Association (NAWSA) in 1890.

Part of NAWSA's efforts in the late 1800s and early 1900s included comparing other countries around the world to the United States. In 1893, New Zealand became the first sovereign state to give women the right to vote. It was followed by Australia in 1902 and Finland in 1906. The United Kingdom granted female suffrage in 1918 to women over age thirty. Austria, Canada, Denmark, Finland, Germany, Norway, Poland, and Russia all approved female suffrage before it was won by American women.

One issue that proved to be contentious in the United States regarding women's right to vote was bound together with racial matters. Some Southern women supported the suffrage movement in the 1870s and 1880s, but organized suffrage efforts did not appear in the South until the 1890s. Women's rights conventions held in the South were usually segregated, while Southern suffrage associations were "composed solely of white women and excluded African American women" (Spruill, 2020).

Although NAWSA did not specifically bar African American women, many state and local NAWSA chapters did, including ones located outside the South. NAWSA also required Black women to march separately from white members during its 1913 parade in Washington, DC. The order of marchers at this and many other NAWSA parade events was white women first, then men, then Black women.

Some suffragist organizations included members of conservative Christian groups such as the Woman's Christian Temperance Union (WCTU), with its charismatic leader, Frances Willard. As the WCTU expanded its role "beyond closing down saloons and calling for an end to liquor sales, the cause for woman's suffrage was high on its list of priorities" ("WCTU Petition for Woman Suffrage," n.d.).

The WCTU aimed at securing women's participation in the political process, so women could better serve in their role as protectors of the home. Despite the common interest of attaining the vote and gaining political parity for females, there was a distinct difference in the philosophical stance between the WCTU and much of the rest of the suffrage movement. The WCTU was interested in obtaining the vote primarily to advance its temperance cause rather than in service to women's rights or gender equality. Although Frances Willard was revered by followers in the WCTU, she occasionally had to justify her position in favor of women's suffrage to her own group. At a WCTU convention held in Arkansas in 1889, for instance, Willard asserted to members that allowing females to vote "did not lower women but instead elevated society and politics" (Johnson, n.d.).

Willard was able to sway members of the WCTU who were not supporters of women's suffrage by emphasizing their traditional duty to protect the family. Allowing women to vote would "promote the social good by removing the scourge of alcohol ... [and] stepping over the threshold from the domestic sphere into public engagement did not subvert their traditional responsibilities" (Johnson, n.d.).

Just as the Civil War impacted the flow of history in America, the nation's entry into the First World War in 1917 created a new dynamic in American society. In order to free men from the workforce so they could go fight overseas, the women of the United States played new roles in the service of their country. Along with vital agricultural, factory, and mining jobs stateside, some women assisted relief organizations, volunteered as medical aides near the front lines, and were allowed to assume some forms of battle zone service, such as ambulance drivers and translators.

Suffragists suspended their voting rights efforts for the duration of the First World War so that the United States could present a unified image to the world. In taking on essential jobs and in risking their lives abroad, American women proved their patriotism, "so it became harder and harder politically for politicians to say women don't deserve the vote" (Pruitt, 2021).

Congress agreed to put forward a proposed suffrage amendment in 1919 for the states to decide. By August of 1920, Tennessee had become vital to the ratification process. It was necessary for the amendment to be passed by thirty-six states; by that time, it had been approved by thirty-five states. Legislatures in several other states—Connecticut, Florida, North Carolina, and Vermont—declined for various reasons to consider the ratification resolution. Therefore, with the 1920 presidential election coming up in November, Tennessee became the focus of both suffrage supporters and opponents. Among the pro-suffrage advocates was Carrie Chapman Catt (1859–1947), the most prominent suffragist figure in the nation following the deaths of Susan B. Anthony and Elizabeth Cady Stanton. The anti-suffrage contingent in Tennessee was spearheaded by Josephine Anderson Pearson (1868–1944), president of the Tennessee State Association Opposed to Women's Suffrage. Along with their disdain for the idea of women's equality with males, "anti-suffragists feared that giving Black women the vote would put them on an equal plane with white women" (Pruitt, 2021).

One of the most awkward situations was the fact that both the suffragists and anti-suffragists had their headquarters at Nashville's Hermitage Hotel, where lawmakers stayed during the legislative session. The all-male legislators could be seen sporting the color of rose that reflected each one's leaning. In what came to be called the War of the Roses, a yellow rose indicated that the wearer was a supporter of women's voting rights; those opposed to female suffrage wore red.

One particular Tennessee lawmaker who wore the red rose of anti-suffrage attained a little-known but important place in history. On August 18, 1920, the bitterly divided Tennessee vote was tied. At age twenty-two, Harry Burn (1805–1977) was the youngest legislator. He wore a red rose, which was not surprising since he came from a conservative district. What shocked many was that when the tie-breaking vote came, Burn startled everyone by voting *for* women's suffrage. In his pocket, he carried a letter from his mother "in which she asked him to 'be a good boy' and vote for the amendment" (Bomboy, 2021). Tennessee thus became the thirty-sixth state to ratify the 19th Amendment, legalizing women's right to vote in the United States. With that vote, "the 70-year-old battle for suffrage was over" (Bomboy, 2021).

The 19th Amendment became part of the US Constitution on August 26, 1920, when America's all-male lawmakers allowed the nation's females to vote. On Tuesday, November 2, 1920, millions of American women went to the polls.

On election day, "some calculations determined that 37% of all registered voters who voted in the 1920 election were women" (Paranic, 2020), although even after female suffrage was legalized by the 19th Amendment, "women faced voter suppression as states used discriminatory measures such as residentiary requirements, poll taxes, literacy tests, and morality clauses" to keep them from the ballot box (Paranic, 2020).

Further Reading

Bomboy, Scott. 2021. "The Vote That Led to the 19th Amendment." *Constitution Daily, National Constitution Center*. Retrieved from https://constitutioncenter.org/blog/the-man-and-his-mom-who-gave-women-the-vote/.

Boyd, Tyler L. 2019. *Tennessee Statesman Harry T. Burn: Woman Suffrage, Free Elections, and a Life of Service*. Charleston, SC: History Press.

Cott, Nancy. 1987. *The Grounding of Modern Feminism*. New Haven, CT: Yale University Press. Retrieved from https://literariness.org/wp-content/uploads/2020/04/Nancy-F.-Cott-The-Grounding-of-Modern-Feminism-1989-Yale-University-Press.pdf.

Debuk (*sic*). 2015. "Ette-ymology." *Language: A Feminist Guide*. Retrieved from https://
    debuk.wordpress.com/2015/08/16/ette-ymology/.
"Declaration of Sentiments." 2015. *Women's Rights National Historic Park* New York,
    National Park Service. Retrieved from https://www.nps.gov/wori/learn/historycult
    ure/declaration-of-sentiments.htm.
"'Don't Forget to Be a Good Boy': Harry T. Burn's Letter from Mom and the Ratification
    of the 19th Amendment in Tennessee." n.d. *Teachtnhisotry.org*. Retrieved from
    http://teachtnhistory.org/File/Harry_T._Burn.pdf.
Grady, Constance. 2018. "The Waves of Feminism, and Why People Keep Fighting
    Over Them, Explained." *Vox*, July 20. Retrieved from https://www.vox.
    com/2018/3/20/16955588/feminism-waves-explained-first-second-third-fourth.
Johnson, Ben. n.d. "Woman's Christian Temperance Union and Votes for
    Women." *Arkansas Women's Suffrage Centennial Project, University of
    Arkansas at Little Rock*. Retrieved from https://ualrexhibits.org/suffrage/
    wctu-and-votes-for-women/.
Maxwell, Angie and Shields, Todd. 2018. *The Legacy of Second-Wave Feminism in
    American Politics*. New York: Palgrave Macmillan. Kindle edition.
"National American Woman Suffrage Association." n.d. *Library of Congress*. Retrieved
    from https://www.loc.gov/collections/national-american-woman-suffrage-associat
    ion/articles-and-essays/the-national-american-woman-suffrage-association/.
Nicholson, Linda. 2010. "Feminism in 'Waves': Useful Metaphor or Not?" *New Politics*,
    Winter 2010, vol. XII, no. 4. Retrieved from https://newpol.org/issue_post/femin
    ism-waves-useful-metaphor-or-not/.
"NWSA and AWSA." 2020. *19th at 100*. Retrieved from https://scalar.case.
    edu/19th-at-100/nwsa-and-awsa.
Paranic, Amber. 2020. "Women Have the Vote!" *Library of Congress*. Retrieved
    from https://blogs.loc.gov/headlinesandheroes/2020/11/women-have-the-
    vote/#:~:text=Still%2C%20some%20calculations%20determined%20that,the%201
    920%20election%20were%20women.
Pruitt, Sarah. 2021. "American Women's Suffrage Came Down to One Man's Vote."
    History.com. Retrieved from https://www.history.com/news/american-womens-suffr
    age-19th-amendment-one-mans-vote.
Spruill, Marjorie. 2020. "Nemesis: The South and the Nineteenth Amendment."
    National Park Service. Retrieved from https://www.nps.gov/articles/000/neme
    sis-the-south-and-the-nineteenth-amendment.htm.
"WCTU Petition for Woman Suffrage." n.d. *History, Art and Archives, United States
    House of Representatives*. Retrieved from https://history.house.gov/HouseRecord/
    Detail/15032436230.
Weiss, Elaine. 2019. *The Woman's Hour: The Great Fight to Win the Vote*.
    New York: Penguin.

Q7: Was Racism a Significant Factor in the Early Women's Equality Movement?

Answer: In the early days of the women's equality movement, many of its adherents originally had roots in anti-slavery organizations. They often sought suffrage and equality in America regardless of race or gender. However, as political developments took place, some suffragist groups distanced themselves from African American women, calculating that it would be the most politically sensible course to winning female suffrage for white women from lawmakers in Congress. A number of alternative suffrage groups sprang up independently in African American communities in response to this rejection.

The Facts: A constitutional amendment proposed in 1869 to give African American men the franchise proved to be a turning point for many women's rights advocates of the first wave, eventually becoming a matter that led to ongoing charges of racism in the female suffrage movement. The proposed 15th Amendment in 1869 read, *"The right of citizens of the United States to vote shall not be denied or abridged by the United States or by any State on account of race, color, or previous condition of servitude."* Failing to address gender, it granted African American males the right to vote while women in the United States remained disenfranchised.

Suffragists who had also been strong abolitionists, such as Elizabeth Cady Stanton, believed that with the Union winning the Civil War and granting enslaved people the right to vote, women would also be included. However, during the Reconstruction and post-Reconstruction era in the late 1860s and 1870s, there were political maneuverings that the suffragists probably could not have foreseen. "The Republican Party saw that if they granted women the right to vote, it might mean white women in the South, who were nearly all Democrats, might outweigh the new political power of freed Black male voters there, who would mostly vote Republican, which was the party of Abraham Lincoln" (Jewell & Raver, 2020). Thus, according to one source, for the politicians in Congress, "it was a calculated decision not to include women in the text of the 15th Amendment" (Jewell & Raver, 2020).

The anger that some suffragists harbored over the exclusion of women from the protections of the 15th Amendment had consequences. It led to the fracturing of decades-old alliances between antislavery groups and supporters of women's rights. Suffragist leader Elizabeth Cady Stanton, who had been a strong abolitionist, called the split among previous allies "one of the saddest divorces in American history" (Dudden, 2011, 3).

Stanton herself publicly claimed that the 15th Amendment would encourage "fearful outrages on womanhood, especially in the Southern states" (Dudden, 2011, 3). Stanton's contemporaries understood that her use of the phrase "fearful outrages" was shorthand for rape.

As the late nineteenth century wore on, Stanton continued to denounce extending voting rights to Black males as long as all women remained disenfranchised. In what appeared to be an attempt to distance the women's rights movement from minority groups, Stanton's writings and speeches increasingly "extolled the virtues of educated white women and warned that new immigrants and African Americans weren't prepared to exercise the full rights of citizenship, or indeed, be citizens at all" (Carlisle, 2020).

The possibility of universal female suffrage that would grant the vote to Black women "was one of the major reasons many Southern lawmakers opposed [female suffrage] legislation" (Carlisle, 2020). Many white suffragists hastened to separate themselves from African Americans—and, in some cases, even used racial fears to argue for their own enfranchisement. "In what is known as 'the Southern Strategy,' white suffragists argued that, by giving white women the right to vote, they could help to further drown out the votes of Black men" (Carlisle, 2020). Suffragist Jeannette Rankin (1880–1973) addressed Congress in 1918 claiming that "there are more white women of voting age in the South today than there are negro men and women together" (Carlisle, 2020).

In the latter 1800s and early 1900s, the emphasis in suffrage groups leaned toward appealing to whites, particularly those in the upper and middle classes whose support was needed in terms of public relations, visibility, and finances. Nonetheless, support for suffrage in Black homes and communities remained strong, especially among women. In fact, African American women—who had even fewer rights than white women or Black men—remained "almost uniformly in favor of the vote" (Trent, 2020). On the local level, many African Americans saw it as a way toward better education for their people by being able to vote on matters such as school board elections. They also sought the right to cast their vote in campaigns for local candidates and state legislators who might be responsive to them.

Black men had technically gained the vote through the passage of the 15th Amendment, but "they had been effectively disenfranchised, particularly in the South. The passage of the 19th Amendment, Black women reasoned, could re-empower the race, carving away at white supremacy" (Trent, 2020).

After the ratification of the 15th Amendment, many suffragists felt that, at the very least, a separate amendment should have followed immediately to include women. One notable supporter of the latter idea was the man who had spoken up for women's suffrage at Seneca Falls: Frederick Douglass. He favored ratifying the 15th Amendment, "arguing that voting rights for Black men were a matter of life and death, while also supporting a separate amendment for women's suffrage" ("Frederick Douglass 1818–1895," n.d.).

After the 15th Amendment became part of the Constitution with no separate legislation for women on the horizon, some supporters of female suffrage remained bitter, spurning Black women who sought the vote. A number of women's rights organizations barred African Americans, "fearing their involvement would turn Southern legislators against the cause" (Trent, 2020).

African American women continued their quest for the vote despite a pattern of racism and being rebuffed by predominantly white suffrage groups. They formed organizations of their own in order to work toward women's rights. The National Association of Colored Women (NACW), founded in 1896, and the Alpha Suffrage Club, founded in 1913, were among the groups that fought for suffrage to be extended to Black women. Part of their strategy was to raise awareness of pressing women's issues in the African American community, such as lack of access to schools and other educational resources. By 1913, though, racism "was tightly stitched into the fabric of the movement for women's votes" (Jones, 2020). At a historic suffrage parade in Washington that year, African American women were told to march at the back of the parade. It was noted that those who did received "courteous treatment on the part of the marshals … and no worse treatment from bystanders than was accorded white women" (Jones, 2020).

Black people were not the only ones who found themselves excluded by racial barriers from women's rights and suffrage groups in the nineteenth and early twentieth centuries. Native Americans and those of Hispanic heritage were usually also left out. Many Asians, such as Chinese people, were barred at that time from becoming American citizens, regardless of how long they had lived in the United States. Therefore, lacking citizenship, they too were unable to vote when the 19th Amendment took effect. A half-century later, the second wave of the women's equality movement is also said by many not to have been free of racism or tendencies toward exclusion. In their quest to win ratification of the ERA, some observers saw the same desperation by mainstream women's groups when the ERA began to stall in the late 1970s. In some second-wave groups, like those of the first wave, that desperation manifested itself in decisions to back away from nonwhites.

Some sources see the second wave's early attempts at inclusion later being superseded by pragmatism. Others maintain that it was a continuation of the same racism in earlier generations rearing its head.

A somewhat more charitable view has also been offered due to the racial realities of America in the latter part of the twentieth century. The voter registration drive in the South that became known as Freedom Summer in 1964 "was the first time Black and white young people had spent so much time together" (Breines, 2007, 19). To some, it was a lack of understanding by "white people, members of the dominant, privileged group [who] inevitably absorb their group's attitudes—which means they are arrogant and ignorant despite themselves" (Breines, 2007, 11). Some second-wave white feminists recognize the racial imbalances of the era of the Freedom Summer, leaving some "to acknowledge differences they did not know they had, did not want to have, and that nevertheless deeply divided them" (Breines, 2007, 17).

Further Reading

Breines, Winifred. 2007. *The Trouble Between Us: An Uneasy History of White and Black Women in the Feminist Movement.* New York: Oxford University Press.

Carlisle, Lois. 2020. "Black Women's Fight for Suffrage." *Atlanta History Center.* Retrieved from https://www.atlantahistorycenter.com/blog/black-womens-fight-for-suffrage/.

Dudden, Faye. 2011. *Fighting Chance: The Struggle over Woman Suffrage and Black Suffrage in Reconstruction America.* New York: Oxford University Press.

"Frederick Douglass 1818–1895." n.d. *Secretary of the Commonwealth of Massachusetts.* Retrieved from https://www.sec.state.ma.us/mus/pdfs/6-Douglass.pdf.

Jewell, Hannah & Raver, Grace. 2020. "How Racism Tore Apart the Early Women's Suffrage Movement." *The Lily.* Retrieved from https://www.thelily.com/how-racism-tore-apart-the-early-womens-suffrage-movement/.

Jones, Martha S. 2020. "The US Suffragette Movement Tried to Leave Out Black Women. They Showed Up Anyway." *The Guardian,* July 7. Retrieved from https://www.theguardian.com/us-news/2020/jul/07/us-suffragette-movement-black-women-19th-amendment.

Trent, Sydney. 2020. "Battle for the Ballot: The Black Sorority That Faced Racism in the Suffrage Movement but Refused to Walk Away." *Washington Post,* August 8. Retrieved from https://www.washingtonpost.com/graphics/2020/local/history/suffrage-racism-black-deltas-parade-washington/.

Q8: Was the Women's Rights Movement Dormant between the First and Second Waves?

Answer: The landmark issue for the first wave of the women's equality movement is generally considered to be the passage of the 19th Amendment in 1920, officially granting women the right to vote in the United States. Observers on both sides of the matter waited expectantly to see how the enfranchisement of half the American people would affect the future of the country. Most scholars agree that there was no radical disruption of either American society or the nation's politics. Many suffrage organizations faded, although some first-wave leaders forged alliances with other groups to promote educated female voters as well as to advocate for the well-being of women and children through the legislative process.

The Facts: The passage of the 19th Amendment in 1920 expanded voting rights "to more people in the United States than any other single measure in American history" (Gidlow, 2020). When the law passed, both supporters and opponents of women's suffrage predicted that major upheavals in American society would follow in the wake of the 19th Amendment's passage. Pro-suffragists predicted that women would clean up politics and pass pro-family laws. Opponents feared the downfall of society as a result of what they viewed as a horrible breach of women's God-given role to be subordinate to their fathers and husbands. Some thought women would organize their own political party; others predicted that most women would just stay home on election day.

In actuality, female suffrage brought neither the positive transformation that women's rights advocates predicted nor the chaos its opponents feared. Furthermore, politicians learned there was no such thing as courting "the women's vote" because there wasn't one. A singular female voting pattern did not exist. For some American women, female suffrage did not initially have much of an impact on their lives. Hattie Caraway (1878–1950) of Arkansas, who in 1932 became the first woman elected to the US Senate (she also won reelection in 1938), recalled that after the 19th Amendment became law, it "simply added voting to cooking, sewing, and other household duties" (Hendricks, 2013, 23).

As was the case of Caraway herself, some females found a few spots for themselves in government, both on the local and national levels. However, while the 19th Amendment was a crucial step for gender equality in American democracy, many women were still denied basic constitutionally protected civil rights, especially if they were not white.

After passage of the 19th Amendment, however, many advocates for women's rights found that lawmakers and journalists had moved on to other issues. For example, suffragists had picketed the White House in 1916 and 1917, resulting in eye-catching newspaper photographs of American women marching and carrying signs in front of the executive mansion. One silent picket led to the arrest of more than two hundred women from twenty-six states, leading to nationwide media attention as the women "were jailed and force-fed at the Occoquan workhouse, a prison in Virginia, and their mistreatment led to public outrage and helped with the campaign" ("History of Marches and Mass Actions," 2022). Women's rights advocates enjoyed no such publicity or coverage after suffrage, even though women still faced an array of discriminatory practices in virtually every sector of American life.

After many suffrage groups disbanded, however, some women made inroads into the political power structure. For example, soon after women gained the right to vote in 1920, a few first wave leaders built an alliance called the Women's Joint Congressional Committee (WJCC) to lobby lawmakers on pertinent issues. It was formed from members of organizations, including the General Federation of Women's Clubs, League of Women Voters, and Woman's Christian Temperance Union. Claiming to represent millions of voters, they forged an agenda to help women and children, pledging to support lawmakers at election time who helped them and to oppose those who did not. Although the mythical "women's vote" was not a single bloc, the WJCC had enough clout to be effective in some demands for action to aid American families.

When post-suffrage women organized, as they did with the WJCC in lobbying for families and children, it "represented a unique moment in U.S. women's political history" (Dukich, 2014). An early success in Congress by the WJCC came in 1921 with the passage of a bill to address the high infant mortality rate in the United States by providing funds for health clinics. So-called "women's issues" such as child labor, health care, and sanitation were not only brought to the forefront, but also addressed with policies that more often reflected the viewpoints of women.

In 1923, an early version of a proposal called the ERA was introduced in Congress. Some women's rights leaders believed that enshrining the principle of gender equality in the Constitution would alleviate many challenges faced by American women. The architects of the 1923 version of the proposed amendment thus included the statement, "*Men and women shall have equal rights throughout the United States and every place subject to its jurisdiction."* The proposed amendment, submitted three years after passage of the 19th Amendment, did not receive much support in Congress.

Although events and marches in support of women's rights subsided during the national economic crisis of the Depression era, some American women were heartened at the increased prominence of women in public life. Frances Perkins (1880–1965) became the first female named to any presidential cabinet in US history after being appointed Secretary of Labor by President Franklin Roosevelt. She served from 1933 to 1945.

Other high-profile women during Roosevelt's "New Deal" era included Mary McLeod Bethune (1875–1955), who led the Office of Minority Affairs at the National Youth Administration (NYA); Hallie Flanagan (1890–1969), directing the Federal Theatre Project; Josephine Roche (1886–1976), Assistant Secretary of the Treasury; and Nellie Ross (1876–1977), Director of the US Mint. In addition, the president's wife, First Lady Eleanor Roosevelt (1884–1962), was a tremendously influential advocate for women's rights and issues.

During the Depression, women across the country sought what work they could find. With many having no prior employment experience outside the home, they often worked in low-paying jobs such as waitressing, taking in laundry, or cleaning other people's houses. With so many males laid off, "women in the 1930s entered the workforce at a rate twice that of men—primarily because employers were willing to hire them at reduced wages" (Donegan, n.d.). Hattie Caraway, the first woman elected and reelected to the US Senate, remained in office from 1932 until 1944. In 1943, Caraway cosponsored another ERA bill— the twelfth such bill introduced in Congress since American independence. This time, its text read, *"Equality of rights under the law shall not be denied or abridged by the United States or by any State on account of sex."* Caraway was in most ways a traditional, conservative woman, but with America fighting the Second World War, she said she wanted to see women take a greater role in serving the nation, and "to work equally with men to build a better world" (Hendricks, 2013, 91). As with the twelve previous ERA bills, however, Caraway's bill failed to gain passage in Congress.

Much has been made of "Rosie the Riveter," a symbol of women who entered the workforce during the Second World War era of the 1940s, stepping in to replace husbands, fathers, and sons serving in the American armed forces. They performed ably in a wide variety of essential industries, but when the war was over and American men returned to civilian life, women were pushed out of their jobs and told to resume their lives of domesticity. These events sowed seeds of discontent for many women, as evidenced in the rise of the second wave of the women's equality movement in the 1960s and beyond.

The postwar years of the 1950s are often seen through two different prisms. One view is that the 1950s were a time of affluence and contentment due to America's vast material wealth. Another view is that after fighting for freedom in the Second World War, millions of Americans were still denied basic civil rights in the United States due to their race, ethnicity, or gender.

With the growth of television in the 1950s and 1960s, a national spotlight was turned on scenes of protest by the civil rights movement. Some women were inspired by this struggle to speak up for women's equality as well. The road to equality for women in mid-twentieth-century America, though, looked impossibly long to many.

Although women comprised 51 percent of the US population in 1950, there were only 9 (or 2 percent of) seats occupied by women out of 435 seats in the US House of Representatives. One woman served in the Senate in 1950, or 1 percent. There were no women on the Supreme Court, nor would there be for decades. Overwhelmingly, government and politics were the domain of males, whose laws and pronouncements affected women in both large and small ways.

An American female in the post–Second World War era could not get a bank loan or a credit card in her own name. This was an enormous handicap for women who were single, divorced, or widowed, especially if they had children to support. One credit card company solicited a household by sending the primary card in the husband's name, although it included "a special '*Hers*' card … in shocking pink." If a marriage ended, "the husband took all the credit standing with him, leaving widows and ex-wives with no credit rating of their own" (Hendricks, 2021, 61).

The arrival of the first oral contraceptive pill in 1959 provided women for the first time in all of human history with a safe, effective, affordable method to avoid pregnancy. However, due to opposition from religious groups and social conservatives, it was not until 1965 that the US Supreme Court approved the legality of married couples using contraception. Unmarried women in America were barred from using birth control until 1972. Certain religious groups continued to forbid birth control for their followers well into the twenty-first century.

Still, even with limitations in the postwar era and beyond, many women were grateful to live in America with all its affluence. Many who had grown up during the deprivations of the Depression and the Second World War were very thankful for living in comfortable homes with no fear of hunger. In addition, achieving one of the goals that first wavers had sought, more women in the postwar era were able to go to college.

However, there were few professional careers that were open to women. Throughout the 1950s, the male president of the elite all-female Radcliffe College told incoming students that "their education would make them 'splendid wives and mothers, and their reward might be to marry Harvard men'" (Hendricks, 2021, 16).

A growing restlessness among many educated women stemmed from the fact that for all their education, they were confined to cooking, cleaning, and child-rearing. Opponents of women's equality believed that the dissatisfaction with traditional gender roles expressed by college-educated women proved their point—that nothing good came from too much education for women.

If white women felt confined to their homes, many minority women spent many of their workdays working in the homes of white people. Jobs as domestic workers were generally the only ones that many African American women and other nonwhites could find. "Earning the right to work outside the home was not a major concern for Black women, many of whom had to work outside the home anyway" (Grady, 2018). With African American and other nonwhite men often limited to low-paying jobs such as janitors or trash collectors, females in those families frequently found themselves forced by economic necessity to hold down jobs outside the home.

A financially disastrous effect of women being unable to obtain jobs with good salaries followed them throughout their lives. Along with those in low-wage domestic labor, "women who had been homemakers and unable to enter the workforce often found there was no financial security at all" (Hendricks, 2021, 45). Medicare did not come into effect until 1966, and homemakers did not have access to health insurance or old-age pension plans through the workplace, since they did not have an employer outside the home. Without the ability to obtain credit in their own name, women who had never married, or who found themselves divorced or widowed, were often left in dire financial straits, especially if they had children to support. With males generally in control of the family finances, women often did not know about the family's lack of savings and/or degree of debt until it was too late.

There had historically been calls for greater economic equity for women, including during the first wave of the equality movement, although women's suffrage tended to take precedence during those years. Books such as Simone de Beauvoir's *The Second Sex*, which was published in the United States in 1953, tackled the status of women, but in the postwar years, female discontent rarely had an outlet. With the publication of *The Feminine Mystique* in 1963, however, that began to change.

Further Reading

Allen, Frederick Lewis. 1986. *Since Yesterday: The 1930s in America*. New York: Harper Perennial.

Donegan, Anne. n.d. "History of Women in the United States since 1877." *Santa Rosa Junior College*. Retrieved from https://canvas.santarosa.edu/courses/24761/pages/women-in-the-1930s-and-1940s.

Dukich, Tamara. 2014. "Women's Organizing after Suffrage: The Women's Joint Congressional Committee and the Sheppard-Towner Act." *Journal of the Newcomb College Institute Research on Women, Gender, and Feminism, Tulane University*, vol. 1 no. 2, 21. Retrieved from https://journals.tulane.edu/NAJ/article/view/200.

Gidlow, Liette. 2020. "Beyond 1920: The Legacies of Woman Suffrage." *National Park Service*. Retrieved from https://www.nps.gov/articles/beyond-1920-the-legacies-of-woman-suffrage.htm.

Grady, Constance. 2018. "The Waves of Feminism, and Why People Keep Fighting over Them, Explained." *Vox*, July 20. Retrieved from https://www.vox.com/2018/3/20/16955588/feminism-waves-explained-first-second-third-fourth.

Hendricks, Nancy. 2021. *Daily Life of Women in Postwar America*. Santa Barbara, CA: Greenwood.

Hendricks, Nancy. 2013. *Senator Hattie Caraway: An Arkansas Legacy*. Charleston, SC: History Press.

Hendricks, Nancy. 2020. "Hattie Caraway, the First Woman Elected to the U.S. Senate, Faced a Familiar Struggle with Gender Politics." *Smithsonian*, January 2. Retrieved from https://www.smithsonianmag.com/history/meet-hattie-caraway-first-woman-elected-us-senate-180973888/.

"History of Marches and Mass Actions." 2022. *National Organization for Women*. Retrieved from https://now.org/about/history/history-of-marches-and-mass-actions/.

"Women and the New Deal." n.d. *The Living New Deal*. Retrieved from https://livingnewdeal.org/what-was-the-new-deal/new-deal-inclusion/women-and-the-new-deal/.

Q9: Did *The Feminine Mystique* Inspire the Second Wave?

Answer: The publication of Betty Friedan's bestselling book *The Feminine Mystique* in 1963 was an important factor triggering the second wave of the feminist movement, but not the only one. The emergence of the National Organization for Women (NOW) and the rising power of television also contributed to spotlighting the women's equality movement, an effort that took place alongside demands for civil rights by racial minorities and others victimized by the nation's many discriminatory institutions and bigoted attitudes. When women's rights supporters revived the proposed ERA, however, a highly effective opposition under conservative activists emerged. As a result of this opposition, the ERA narrowly failed to gain ratification at the state level.

The Facts: In the first years of the postwar era, women's rights seemed to subside as an issue in American life. In the mid-1960s, however, three events combined to ignite the second wave of feminism and women's rights.

The first was the release of Betty Freidan's bestselling book *The Feminine Mystique* in 1963. While it was not the first publication to address gender inequality, it was the one that became a cultural phenomenon, selling millions of copies in the United States and often being shared among friends. *The Feminine Mystique* touched a nerve among women because "it gave them permission to be angry" for the gendered limitations imposed on them (Grady, 2018). Women who felt guilty for being dissatisfied amid America's bounty were reassured by the book that it was not because something was wrong with them. For many, it not only identified what Friedan called "the problem that has no name" among women, but also asserted that it was not inevitable for things to stay the way they were simply because that was just the way things always were. As one scholar noted, the book "rebukes the pervasive post-World War II belief that stipulated women would find the greatest fulfillment in the routine of domestic life, performing chores and taking care of children. … [It] showed them a systemic analysis of how society was undermining women in order to keep them at home under the moniker 'occupation: housewife'" (Muñoz, 2021, n.p.).

Apart from *The Feminine Mystique*, the second factor spurring the second wave of the women's rights movement was the creation of the National Organization for Women (NOW) in 1966. Cofounded by Friedan, who served as its first president, NOW was the first popular unified women's rights organization since first-wave suffrage groups were founded in the 1800s. NOW not only denounced the general treatment of women in America, but specifically objected to the lack of enforcement of the Civil Rights Act of 1964 and the ineffectiveness of the Equal Employment Opportunity Commission (EEOC), which was created in 1965. For example, NOW members claimed that employers were still discriminating against women in hiring practices as well as paying them less than men for doing the same job.

The third element was the juggernaut of television, which was reaching most American homes by the mid-1960s. Especially among younger people who did not know a world before TV, there was a growing sense in the 1960s that if something was not seen on television, it didn't happen—or at least it wasn't important. Therefore, in order to reach the widest possible audience, any message or form of protest had to deliver striking visual images in order to be captured by TV cameras.

In America, the 1960s are usually considered a decade of advances in civil rights. However, "the laws, practices and attitudes of 1963 had more in common with the first fifty years of the century" (Coontz, 2012).

In 1968, an article by Martha Lear in *The New York Times* titled "The Second Feminist Wave" gained widespread attention. It was the earliest known public reference to emerging female activism in the 1960s being called the "second wave."

Along with the ERA, second-wave attention turned to matters such as domestic violence, economic issues, legal bias, and sociopolitical disparity, along with the need for rape crisis centers and women's shelters nationwide.

Opponents of the women's movement countered by saying that American women were already the most privileged on Earth and were fortunate to play their traditional God-given feminine role, even if it was seen by some as being submissive to males.

As the second wave grew in strength, there were women's rights demonstrations such as protest marches that were often localized. In 1967, for example, picketers targeted newspapers that segregated classified ads into "Help Wanted-Male" and "Help Wanted-Female." Jobs for men were described in terms of skills needed and opportunities for advancement. However, jobs for women were generally lower paying, such as clerical positions, often specifying that "applicants must be attractive and well-groomed, attributes that were never required in ads for men" (Hendricks, 2021, *Ruth Bader Ginsburg*, 83).

Despite opposition, a number of gains were made toward women's equality during the second wave. In 1963, the Equal Pay Act was passed by Congress, theoretically guaranteeing equal pay for equal work regardless of gender, national origin, race, or religion. Title VII of the Civil Rights Act, prohibiting gender discrimination in employment, was enacted in 1964; the next year, the Equal Employment Opportunity Commission was created.

President Lyndon Johnson's executive order of 1968 prohibited gender discrimination by government contractors, also requiring affirmative action plans for hiring women. Title IX of the Education Amendments in 1972 prohibited sex discrimination in educational programs that received federal support. The Supreme Court banned gender-segregated "Help Wanted-Male" and "Help Wanted-Female" advertising in 1973.

Throughout this period, women's rights protests and activism emerged as regular sources of news and public debate. In 1968, for example, women's rights advocates targeted the annual Miss America pageant for protests, claiming that such beauty contests objectified women. Protesters created what they called the Freedom Trash Can on the Boardwalk outside the Miss America venue in Atlantic City, New Jersey. In this trash can, they threw items considered to be demeaning to women such as copies of risqué magazines, plus objects that they felt enforced male standards of femininity, including girdles and high-heeled shoes. Some brassieres were also tossed into the Trash Can, from which came the myth of "bra-burning." Nothing was actually burned because of the risk of fire on the Boardwalk, which was made of wood. The falsehood was inspired by a reporter who stated that bra-burning might have been a compelling visual image similar to the era's antiwar protestors burning their draft cards. However, other journalists repeated it as fact, and humor columnist Art Buchwald disseminated the myth in his syndicated national column (Gay, 2018).

Another national story was sparked in 1969 when journalist Gloria Steinem (1934–) referenced the civil rights movement by publishing an article in *New York* magazine titled "After Black Power, Women's Liberation." It brought recognition to Steinem as a feminist leader as well as helping to popularize the phrase "women's liberation." In 1971, Steinem cofounded the feminist-based *Ms. Magazine*, which sold out its first 300,000 issues in about a week, a fact that was carried by national news media.

The increased prominence of women's voices, though, coincided with the rise of "shock jocks," predominantly male radio personalities who inflamed controversy and provoked angry debate to boost their ratings with their primarily male listening audiences. Many critics of the women's rights movement, whether their forum was radio, television, or the printed page, characterized feminists and the women's liberation movement using a wide range of dismissive and hostile terms; one, for example, described women's rights advocates as "humorless, hairy-legged shrews ... probably to distract themselves from the loneliness of their lives, since no man would ever want a feminist" (Grady, 2018).

A number of Supreme Court rulings during the second wave in the 1970s were decided based on legal arguments by one person, attorney Ruth Bader Ginsburg (1933–2020). Often known by her initials "RBG," she had personal knowledge of gender-related issues based on her own life experiences. As one of nine females admitted to her Harvard Law School class with 552 men, she and the other eight women had to make a statement that justified their taking the place of a male. Although she graduated at the top of her class in 1959, she could not find a job, with law firms stating openly that they would not hire a woman. She eventually took a college teaching position in 1963, at a salary less than male faculty of the same rank.

In the 1970s, when RBG was teaching law, she argued successfully before the US Supreme Court on several landmark decisions. In 1971, she won *Reed v. Reed*, the first major suit addressing discrimination based on gender. She won further gender-related victories, including *Moritz v. Commissioner of Internal Revenue* in 1972, citing the Constitution's equal protection clause. Other wins for RBG include *Frontiero v. Richardson* in 1973, regarding gender discrimination in the military, and *Edwards v. Healy* in 1974, which pertained to excluding women from serving on juries. Two others, *Weinberger v. Wiesenfeld* (1975) and *Califano v. Goldfarb* (1976), concerned gender discrimination under the Social Security Act. In 1974, Ginsburg published *Text, Cases, and Materials on Sex-Based Discrimination*, America's first legal casebook on gender inequity.

Unbowed by the attacks, women's rights advocates continued to press for their cause, encouraged by concrete signs of progress in the quest for gender equality. In 1981, President Ronald Reagan appointed Sandra Day O'Connor (1930–) as the first woman to serve on the US Supreme Court since it was created in 1789. O'Connor was joined in 1993 by President Bill Clinton's appointee, the second woman on the Supreme Court in its 204-year history: Ruth Bader Ginsburg.

Despite legislative and judicial advances, though, the primary issue associated with the second wave became the ERA. In 1970, congressional hearings began on the proposed amendment, which read, "*Equality of rights under the law shall not be denied or abridged by the United States or by any State on account of sex.*"

By the end of the second wave, the ERA had not gathered enough votes to pass. "Some have wondered whether, if the text had been written using the word 'gender' instead of 'sex,' things might have turned out differently" (Hendricks, 2021, 104).

Regardless of the eventual fate of the ERA, some observers of the second wave perceived that a change was in the air. Amid feminist demands regarding equal pay for equal work as well as equal opportunity in education and athletic programs, the Hollywood movie industry sensed the possibility of profit in what was being called the sexual revolution.

The second-wave era saw such popular female-centered films as *Diary of a Mad Housewife* (1970), *The Way We Were* (1973), *A Woman Under the Influence* (1974), *Alice Doesn't Live Here Anymore* (1974), *Annie Hall* (1977),

An Unmarried Woman (1978), *Coming Home* (1978), *Norma Rae* (1979), and *9 to 5* (1980). A film genre known as "Blaxploitation" featured strong African American women as lead characters in movies such as *Coffy* (1973), *Cleopatra Jones* (1973), and *Foxy Brown* (1974).

These movies were part of discussions in the mid-1970s about the term "male gaze" as being central to the entertainment industry. The terminology "emphasized how much films were angled toward men, and a trickle of edgier, female-directed stories began" (Frankel, 2019). However, "female-directed" did not mean "directed by females," merely that the films were aimed toward ticket-buying women by having a woman as a central character. All of the movies cited above were directed by men.

Further Reading

Coontz, Stephanie. 2012. *A Strange Stirring: The Feminine Mystique and American Women at the Dawn of the 1960s*. New York: Basic Books.

Frankel, Valerie. 2019. *Fourth Wave Feminism in Science Fiction and Fantasy: Volume 1. Essays on Film Representations, 2012–2019*. Jefferson, NC: McFarland. Kindle edition.

Friedan, Betty. 2013. *The Feminine Mystique, 50th Anniversary edition*. New York: W.W. Norton.

Gay, Roxane. 2018. "Fifty Years Ago, Protesters Took on the Miss America Pageant and Electrified the Feminist Movement." *Smithsonian*, January. Retrieved from https://www.smithsonianmag.com/history/fifty-years-ago-protestors-took-on-miss-america-pageant-electrified-feminist-movement-180967504/.

Grady, Constance. 2018. "The Waves of Feminism, and Why People Keep Fighting Over Them, Explained," *Vox*, July 20. Retrieved from https://www.vox.com/2018/3/20/16955588/feminism-waves-explained-first-second-third-fourth.

Hendricks, Nancy. 2021. *Daily Life of Women in Postwar America*. Santa Barbara, CA: Greenwood.

Hendricks, Nancy. 2021. *Ruth Bader Ginsburg: A Life in American History*. Santa Barbara, CA: ABC-CLIO.

Lear, Martha. 1968. "The Second Feminist Wave." *New York Times*, March 10. Retrieved from https://www.nytimes.com/1968/03/10/archives/the-second-feminist-wave.html.

Maxwell, Angie & Shields, Todd. 2018. *The Legacy of Second-Wave Feminism in American Politics*. New York: Palgrave Macmillan. Kindle edition.

Muñoz, Jacob. 2021. "The Powerful, Complicated Legacy of Betty Friedan's 'The Feminine Mystique.'" *Smithsonian*, February 4. Retrieved from https://www.smithso

nianmag.com/smithsonian-institution/powerful-complicated-legacy-betty-friedans-feminine-mystique-180976931/.

Napikoski, Linda. 2020. "What Is 'The Second Feminist Wave?'" *ThoughtCo.* Retrieved from https://www.thoughtco.com/the-second-feminist-wave-3528923.

Spruill, Marjorie. 2017. *Divided We Stand: The Battle over Women's Rights and Family Values That Polarized American Politics.* New York: Bloomsbury.

Q10: Did Women Lead the Opposition to the First Two Waves of the Women's Equality Movement?

Answer: Female suffrage was granted in 1920 when the 19th Amendment was added to the US Constitution. However, before that happened, there had been significant opposition to women having the right to vote. Although millions of men opposed female suffrage, many of the Americans most vociferously opposed to the idea were women.

In the 1970s, significant opposition was mounted to what most historians consider the flagship issue of the second wave of the feminist movement: the proposed ERA. Much of this opposition came from the same constituencies that had opposed giving women the vote a half century earlier: culturally conservative men and women who believed that traditional gender roles and family relationships were pillars of societal stability.

The Facts: When America won its independence from England in 1783, most states continued to tie voting rights to men's property ownership, just as the former colonies had done when they were under British rule. Therefore, in the early days of the American republic, the vote was generally granted only to land-owning males, the vast majority of whom were white.

Toward the mid-1800s, a progressive spirit became more pronounced in the United States. Even so, "when some women began agitating for the right to vote in the 1840s, most observers expressed revulsion, contempt, or disbelief" (Goodier, 2013, 1). Nonetheless, women's rights—including the right to vote—became a rallying cry for growing numbers of women (and their male allies). By the early 1900s, the suffrage movement had emerged as a genuine force in American society. Not all Americans welcomed this development. Opponents to women's suffrage were called by a variety of terms, including "anti-suffragists," or simply "antis." Female leaders of the anti-suffrage campaign in the United States "were generally women of wealth, privilege, social status and even political power" (Weeks, 2015).

They held enviable positions in American society—especially for women of the era—and they much preferred to maintain the status quo rather than face the potential for its disruption. Female anti-suffrage leaders were frequently the wives or daughters of men who were powerful figures in business, finance, and/or politics.

These women appealed to less affluent women by warning them that female suffrage was a threat to femininity. They claimed that if women gained the right to vote, they would lose the protection of males within the home as well and their God-given role of motherhood.

There was often an additional element among anti-suffragists in the South, who "were generally planter class, and so their resistance was also tied more explicitly to worries about disruption of the racial order" (Weeks, 2015).

Many anti-suffragists in both the Northern and Southern states claimed that women were intended to serve the nation not by voting or being part of the political process, but by being wives and mothers who focused on their duties at home. If being confined to caring for their house and children was seen by some women as a life that was limited, they "were encouraged to consider their self-sacrifice as self-fulfillment" (Goodier, 2013, 3). Female suffrage opponents were often privileged white women who employed servants responsible for tending to the anti-suffragists' homes and children.

For men, the idea of any woman voting and being part of the governmental process struck a deep chord of uneasiness pertaining to a basic perception of the importance of their own manhood and patriarchal models of home and society. Just as the concept of "true womanhood" involved confining females to the domestic sphere, "participation in politics, especially the right to vote, was a powerful symbol of manhood" (Goodier, 2013, 1). Men opposed to women's suffrage were often content to let their female counterparts take the lead in speaking out publicly against women voting. When they did speak up, they usually relied on Bible scripture to support their position, calling on women to prove their belief in God's law as true Christians by scorning suffrage.

Many suffragists believed voting was not just a political right, but the way for women to "change the world, counter the undesirable effects of industrialization, improve women's wages, and combat corruption and wrongdoing." For people who opposed suffrage, that was a vision of chaos. "Conservative men and women argued that the family structure, necessitating the 'subordination of women,' was critical to the preservation of the social order" (Goodier, 2013, 2).

The concern about preserving the social order was not only a response to the newfound freedom of formerly enslaved African Americans but also a reaction to the rise in immigration. Some scholars cite a fear among antis that women and recent immigrants would band together against the native born, and that "a women's 'bloc' [of votes] would curtail the oppositional groups' profits or other interests" (Goodier, 2013, 9).

Some opponents made speeches against female suffrage while others published broadsides. An anonymous pamphlet addressed to the "Men of Massachusetts" cites reasons why women were "inherently unqualified to vote, such as inferior knowledge and reasoning skills compared to men, and the magnitude of the responsibility" ("Men Against Suffrage," 2014).

In the early 1900s, a group called the Massachusetts Anti-Suffrage Committee published "The Case Against Woman Suffrage" around the same time when another document, "Woman Suffrage a Menace to the Male Population," was released under the name Herbert N. Carleton. Those writers claimed sovereignty of voting rights for males only, citing the threat of the effect that female suffrage would have on the patriarchal hierarchy, which they claimed was the very bedrock of civilized society. Some male anti-suffragists called women's enfranchisement unconstitutional. Others saw it as blasphemy, claiming that "gender equality was unlawful in the eyes of God" ("Men Against Suffrage").

Female anti-suffragists were no less fervent in their beliefs. One prominent anti-suffrage leader was Alice Hill Chittenden (1869–1945) of the New York State Association Opposed to Woman Suffrage. Her father was a well-to-do attorney, and when she became involved with denying women the vote and keeping them out of politics, Chittenden was in a position of influence among her father's peers. She "learned and utilized political behavior, whether or not [she] recognized it as such" (Goodier, 2007). Chittenden met regularly with lawmakers, and her resulting tactics "account for the increased politicization of the anti-suffrage movement" (Weeks, 2015).

One of the best-known antis was Josephine Jewell Dodge (1855–1928), who served as president of the National Association Opposed to Woman Suffrage. Married to a prominent businessman, she was also the daughter of a high-ranking diplomat who became US postmaster general. Josephine Dodge believed female suffrage would jeopardize the home, forcing women into what she considered to be the lowered status of taking part in the corrupt world of politics.

Two antis with well-known names during the first-wave era were Catharine Beecher (1800–1878) and Susan Fenimore Cooper (1813–1894). Catharine Beecher was the daughter of famed minister Lyman Beecher. She believed in higher education for women as an extension of the female domestic role, since women were held responsible for raising virtuous sons capable of running the country. Catherine Beecher felt that education "would solve all women's 'wrongs' with no need for the ballot box" (Goodier, 2013, 19).

Susan Fenimore Cooper, daughter of author James Fenimore Cooper, wrote, "A Letter to the Christian Women of America" in *Harper's* magazine stating that a woman was historically and logically subordinate to man for three main reasons: (1) she was "his physical inferior, making her incapable of self-defense and relying on his protection," (2) women were "inferior to men intellectually," and (3) women "were subordinate to men through the directives of Christianity and no woman could call herself a Christian if she denied her subordinate role because she was defying God" (Goodier, 2013, 18).

Another prominent opponent of suffrage was Helena de Kay Gilder (1846–1916). She felt that men could claim the sole right to vote since only a male was "able to sacrifice himself on the battlefield" (Goodier, 2013, 24)—a position that ignored the fact that many men did not serve in the military.

Antis such as Eleanor Hewitt, Anna Maxwell, and Annie Nathan Meyer felt that education for women would make up for their lack of legal rights or being denied employment, so they did not need the vote. Lucy Parkman Scott, who was married to a New York Supreme Court judge, espoused the belief that "any legal wrongs that women bore could be ameliorated without resorting to the ballot" (Goodier, 2013, 29).

Another suffrage opponent, Mrs. William Force Scott, who always referred to herself by her husband's name ("Mrs. William Force Scott"), claimed that if women voted, they might "form a new party of their own—a Woman's Party— and that would be women against men, and more dangerous than labor against capital" (Weeks, 2015). Kate Douglas Wiggin (1856–1923), author of the best-selling children's book *Rebecca of Sunnybrook Farm*, publicly stated that her opposition to women's suffrage was due to her belief that women should stay in the background and influence the men in their lives indirectly because it was "more difficult to be an inspiring woman than a good citizen and an honest voter" (Weeks, 2015).

Josephine Pearson and Nina Pinckard led the anti-suffrage battle in Tennessee. Kate Gordon (1861–1932) of New Orleans was not entirely anti-suffrage but wanted individual states to control voting rights in order to maintain local standards. In the face of growing support for a national amendment granting voting rights for women, Kate Gordon formed the Southern States Woman Suffrage Conference in 1913. "The motto of its journal, '*Make the Southern States White*,' underlined its view of the goal of enfranchising white women" (Case, 2019).

Mildred Lewis Rutherford (1851–1928) of Georgia was another noted Southern anti-suffragist. She felt that preserving a woman's place in the home would give females the power to help solidify traditional Southern society after the upheaval of the Civil War, shoring up "'Old South' ideals about a woman's proper sphere" (Marshall, 2019).

While many anti-suffragists would generally be considered conservatives, there were some opponents of women's suffrage who definitely were not. Originally a communist, Emma Goldman (1869–1940) was a self-described anarchist, someone who promotes the violent overthrow of the government. Goldman opposed female suffrage on the grounds that it would not make a difference in what she considered to be the corrupt American system and that the battle for female suffrage was merely a diversion from the more important struggle against capitalism. She claimed that women should "advocate revolution rather than seek greater privileges within an inherently unjust system" ("Life Story: Emma Goldman," n.d.).

Although there was substantial opposition to female suffrage by influential adversaries during the first wave, some women's rights activists felt there was an even greater opponent: indifference by many of the average American women whom the suffragists were working to enfranchise. Some women who were indifferent to female suffrage lacked interest "because it was not part of their citizenship responsibilities; it was not how they were taught to serve society" (Poinsatte, 2020). Others reflected, "the general attitude of the public toward women voting [which] was more amused, indifferent and incredulous than hostile" (Weber, 2022).

Ultimately, in 1920, women did indeed receive the right to vote. At that point, many first-wave groups—both pro- and anti-suffrage—disbanded or directed their energies elsewhere. It would take a half century for another flagship issue of the women's equality movement to stir passionate reactions, bringing "pro" and "anti" forces once again into a collision course. That issue was the ERA.

The latter confrontation took place in the 1970s during what became known as the second wave. Any look at opposition to the second wave of the women's rights movement, specifically to the ERA, must stress the importance of Phyllis Schlafly (1924–2016). While there were others who endorsed the opposition, Schlafly became its face and its voice. She led one of the most effective issue-based campaigns in history by merging disparate groups that seemed on the surface to have had nothing in common; in fact, some traditionally harbored mutual animosity. Schlafly was able to persuade them to put aside their differences to fight against a common foe: the proposed ERA.

Phyllis Stewart Schlafly of Illinois was a long-time conservative political activist who presented herself as a "wife, mother, and devout Catholic" (Granat, 1997). Along with being a highly effective speaker, she also wrote a conservative newsletter and published a number of books. By 1972, Schlafly was recognizing what appeared to be a growing conservative backlash to the vast social and cultural changes taking place in America during the late 1960s and early 1970s. Through her newsletter, speeches, television appearances, and word of mouth, the charismatic Schlafly rallied support.

Critics, though, pointed out that even though Schlafly claimed to represent average housewives, she was not one herself, being married to a prosperous attorney. Schlafly "justified the contradiction between her career and her insistence that women should be wives and mothers above all by saying that women should work only if they can put home and family first" (Granat, 1997).

Schlafly's organization, the Eagle Forum, attracted conservative Catholics, fundamentalist Protestants, Orthodox Jewish people, and members of the Church of Jesus Christ of Latter-Day Saints (sometimes called Mormons). Her arguments appealed to the belief among those groups that the women's rights movement, particularly the ERA, went against the God-given roles intended for males and females. She claimed that each gender had a certain function, and while females were directed to be subordinate to males, a woman had a specific role in the home as a wife and mother who saw to the nurturing and spiritual guidance of the family as ordained by the Almighty. Schlafly, though, also tailored her message to appeal to average housewives and others who might not have been members of fundamentalist religious groups. "Many women came to feel that the ERA was a personal attack on them, their lifestyles, and their values" (Granat, 1997).

Although the military draft was discontinued in 1973, Schlafly and fellow members of the opposition stated that female equality meant that a woman could be drafted and sent to the front lines as a combat soldier if the draft was ever reinstated.

In addition, ERA opponents falsely claimed that under women's equality, housewives would be forced to take jobs outside the home in order to contribute half of the household's income. The claim was untrue, but it shook many women who had no work experience outside the home. Another effective falsehood spread by Schlafly and her allies was that mothers who worked at home would be compelled to put their children into government-run day care centers and forced to get an outside job.

Although there were various state and local leaders of the opposition, most looked to Schlafly for direction and tended to follow a very consistent plan.

Their unswerving message was relayed via the opposition's demand for equal time in local and national media if an ERA supporter was being interviewed. That consistency was a significant weapon for the opposition when the pro-ERA forces started to face dissension in the ranks.

At first, women's equality supporters in the second wave "pursued collective action across myriad differences and forged coalitions to make change real" (Gilmore, 2008). However, things began to unravel. There were differences of opinion within the various women's rights groups as to what tactics to pursue, which causes to prioritize, and who would speak for them. In an echo of what happened to prominent female suffrage organizations a half century earlier, women's equality groups of the second wave began to splinter.

By the time representatives of the National Women's Political Caucus (NWPC) were present at the 1972 Democratic Convention, relationships between some top women's rights leaders had reportedly become strained. The NWPC, along with much of the equality movement, was "pretending to a unity that did not exist" (Ephron, 1984). Opponents such as Schlafly saw this disarray among their feminist adversaries as a sign from God. Ultimately, whether due to the nature of the ERA itself or the effectiveness of its opponents' false claims, "the sight of traditional women vocalizing their opposition to the amendment altered the political dynamic in enough states to cause the ERA's failure" (Granat, 1997).

Further Reading

"Anti-Suffrage Views." n.d. *University of North Carolina Libraries*. Retrieved from https://exhibits.lib.unc.edu/exhibits/show/organized-womanhood/suffragenc/antis uffrage.

Case, Sarah. 2019. "Woman Suffrage in the Southern States." *National Park Service*. Retrieved from https://www.nps.gov/articles/woman-suffrage-in-the-southern-sta tes.htm?utm_source=article&utm_medium=website&utm_campaign=experien ce_more&utm_content=small.

Ephron, Nora. 1984. *Crazy Salad Plus Nine*. New York: Pocket Books.

Gilmore, Stephanie. 2008. *Feminist Coalitions: Historical Perspectives on Second-Wave Feminism in the United States*. Urbana: University of Illinois Press.

Goodier, Susan. 2007. "Anti-Suffragists." *New York Archives*. Retrieved from https://www.nysarchivestrust.org/application/files/7215/6510/3210/archivesmag_fall2 007.pdf.

Goodier, Susan. 2013. *No Votes for Women: The New York State Anti-Suffrage Movement*. Urbana: University of Illinois Press.

Granat, Jennifer. 1997. "The Failure of the Equal Rights Amendment." *Georgetown University*. Retrieved from http://hdl.handle.net/10822/1051268.

Lange, Allison. 2015. "National Association Opposed to Woman Suffrage." *National Women's History Museum*. Retrieved from http://www.crusadeforthevote.org/naows-opposition.

"Life Story: Emma Goldman." n.d. *Women & the American Story, New York Historical Society*. https://wams.nyhistory.org/modernizing-america/fighting-for-social-ref orm/emma-goldman/.

Marshall, Anne. 2019. "Mildred Lewis Rutherford." *New Georgia Encyclopedia*. Retrieved from https://www.georgiaencyclopedia.org/articles/history-archaeology/ mildred-lewis-rutherford-1851-1928/.

McConnaughy, Corrine. 2013. *The Woman Suffrage Movement in America: A Reassessment*. New York: Cambridge University Press.

"Men Against Suffrage." 2014. *Boston Athenaeum*. Retrieved from https://www.bostonat henaeum.org/exhibitions/antisuffrage/men-against-suffrage.

Poinsatte, Marie. 2020. "History Major's Surprise Discovery: Anti-Suffrage." *University of Dayton*. Retrieved from https://udayton.edu/blogs/libraries/2020-10-05-suffr age.php.

Spruill, Marjorie. 2020. "Nemesis: The South and the Nineteenth Amendment." *National Park Service*. Retrieved from https://www.nps.gov/articles/000/neme sis-the-south-and-the-nineteenth-amendment.htm.

Weber, Shirley. 2022. "History of Women's Suffrage in California." *California Secretary of State*. Retrieved from https://www.sos.ca.gov/archives/women-get-right-vote/hist ory-womens-suffrage-california.

Weeks, Linton. 2015. "American Women Who Were Anti-Suffragettes." *National Public Radio*, October 22. Retrieved from https://www.npr.org/sections/npr-hist ory-dept/2015/10/22/450221328/american-women-who-were-anti-suffragettes.

Q11: Who Supported the First Two Waves of the Women's Equality Movement?

Answer: In both the first and second waves of the women's equality movement in America, there were a number of supporters who became well known as leaders. During the first wave's pursuit of female suffrage, women such as Susan B. Anthony, Carrie Chapman Catt, Matilda Joslyn Gage, Lucretia Mott, Alice Paul, Elizabeth Cady Stanton, Lucy Stone, and Victoria Woodhull carved their names into the history books. But that was only half the story. African American women were generally kept apart from the predominantly white women's suffrage groups, even having to march at the rear of suffrage parades. Nevertheless, Black women mounted a tireless quest for women's rights alongside their goal of racial equity. Ida B. Wells-Barnett, Sojourner Truth, and Harriet Tubman were prominent leaders among Black suffrage advocates.

During the second wave, a number of well-known supporters emerged, such as Bella Abzug, Betty Friedan, and Gloria Steinem, although by the 1970s, women of color joined the ranks of second-wave women's rights advocates, including Shirley Chisholm, Dolores Huerta, Dorothy Pitman Hughes, and Patsy Mink. Illuminated by the media, those were people who made it into the spotlight. However, during the second wave, as in the first, untold numbers of individuals worked anonymously behind the scenes in their own fight for women's rights.

The Facts: The most recognizable names of the first wave are usually those who were associated with the Seneca Falls Convention of 1848. When the multivolume *History of Woman Suffrage* was published in the late 1800s it quickly came to be regarded as the "official" story of the women's equality movement. The series was written by people linked to Seneca Falls, such as Elizabeth Cady Stanton, and those were the names that were at the forefront.

In addition, concentrating solely on the leaders associated with Seneca Falls omits a major group of people. Frederick Douglass was in attendance at the conference, but Black women were not invited to attend.

African American women are often overlooked in the history of female suffrage, although they "engaged in significant reform efforts and political activism leading to and following the ratification in 1920 of the 19th Amendment ... They had as much—or more—at stake in the struggle as white women" (Harley, 2019).

In the early years of the suffrage movement, Black women worked alongside their white counterparts. However, the issue of race became more pronounced after the Civil War, leading to the splintering of major suffrage groups. After being excluded from many women's equality groups, African American women began forming their own organizations to pursue their rights. Those included the National Association of Colored Women (NACW) in 1896 and the Alpha Suffrage Club of Chicago in 1913, the latter being "the nation's first Black women's club focused specifically on suffrage" (Bailey, 2020).

In the 1830s, prior to Seneca Falls, abolitionist sisters Angelina and Sarah Grimké were two prominent women's rights activists in the early days of the movement. They broke gender norms by speaking about the evils of slavery to mixed audiences of males and females, attracting scathing criticism and often risking violence for that bold act. They began defending women's rights in order to secure their right to speak out publicly about abolition. In 1838, Sarah Grimké published the book, *Letters on the Equality of the Sexes, and the*

Condition of Women in response to Catherine Beecher's writings that promoted the subordinate role of women.

The women who are generally placed at the forefront of the early women's equality movement were Elizabeth Cady Stanton and Lucretia Mott, organizers of the 1848 Seneca Falls Convention, along with colleague Susan B. Anthony. In addition to being considered the driving forces behind the Seneca Falls Convention and its aftermath, they were also powerful lecturers who devoted their lives to traveling around the country, speaking for gender equality.

Another leading supporter of women's rights of that era was Lucy Stone. She was a staunch abolitionist and suffragist who publicly defied centuries-old traditions by refusing to take her husband's last name when she married. In 1869, Lucy Stone was one of the founders of the National Woman Suffrage Association (NWSA).

Feminist leaders Anthony and Stanton did not support the 15th Amendment, which gave the vote to Black males. Abolitionist Stone supported the 15th Amendment as it was written, giving Black males the right to vote regardless of the fact that women still could not. In late 1869, Stone and others broke away from NWSA to form their own national organization, the American Woman Suffrage Association (AWSA). Being formed in the same year as NWSA, Stone's group—AWSA—was confusing for many as the two organizations competed with each other for support. Although they later merged in 1890 into the National American Woman Suffrage Association (NAWSA), some historians feel the schism created discord and disorganization during the early years of the women's suffrage campaign when efforts might have been spent more constructively.

Three years after the Seneca Falls Convention, another leading figure in the women's equality movement, Sojourner Truth, made a speech that caused a ripple and was one of the first examples of what is today called intersectionality. Sojourner Truth was a leading advocate of abolition, civil rights, temperance, and women's equality in the United States. In 1851, she delivered what is known today as the "Ain't I a Woman" speech, espousing the belief that suffrage for females and African American males should be granted simultaneously.

While often remembered primarily for her work with the Underground Railroad to lead enslaved people out of bondage, Harriet Tubman was also an ardent supporter of women's voting rights, giving speeches on abolitionism and women's suffrage in Northern cities during the 1850s. To protect her from being captured and returned to slavery under the Fugitive Slave Act, she was often presented at speaking engagements under false names such as "Harriet Garrison," "Harriet Tribbman," and "Harriett Tupman" (Balkansky, 2020).

During the mid-1800s, women's equality leader Matilda Joslyn Gage included a quest for Native American rights along with her efforts toward abolitionism and women's suffrage. She was rebuked for criticizing organized Christianity due to its role in the oppression of women. In 1886, her fame spread for leading a protest at the unveiling of the Statue of Liberty in New York City, arguing that it was hypocritical to depict the concept of Liberty as a woman when actual American women were denied their rights, curtailing *their* liberty.

Victoria Woodhull shocked many Americans in the late 1800s by not only fighting for women's equality but actually running for president of the United States in the 1872 election on what was called the Equal Rights Party ticket. Even though she could not vote and her campaign was not taken seriously by most Americans, earning very few votes, she is regarded by many historians as the first woman to run for president.

In the early 1900s, Ida B. Wells-Barnett (1862–1931) was a prominent African American journalist and activist, fighting both sexism and racism. In 1913, Wells-Barnett founded the Alpha Suffrage Club in Chicago, Illinois, to help elect candidates who would best serve the Black community. When she traveled to Washington, DC, for the 1913 Suffrage Parade, she and other African Americans "were met with an unexpected choice: march at the back or not at all" ("The March of 1913," 2014). Wells-Barnett refused to march with the segregated Black suffragists at the rear of the parade, standing on the sidelines until the Illinois contingent of white women was passing. Suddenly, she emerged from the crowd to take her place at the front of the Illinois delegation. For Ida B. Wells-Barnett, "the suffrage parade of 1913 was just another opportunity to live by her motto: 'One had better die fighting against injustice than die like a dog or a rat in a trap'" ("The March of 1913").

Carrie Chapman Catt (1859–1947) directed the National American Woman Suffrage Association (NAWSA) in the early 1900s. A forceful advocate of women's right to vote, just before suffrage was granted in 1920, she founded the League of Women Voters to educate and involve women in the political process.

Alice Stokes Paul (1885–1977) was a leading figure in the women's suffrage movement and in the eventual passage of the 19th Amendment. She organized the Silent Sentinels, a peaceful protest in front of the White House, which was entirely legal. However, she and others were jailed and suffered abuse while incarcerated.

Not only was she able to vote in the 1920 presidential election, but Alice Paul also became the author of the first proposed ERA in 1923. However, after suffrage was won, the momentum of the women's rights movement seemed to ebb. "As Alice Paul learned after the ratification of the suffrage amendment, women retired from participation in public life for nearly half a century" (Baker, 2005). She was able to live long enough to see the second wave of the women's rights movement emerge in the 1960s and 1970s, but at the time of her death in 1977 at age 92, the ERA still had not passed.

When Alice Paul died, leaders of the second wave included Betty Friedan, author of the landmark 1963 book, *The Feminine Mystique*, which many feel set the mid-century women's rights movement in motion. Friedan remained an activist for women's equality in the 1960s and beyond, serving as a cofounder of the National Organization for Women (NOW) in 1966 and the National Women's Political Caucus (NWPC) in 1971.

In 1968, women's rights advocate Shirley Chisholm (1924–2005) became the first African American woman to be elected to the US Congress, going on to serve for seven terms in the House of Representatives as a Democrat. In 1972, she became the first African American woman to pursue the nomination for President of the United States from one of the two major political parties. With her friend Gloria Steinem, pioneering African American business owner Dorothy Pitman Hughes (1938–) cofounded the Women's Action Alliance, a national information center to assist local groups in the pursuit of women's rights. Along with Steinem, she envisioned the creation of a female-run publication, which grew to become *Ms. Magazine* when it was first published in 1971. The two women toured the country together throughout the 1970s, speaking about the intersection of gender, race, and socioeconomic issues.

Gloria Steinem was one of the most recognized figures of the second wave, in part because media sources were attracted both to her photogenic physical appearance and her sharp wit and bold words. Journalist Steinem published an article in 1969 titled "After Black Power, Women's Liberation," which brought her national fame as well as helping to popularize the term "women's liberation." She campaigned in favor of the proposed ERA, testifying before the Senate Judiciary Committee in 1970. In 1971, Steinem was a cofounder of the National Women's Political Caucus (NWPC). That same year, she cofounded the Women's Action Alliance to support causes and legislation centering on women's rights in such areas as equal pay, reproductive rights, and combating sexual harassment. "'Sexual harassment' didn't even exist [as a term] until the mid-1970s," Steinem later said. "Until then, it was just called 'life'" (Sermaker, 2017). Steinem also helped establish Take Our Daughters to Work Day in 1992, an annual event to give young girls opportunities to learn about possible career paths outside the home.

A number of second-wave leaders advocated various degrees of inter-sectionality among such factors as gender and race. They included African American activists such as Bettina Aptheker, Angela Davis, Audre Lorde, bell hooks, Michele Wallace, and Mary Ann Weathers. Another, Alice Walker (1944–), authored the Pulitzer Prize winning book, *The Color Purple*. She was also the mother of Rebecca Walker (1969–), who later became a feminist leader in her own right during what became known as the third wave of the women's rights movement.

The second wave brought forth voices from a number of groups, such as Native American women who faced racial and ethnic stereotypes along with gender-related issues, including violence against women in their communities. Among indigenous leaders during the second wave were Sarah Deer, Renya Ramirez, Audra Simpson, Leanne Simpson, and the poet Chrystos. Women of Hispanic descent were also notable for their involvement as second-wave leaders. Although Puerto Rican poet Julia de Burgos died in 1953, one of her most famous lines, "Don't let the hand you hold, hold you down," resonated with second-wave feminists in challenging whether womanhood and motherhood were synonymous. While labor leader Dolores Huerta was one of the most well-known figures of this era for her work as cofounder of the United Farm Workers, writers Sandra Cisneros and Martha P. Cotera and activist Aurora Levins Morales were also leaders in addressing second-wave issues.

Women, including writer Maxine Hong Kingston, activist Yuri Kochiyama, and journalist Helen Zia, used their talents to champion the Asian American community. Some observers feel that the most prominent Asian American figure during the second wave was Patsy Mink, the first woman of color elected to the US House of Representatives, where she served from 1965 to 1977. Throughout her career in public service, Mink drove legislation promoting gender and racial equity, including her role in the enactment of the landmark Title IX and the Women's Educational Equity Act.

Some historians interpret the multiplicity of voices and the number of diverse women's rights leaders during the second wave to be a positive development, far removed from the first wave in which the most visible leaders, both anti- and pro-suffrage, were usually white women of privilege. The variety of second-wave viewpoints and preferred strategies, from writing articles to staging highly visual protests, tended to stimulate involvement by people whose forebears felt excluded during the first wave. Some felt that opportunities for leadership tended to spur excitement and optimism among various supporters of the women's equality movement by virtue of having the chance to state their case.

However, everything did not always go according to plan. In the words of writer Peggy Orenstein, "We thought if you just explained the injustice of discrimination, it would go away because everyone would see it's not nice to discriminate against women. We were naïve, to say the least" (2018).

Further Reading

Bailey, Megan. 2020. "Between Two Worlds: Black Women and the Fight for Voting Rights." *National Park Service*. Retrieved from https://www.nps.gov/articles/ black-women-and-the-fight-for-voting-rights.htm#:~:text=In%201913%2C%20 Ida%20B.,elections%20and%20held%20political%20offices.

Baker, Jean H. 2005. *Sisters: The Lives of America's Suffragists*. New York: Hill and Wang.

Balkansky, Arlene. 2020. "Harriet Tubman: Conductor on the Underground Railroad." *Library of Congress*. Retrieved from https://blogs.loc.gov/headlinesandher oes/2020/06/harriet-tubman-conductor-on-the-underground-railroad/.

Ephron, Nora. 1984. *Crazy Salad Plus Nine*. New York: Pocket Books.

Greenridge, Kerri. 2023. *The Grimkes: The Legacy of Slavery in an American Family*. New York: Liveright.

Harley, Sharon. 2019. "African American Women and the Nineteenth Amendment." *National Park Service*. Retrieved from https://www.nps.gov/articles/african-ameri can-women-and-the-nineteenth-amendment.htm?utm_source=article&utm_med ium=website&utm_campaign=experience_more&utm_content=large.

"The March of 1913." 2014. *PBS History Detectives*. Retrieved from https://www.pbs.org/ opb/historydetectives/feature/the-march-of-1913/.

Norwood, Arlisha. 2017. "Ida B. Wells-Barnett." *National Women's History Museum*. Retrieved from https://www.womenshistory.org/education-resources/biograph ies/ida-b-wells-barnett#:~:text=Wells%2DBarnett%20traveled%20internationa lly%2C%20shedding,organizations%20in%20the%20United%20States.

Orenstein, Peggy. 2018. *Don't Call Me Princess: Essays on Girls, Women, Sex, and Life*. New York: Harper.

Ramirez, Renya. 2007. "Race, Tribal Nation, and Gender: A Native Feminist Approach to Belonging." *Meridians*, March 1, Volume 7, Issue 2. Retrieved from https://read. dukeupress.edu/meridians/article-abstract/7/2/22/138375/Race-Tribal-Nation-and- GenderA-Native-Feminist?redirectedFrom=fulltext.

Sernaker, Emily. 2017. "The Ms. Q&A: Gloria Steinem on #MeToo and Believing Women After Weinstein." *Ms. Magazine*, October 23. Retrieved from https://msm agazine.com/2017/10/23/ms-qa-gloria-steinem-metoo-believing-women-weinstein/.

Spruill, Marjorie. 2017. *Divided We Stand: The Battle Over Women's Rights and Family Values That Polarized American Politics.* New York: Bloomsbury.

Wagner, Sally Roesch. 2019. *The Women's Suffrage Movement.* New York: Penguin Books.

3

Women's Equality and the Equal Rights Amendment

The proposal to add an Equal Rights Amendment (ERA) to the Constitution was approved by the US Congress on March 22, 1972. It read, *"Equality of rights under the law shall not be denied or abridged by the United States or by any state on account of sex."* The amendment was then submitted to the fifty individual state legislatures, three-quarters (thirty-eight) of which would have to ratify the amendment for it to be incorporated into the US Constitution. There was a seven-year time limit for the ERA to be ratified by the proper number of states, but thirty states approved the proposed amendment within a year.

By 1975, however, doubts about whether the ERA would gain the necessary state support for ratification began to increase. This gradual shift in momentum was symbolized by a ninety-minute debate that took place on February 14, 1975, at the Arkansas state capitol in Little Rock, where the ERA was due for a ratification vote by the legislature. Dubbed by the news media as the "Valentine's Day Debate" because it took place on the date of that holiday, the event received national attention. The debate did not take place between elected officials, however. On one side was ERA supporter Diane Kincaid (1938–2000), a political science professor at the University of Arkansas, the state's flagship university. On the other side was ERA opponent Phyllis Schlafly (1924–2016) of Illinois, head of the STOP ERA coalition.

At the time of the debate in 1975, the ERA had already been approved by thirty-four of the necessary thirty-eight states. After the Valentine's Day debate took place in Arkansas, only four other states approved the ERA—while six states eventually revoked their earlier ratification.

During the debate, Kincaid emphasized all the points that supporters of the ERA had been making. She said that passage would be an enormous financial benefit for women, both in terms of combating gender discrimination in employment and giving women the same access to credit and other financial tools that men had always enjoyed "as a birthright" ("ERA Debate Starts with State Solons," 1975).

Kincaid stated that statistics on economic conditions showed that women exceeded men in only two categories: "unemployment and poverty" ("ERA Debate Starts with State Solons"). She added that facts showed discrimination based on gender to be widespread and that economic problems are compounded for women who are unmarried, divorced, widowed, or abandoned by spouses.

Schlafly waived off all of these purported benefits, insisting that jobs were available to women if they wanted them and that the pro-ERA movement promoted the issue with a "tedious, tried, tearjerking recitation of injustices that no longer exist." Rather than granting rights to women, Schlafly said that the ERA "would take away privileges that women enjoy under existing law" ("ERA Debate Starts with State Solons," 1975).

Schlafly also made the untrue claim that in Colorado and Pennsylvania, where equal rights proposals had been approved, courts were revoking benefits such as child support that many women relied on for the economic survival of their children and themselves. Kincaid stated she had letters from the attorneys general of both states that "absolutely refute" Schlafly's statements ("ERA Debate Starts with State Solons," 1975). However, when it came time for the ratification vote, Kincaid's arguments "appeared to have little impact" (Pruden, 2020). Arkansas legislators rejected the ERA, becoming one of fifteen states that ultimately failed to ratify the proposed amendment before the deadline.

Q12: Is the Equal Rights Amendment Part of the Constitution?

Answer: No, although the proposed Equal Rights Amendment *was* approved by the US Congress on March 22, 1972. From there, it was sent to America's fifty states for ratification. Thirty states ratified the proposed amendment within a year, well in advance of the seven-year deadline required for the ERA to pass. After a slowdown in approvals, the original deadline of March 22, 1979, was extended to an expiration date of June 30, 1982. When the extended deadline date arrived, the required thirty-eight states had still failed to ratify the ERA. As a result, it never became a legal amendment to the Constitution.

The Facts: Constitutional amendments are official additions to the US Constitution. As time has passed, a number of amendments have been added to the nation's governing document after it was enacted in 1789. A proposed amendment must be ratified, meaning it has to be approved, by the legislatures of three-quarters of the states. With there currently being fifty states in the Union, an amendment would need to be ratified by 37.5 states, rounded up to thirty-eight.

The first ten amendments, usually known as the Bill of Rights, guarantee such rights to American citizens as freedom of speech and freedom of religion. These ten amendments were all ratified in 1791, soon after the Constitution became the official framework for the government of the United States.

Proposed amendments must be officially presented to the states for ratification after approval by the US Congress. Not all amendments put forward by Congress have received ratification from the states. Failed amendments over the years have included banning American citizens from accepting titles of nobility from foreign governments, a measure treating the District of Columbia as if it were a state, and a child labor law.

In March of 1972, the Equal Rights Amendment was passed by a large margin in both houses of Congress. Its stated aim was to secure full equality for American women nationwide by seeking to end distinctions between males and females in terms of education, employment, and property as well as in matters such as child custody, divorce, domestic violence, and sexual assault.

Following its passage in Congress, the ERA was put before the states for ratification, requiring the approval of legislatures in thirty-eight states. Although some amendments (such as the 27th, concerning congressional salaries) had no ratification deadline, the ERA's deadline to be ratified by the states was set by Congress at seven years, which would be 1979.

After a slowdown in approvals, the original deadline was extended to an expiration date of 1982. When the extended deadline date arrived, the required number of states that were needed to approve the ERA still had not been reached.

At the current time, there are said to be legal and political challenges to the ratification process that would need to be resolved before the Equal Rights Amendment could potentially be revived and go further toward becoming part of the Constitution. These issues include whether the original deadline can be waived as well as whether states can rescind their support. Congress confronted the latter question twice before, during the ratification of the 14th and 15th Amendments. In those instances, Congress declared the amendments to be ratified, ignoring any state rescissions. "But in 1980, a federal district court in Idaho ruled that the state's rescission of the ERA was valid" (Cohen & Codrington, 2020).

Some say that any form of a proposed Equal Rights Amendment would have to start completely over, with members of Congress sponsoring it as a new bill.

It would then have to be approved by both the US Senate and the House of Representatives before being ratified individually by thirty-eight states.

If the ERA were to pass in the twenty-first century or beyond, it would classify gender for the first time, along with other factors such as race, as a class of people who have traditionally been subject to discrimination and worthy of constitutional protection.

Further Reading

"Arkansas." 2021. *Equal Means Equal*. Retrieved from https://equalmeansequal.org/states/arkansas.

Cohen, Alex & Codrington, Wilfred. 2020. "Equal Rights Amendment Explained." *Brennan Center for Justice*. Retrieved from https://www.brennancenter.org/our-work/research-reports/equal-rights-amendment-explained.

"Equal Rights Amendment." n.d. *Rep. Carolyn B. Maloney*. Retrieved from https://maloney.house.gov/issues/womens-issues/equal-rights-amendment.

"ERA Debate Starts with State Solons." 1975. *Hot Springs (Arkansas) Sentinel Record*, February 15.

Hendricks, Nancy. 2013. *Senator Hattie Caraway: An Arkansas Legacy*. Charleston, SC: History Press.

"History of the Equal Rights Amendment." 2018. *ERA*. Retrieved from https://www.equalrightsamendment.org/the-equal-rights-amendment.

"History of Women in the U.S. Congress." 2021. *Center for American Women and Politics (CAWP)*. Retrieved from https://cawp.rutgers.edu/history-women-us-congress.

"Proposed Amendments Not Ratified by the States." 1992. *Authenticated U.S. Government Information*, GPO. Retrieved from https://www.govinfo.gov/content/pkg/GPO-CONAN-1992/pdf/GPO-CONAN-1992-8.pdf.

Pruden, William. 2020. "Equal Rights Amendment." *Encyclopedia of Arkansas*. Retrieved from https://encyclopediaofarkansas.net/entries/equal-rights-amendment-13669.

"Ratification Info State by State." 2020. *ERA*. Retrieved from https://www.equalrightsamendment.org/era-ratification-map#:~:text=The%20Equal%20Rights%20Amendment%20was,38)%20of%20the%2050%20states.

Q13: Does the Constitution Already Provide Women's Equality?

Answer: As of 2023, no specific protection against gender discrimination exists in the Constitution. Through the years, laws and judicial rulings have evolved in the United States regarding gender equality that opponents of the Equal Rights Amendment contend are sufficient, rendering passage of the ERA unnecessary. However, ERA supporters claim those rulings are not enough and/or could be overturned at any time, making the Equal Rights Amendment a necessary part of the Constitution to ensure gender equality under the law.

The Facts: When the Equal Rights Amendment, based on gender, was proposed in 1972, its opponents stated that the ERA was not necessary because women were already assured of their constitutional rights. However, some legal experts, including conservative Supreme Court Justice Antonin Scalia, expressed a belief that "there is no explicit guarantee of protection against sex discrimination in the U.S. Constitution" (Rodriguez, 2021).

ERA supporters claimed that even though laws had been passed that gave women some protections, those laws could be unenforced or overturned at any time. They also marshaled extensive data underscoring the continued economic and social disadvantages experienced by women as a result of gender discrimination, especially in male-dominated industries and other groups. Proponents of the ERA stated that the best way to address those problems was through a constitutional amendment.

Some supporters said the Equal Rights Amendment would guarantee "Equal Justice Under Law," the slogan that is inscribed over the entrance to the US Supreme Court. Other ERA advocates emphasized that a constitutional amendment would warn against any future laws being passed that dealt unfairly with Americans on the basis of gender.

Those opinions were supported by Supreme Court Justice Ruth Bader Ginsburg, who believed the ERA reflected a basic principle in American society "that women and men are persons of equal stature" (Stewart, 2018). On another occasion, Justice Ginsburg, who did much to advance the cause of women's rights as both a lawyer and a jurist, remarked that "every constitution in the world written since the year 1950, even Afghanistan, has the equivalent of an equal rights amendment, and we [in the United States] don't. ... Even if the argument is that [passage of the ERA] is largely symbolic, it is a very important symbol" (Walsh, 2020).

Further Reading

Bleiweis, Robin. 2020. "The Equal Rights Amendment: What You Need to Know." *Center for American Progress*, January 29. Retrieved from https://www.americanp

rogress.org/issues/women/reports/2020/01/29/479917/equal-rights-amendm
ent-need-know/.

Rodriguez, Barbara. 2021. "The 19th Explains: What Is the Equal Rights Amendment
and Will It Become Part of the Constitution?" *The 19th*. Retrieved from
https://19thnews.org/2021/03/equal-rights-amendment-19th-explains/.

"Ruth Bader Ginsburg." n.d. *Oyez*. Retrieved from https://www.oyez.org/justices/ruth
_bader_ginsburg.

Stewart, Emily. 2018. "The Equal Rights Amendment's Surprise Comeback,
Explained." *Vox*, May 31. Retrieved from https://www.vox.com/policy-and-polit
ics/2018/5/31/17414630/equal-rights-amendment-metoo-illinois.

Walsh, Mark. 2020. "Justice Ginsburg Calls for Renewed Effort to Pass Equal Rights
Amendment." *ABA Journal*, February 11. Retrieved from https://www.abajournal.
com/web/article/justice-ginsburg-calls-for-renewed-effort-to-pass-equal-rights-
amendment.

Q14: What Arguments Were Used by Opponents of the Equal Rights Amendment?

Answer: According to opponents of the Equal Rights Amendment, a substantial number of American women—possibly a majority—did not want the ERA, and many actively campaigned against it. There was strong opposition to the Equal Rights Amendment by such organizations as STOP ERA and other groups. They based their opposition on claims that the ERA would upset traditional God-given gender norms, that women could lose existing privileges and protections, that there might be the potential for unintended effects of the amendment, and that the ERA was unnecessary since there were protections for women that were already in place.

The Facts: There were a number of arguments from various groups against ratifying the Equal Rights Amendment when Congress forwarded it to the states in 1972. After an initial flurry of state legislatures that ratified the ERA, waves of objections began to slow the process.

A major source of opposition was from a conservative organization calling itself STOP ERA, in which STOP was an acronym for Stop Taking Our Privileges. There were also groups on the other end of the political spectrum, such as self-described radical feminists, who thought the ERA did not go far enough.

Opposition to the Equal Rights Amendment was especially strong among those who considered themselves to be religious conservatives. They argued that the amendment would guarantee such things as unrestricted, taxpayer-funded abortions and the right for same-sex couples to marry, which went against their religious beliefs. Therefore, a number of otherwise dissimilar groups found themselves under the umbrella of STOP ERA. They included men and women such as evangelical Christians, members of the Church of Jesus Christ of Latter-Day Saints (Mormons), Roman Catholics, and Orthodox Jewish people, religious communities that were not ordinarily closely aligned. Various arguments were felt more strongly among different groups, such as the claim that under the ERA, women would be able to become Roman Catholic priests, defying the authority of the Vatican. While different objections were more important than others to various opponents, on the whole, the groups were united in one thing: staunch opposition to the ERA.

A common argument against the Equal Rights Amendment was that it was unnecessary since the US Constitution already includes the 14th Amendment, which was passed in 1868 after the Civil War. The 14th Amendment contains the statement, "*No state shall make or enforce any law which shall abridge the privileges or immunities of citizens of the United States; nor shall any state deprive any person of life, liberty, or property, without due process of law; nor deny to any person within its jurisdiction the equal protection of the laws.*" Those who advocated this argument against the need for the Equal Rights Amendment stated that if a woman is a citizen of the United States, she would therefore fall under the category of "equal protection" as much as anyone else.

ERA opponents also noted that if individual states wanted to pass their own version of the Equal Rights Amendment, there was nothing that stopped their lawmakers from doing so. Their argument was that if gender equality was something a majority of the people in a particular state wanted, they could lobby their own state legislature to pass appropriate laws. Since each state has its own constitution, protections against gender discrimination could be enacted in each individual statewide jurisdiction if so desired.

Another argument against ratification of the Equal Rights Amendment was that the ERA would mean laws could not be passed to protect men and women differently. The ERA states that equality of rights under the law shall not be denied or abridged by the United States or by any state on account of sex, "implying all laws must affect men and women equally" (Hamilton, 2019). Those who opposed the ERA noted a 1923 US Supreme Court case, *Adkins v. Children's Hospital*, in which the Court ruled that it was unconstitutional to guarantee a minimum wage to women because in an earlier decision, the court ruled that men could not be guaranteed a minimum wage.

An additional argument against the ERA came from those who stated that it has the potential for unintended consequences to women's rights as a whole. They cite the Supreme Court's decision in the 1896 *Plessy v. Ferguson* case. In that decision, the Court ruled that as long as racially segregated entities were equivalent, the situation would adhere to the Constitution under the 14th Amendment. This paved the way for the legality of the "separate but equal" standard under Jim Crow statutes, since African Americans were not being deprived of equal protection under the 14th Amendment. As in the case of racial discrimination, opponents claimed that approving the ERA would make it more difficult to pass laws that specifically protect women. Just as the 14th Amendment was ultimately interpreted to uphold segregation under the "separate but equal" doctrine, opponents claimed that the same interpretation could conceivably be applied to potential issues regarding gender, having unforeseen consequences.

There were also those who favored the Equal Rights Amendment in spirit but had concerns that its passage might foster a false sense of security among supporters of the women's rights movement. These opponents felt that passing the ERA could be falsely perceived by some as the end of the struggle for gender equality. Some of the most stringent opposition to the ERA came from the pro-life movement, which asserted that the amendment would overturn all restrictions on abortion and mandate taxpayer funding (through Medicaid) of elective abortion procedures. It was difficult for ERA supporters to counter the abortion issue, since many women's rights advocates concurred that opponents were "correct in sensing that women's equal status in society requires some measure of reproductive freedom, and some measure of reproductive freedom includes access to abortion, under at least some circumstances" (Mueller & Ollstein, 2020).

Another argument that was raised against adopting the Equal Rights Amendment was that it would strike down laws and regulations that actually benefited women.

ERA opponents argued that protections were already in place under state labor laws and guidelines that benefit women who do heavy, manual work. In addition, they said the ERA would overturn the Women, Infants, and Children nutritional program (WIC) and other state and federal social welfare programs beneficial to women and mothers.

Opposition groups also claimed that if the ERA became law, all incentives for women-owned businesses would be ended, along with scholarships specifically for women. There were arguments against the ERA that were centered on the amendment upsetting traditional gender norms. Opponents asserted that the ERA would end guidelines for alimony and child support. They said it would also nullify Social Security benefits based on a husband's income, which opponents said would harm middle-aged women such as divorcées and widows who did not have the skills to join the labor force late in life. In reality, no such proposal to nullify Social Security benefits in that way was ever introduced.

Opponents claimed that athletics would be impacted under the Equal Rights Amendment by compelling women and girls to compete against males in sports. Under the ERA, they said, it stood to reason that equality would mean the end of women's sports programs. However, no known athletic programs ever indicated that such women's programs would be jeopardized if the ERA passed.

Opponents predicted that the ERA would mean "coed everything—whether you like it or not" (Thulin, 2020). They falsely claimed it would mandate abolishing female privacy in everything from locker rooms to hospitals, from nursing homes to women's shelters to prisons. Two of the most frequently employed claims by ERA opponents were that women would be drafted by the military to fight in combat since they would be equal to men and that males and females would have to use the same bathrooms. Those claims, like many other objections, were dismissed as spurious and ridiculous by ERA supporters. However, opponents stated that they were not willing to gamble on decisions by the courts as to whether or not their assertions could potentially come to pass.

Amid the tumultuous social and cultural changes of the 1960s and 1970s, activist Phyllis Schlafly sensed a growing conservative backlash against the ERA. She recognized the discontent of those who saw themselves as traditional Americans, especially religious conservatives, perceiving that this discontent could grow into a powerful political movement.

Schlafly was the founder of the conservative Eagle Forum, publishing a newsletter in which she pointed out what she saw as the changes threatening traditional American values. In what many historians consider one of the most successful campaigns in American history, Schlafly skillfully organized widespread resistance to the Equal Rights Amendment.

She was able to mobilize women who identified with her in the role of housewives and mothers, as well as a cadre of men who supported her espousal of traditional family values and hostility to the feminist movement. Schlafly warned her supporters that the ERA threatened women's special status as wives, mothers, and homemakers and would eventually lead to the destruction of the traditional heterosexual family. That would happen, she claimed, through the legalization of taxpayer-supported abortion on demand as well as the prevalence of homosexual marriage.

One of Schlafly's strengths was being able to unite followers of disparate religions who were not usually aligned with each other. Those groups generally believed that gender roles were assigned by God and claimed that to support the ERA meant going against God's will. Although the coalition that came together under Schlafly's leadership was broadly Christian in nature, she convinced the factions to be respectful of religious differences among non-Christian allies when they needed to be, since they shared conservative principles of faith, family, and traditional gender roles. Schlafly's warnings about the Equal Rights Amendment are perhaps best exemplified in an essay that was published in her newsletter, *The Phyllis Schlafly Report*, on January 1, 1972, two months before the proposed Equal Rights Amendment was approved by Congress. Her essay was adapted for speeches and debates on behalf of STOP ERA throughout the ten-year ratification process not only by Schlafly herself but also by public speakers who were fellow ERA opponents, who obtained consistent talking points from it. Schlafly's essay titled "What's Wrong with 'Equal Rights' for Women?" asserted that of all the classes of people who ever lived, "the American woman is the most privileged." She further stated that any complaints about gender roles would have to be taken up with God "because He created us this way" and mocked supporters of the ERA as "straggly-haired women … on television talk shows yapping about how mistreated American women are" (Schlafly, 1972).

Schlafly allowed that any woman who wanted to reject marriage and motherhood could do so because America is a free country. However, she called on her followers to reject the arguments of ERA supporters, whom she called a "tiny minority [who would] degrade the role that most women prefer. Let's not let these women's libbers deprive wives and mothers of the rights we now possess" (Schlafly, 1972). She called on her followers to demand equal time on television and to tell their legislators to vote NO on the Equal Rights Amendment, concluding her essay with words in bold capital letters, "WOMEN'S LIBBERS DO NOT SPEAK FOR US."

Day after day, Schlafly asserted that the people lining up in opposition to the ERA represented traditional American values and God-given gender norms. "ERA opponents took care to present themselves as feminine rather than feminist … They adopted pink as their trademark color, aggressively distributed anti-ERA literature, and charmed legislators with baked goods and earnest pleas to maintain the gender status quo" (Spruill, 2018).

While Phyllis Schlafly was the best-known opponent of the Equal Rights Amendment, she was not alone. Working with Schlafly in STOP ERA and the Eagle Forum was Lottie Beth Hobbs (1921–2016), a conservative evangelical Christian activist, Bible teacher, and author. Hobbs was a leader in the national pro-family movement, serving as president of the National Pro-Family Forum and editor of *The Family Educator* newsletter. Hobbs, who directed a Christian group called "Women Who Want to be Women," authored and published a number of religious-themed books, including *Daughters of Eve: Strength for Today from Women of Yesterday*. Hobbs was something of an anomaly in the opposition movement, being both single and childless.

It was Hobbs, a native Texan, who organized a National Pro-Family Rally in Houston in 1977. Taking place just a few miles from the site of the National Women's Conference, it included declarations against abortion, lesbian rights, and the Equal Rights Amendment. Through Hobbs's efforts, "the sudden visibility of Schlafly's counter-protest and her vocal followers led to a schism in political support for the women's rights movement that has continued to this day" (Boissoneault, 2017).

Ann Patterson, a conservative housewife and member of STOP ERA, led anti-ERA forces in Oklahoma. Chairing Women for Responsible Legislation, she fought diligently for her cause. If Oklahoma approved it, her home state was in line to be one of the last few critical votes needed to ratify the Equal Rights Amendment before its deadline. Both pro- and anti-ERA forces saw Oklahoma as a battleground state. Eleanor Smeal (1939–), president of the National Organization for Women, visited Oklahoma's state capital, urging legislators to approve the amendment. Although the proposed amendment initially had widespread support in Oklahoma, lawmakers in Oklahoma City ultimately did not ratify the amendment before time ran out.

Conservative activist Rosemary Thomson was also a staunch supporter of the fight against the ERA. She served as the Illinois director of Phyllis Schlafly's Eagle Forum as well as being a member of the STOP ERA campaign.

While many people were involved with STOP ERA, they generally looked to Phyllis Schlafly for leadership and guidance because of her ability to unite people in the anti-feminist cause and maintain their loyalty: "Agree or disagree with Schlafly, her role in marshalling conservative women to be part of American politics had never been done before and was a remarkable accomplishment considering the whole operation was run out of her home and overseen by volunteers" (Duin, 2020).

Many of the men and women who drove STOP ERA felt that the Equal Rights Amendment was a personal attack on their choices, lifestyles, values, and religious beliefs. State lawmakers became particularly wary of angering local churches.

Supporters of the Equal Rights Amendment tried to offer assurances that the ERA would actually benefit women who were more traditional wives and mothers, claiming it would compel states to recognize the contributions that homemakers provide to family life. However, supporters of the amendment often found it difficult to make headway against anti-ERA rhetoric and warnings.

Supporters of the Equal Rights Amendment often found themselves spending their time responding to false or exaggerated claims from anti-ERA statements and condemning groups such as STOP ERA for fearmongering. Ultimately, however, the attacks took their toll, in part because pro-ERA forces did not have an advocate for their positions who could match the stature or effectiveness of the charismatic Schlafly.

Those who opposed the Equal Rights Amendment were able to convince state legislators that not all American women wanted the ERA, that those numbers might be higher than lawmakers expected, and that the backlash by those who did not want the ERA could be severe.

Further Reading

Boissoneault, Lorraine. 2017. "The 1977 Conference on Women's Rights That Split America in Two. *Smithsonian*, February 15. Retrieved from https://www.smithsonianmag.com/history/1977-conference-womens-rights-split-america-two-180962174/.

Duin, Julia. 2020. "Review: 'Mrs. America' Series More Drama Than Truth. *Christian Chronicle*, June 11. Retrieved from https://christianchronicle.org/review-mrs-america-series-more-drama-than-truth/.

"Equal Rights Under the Law, What's Wrong with That?" 2020. *League of Women Voters*. Retrieved from https://www.lwv.org/blog/equal-rights-under-law-whats-wrong.

Hamilton, Sydney. 2019. "Arguments for and against the Equal Rights Amendment." *Brief Policy Perspectives*, November 21. Retrieved from https://policy-perspectives.org/2019/11/21/arguments-for-and-against-the-equal-rights-amendment/.

Lange. Allison. 2018. "The Equal Rights Amendment Has Been Dead for 36 Years. Why It Might Be on the Verge of a Comeback." *Washington Post*, June 18. Retrieved from https://www.washingtonpost.com/news/made-by-history/wp/2018/06/18/the-equal-rights-amendment-has-been-dead-for-36-years-why-it-might-be-on-the-verge-of-a-comeback/.

Mueller, Eleanor & Ollstein, Alice. 2020. "How the Debate over the ERA Became a Fight over Abortion." *Politico*, February 11. Retrieved from https://www.politico.com/news/2020/02/11/abortion-equal-rights-amendment-113505.

Schlafly, Phyllis. 1972. "What's Wrong with 'Equal Rights' for Women?" *Iowa State University Archives of Women's Political Communication*. Retrieved from https://awpc.cattcenter.iastate.edu/2016/02/02/whats-wrong-with-equal-rig hts-for-women-1972/.

Spruill, Marjorie. 2017. *Divided We Stand: The Battle over Women's Rights and Family Values That Polarized American Politics*. New York: Bloomsbury.

"10 Reasons to Oppose the Equal Rights Amendment." n.d. *Eagle Forum*. Retrieved from https://eagleforum.org/topics/era/10-reasons-to-oppose-equal-rights-amendm ent.html.

Thulin, Lila. 2020. "Why the Equal Rights Amendment Is Still Not Part of the Constitution." *Smithsonian*, January 15. Retrieved from https://www.smithsonian mag.com/history/equal-rights-amendment-96-years-old-and-still-not-part-const itution-heres-why-180973548/.

Young, Neil J. 2016. "Sermonizing in Pearls: Phyllis Schlafly and the Women's History of the Religious Right." *Los Angeles Review of Books*, September 7. Retrieved from https://www.lareviewofbooks.org/article/sermonizing-pearls-phyllis-schlafly-wom ens-history-religious-right.

Q15: What Were the Main Arguments Raised by Supporters of the Equal Rights Amendment?

Answer: Those who supported ratification of the Equal Rights Amendment urged its passage on the grounds that even though the 14th Amendment of the US Constitution states that equal protection under the law is to be granted for all American citizens, gender discrimination tended to be less strictly interpreted than other forms of bias. This inequity, they felt, would be addressed by the ERA.

In addition, ERA advocates argued that the amendment would meaningfully address long-standing and deeply entrenched issues of gender discrimination and gender-based income and professional inequities. Supporters recognized that if the ERA was enshrined in the Constitution, it would have a major impact on federal laws and policies impacting every corner of American life. It would also therefore be subject to a higher level of judicial protection and review than at the state level.

The Facts: According to supporters of the Equal Rights Amendment, there was a false claim by ERA opponents that it was unnecessary since the Constitution already covered women's rights via the 14th Amendment. Passed in 1868 after the Civil War, the 14th Amendment includes the clause, "No state shall make or enforce any law which shall abridge the privileges or immunities of citizens of the United States; nor shall any state deprive any person of life, liberty, or property, without due process of law; nor deny to any person within its jurisdiction the equal protection of the laws."

ERA supporters claimed that even though what came to be called the equal protection clause existed as part of the 14th Amendment, gender discrimination is viewed less strictly than other types of discrimination based on factors such as race. Supporters of the ERA stated that women were indeed deprived of liberty or property since they remained controlled by men, whether those men were husbands, fathers, or authority figures such as virtually all-male lawmakers.

Advocates of the ERA also claimed that under the 14th Amendment, an individual has to prove the intent to discriminate in order to be subject to penalties. Some legal experts have interpreted this to mean that "discrimination is not illegal if it is unintentional" (Castile, 2017). However, if the Constitution explicitly specified that discrimination based on gender is prohibited, individuals could find legal recourse even if it can be asserted that the discrimination was unintentional, which observers say it often is not. ERA supporters claimed that "the first—and still the only—right that the U.S. Constitution specifically affirms equally for women and men is the right to vote" ("Why We Need the Equal Rights Amendment," 2018).

Insofar as assertion by ERA opponents that the Equal Rights Amendment would take away women's privileges and protections, ERA supporters stated that those "'protections' are actually limitations" (Castile, 2017).

As a corollary to that argument—opposition to the ERA based on women losing protections against being drafted into frontline combat—pro-ERA factions stated that females who wished to serve their country in the military have traditionally struggled to be allowed to perform the same jobs as men in the armed forces. It was not until 2015 that military roles such as combat were opened to women if they so desired. The restriction on performing all types of jobs in the armed services often hobbled women in terms of promotions and higher pay grades, which would in turn impact retirement benefits that a woman might need to support herself in old age.

When the Equal Rights Amendment was undergoing the ratification process in the 1970s, the Selective Service System, generally known as "the draft," was undergoing changes. On July 1, 1973, the draft officially ended, with an all-volunteer force being established. Subsequent to that time, "only men and women who volunteered are serving in the nation's armed forces" (Vergun, 2020). ERA supporters stated that the opposition's assertion of women being drafted into frontline combat under the Equal Rights Amendment was both outdated and false. Whether or not the Equal Rights Amendment is in place, they say, "the Constitution gives Congress the power to raise armies without any indications as to age or gender" ("Equal Rights Under the Law, What's Wrong with That?" 2020).

Along with the potential for drafting women into frontline combat duty, a pervasive argument among ERA opponents was that under the amendment, women would be forced to use unisex restrooms along with men. ERA supporters accurately stated that the Equal Rights Amendment would not require unisex bathroom facilities and that restroom usage would be "covered by citizens' right to privacy" (Castile, 2017).

The same right to privacy "would protect gender-segregated dorms and locker rooms" (Castile, 2017), something on which the ERA would have no bearing, its supporters argued. They pointed out that unisex public restrooms had already been a fact of life for years—on airplanes, for example. Supporters stated that the ERA was meant to ensure that people "cannot be fired, denied housing, or denied public services based on gender, and that if there were cases of unrestricted bathroom access, it would not be because of the ERA" ("Equal Rights Under the Law, What's Wrong with That?" 2020).

Opponents also objected to passing the Equal Rights Amendment on the premise that it would lead to same-sex marriages—an idea that had little public support during the 1970s. ERA supporters insisted that such an amendment would have no bearing on whether homosexual couples could marry. The Equal Rights Amendment did not explicitly address same-sex marriage, nor did the issue become prominent in the United States until 1993, well after the ERA failed to be ratified. That was the year the Supreme Court of Hawaii *Baehr v. Miike*, in a milestone ruling, found that abridging marriage on the basis of sex violated the state constitution.

As it turned out in the decades that followed the failure of the Equal Rights Amendment to win ratification, same-sex marriages became common throughout the United States through popular votes and state legislation as well as state and federal court rulings.

Many of the arguments advanced by supporters of the EPA concerned the huge economic gap that existed between American men and women, the latter of whom were routinely paid less than men for the same job, discouraged from pursuing more lucrative careers traditionally dominated by men, and subject to sexual harassment and hostile workplace environments due to their gender.

Some progress in wage equity was being made in the 1970s, although ERA supporters emphasized that women were still paid less than men for comparable labor. In 1972, when the ERA was proposed, women earned 57.9 cents per dollar compared to men for comparable work (National Committee on Pay Equity, n.d.).

In 1975, by the time the rate of approval for the ERA by state legislatures had slowed, women were being paid 58.8 cents per dollar earned by men. By 1982, when the deadline ran out on approving the ERA, women were still earning 61.7 cents to every dollar earned by males for doing the same type of job (National Committee on Pay Equity, n.d.).

ERA supporters emphasized that as a result of this gender-based disparity, "women working full time are able to afford less education, housing, transportation, food, and health care for themselves and their families than their male counterparts" (Separa, 2012). In addition, individual women and female-headed households "are more likely to be in poverty and less likely to have health insurance" (Separa, 2012).

Insofar as the opposition's argument that individual states could draft their own version of the Equal Rights Amendment to guarantee protections against gender discrimination if they so desired, ERA supporters said that was exactly the problem. With each state having its own constitution, they could draft a full version of the ERA, a partial version, or none at all. There would be no nationally consistent standard.

Supporters said that an amendment in the US Constitution would mean a higher judicial standard for determining questions of equal treatment for women and men since it would exist on the federal level rather than that of individual states. With the ERA in place, they said, there would be a greater degree of legal recourse for men and women who feel they have experienced gender discrimination. Supporters said the ERA would provide constitutional protection from future gender discrimination on the national level in contrast to state laws that might be passed in the future, a rollback of current laws, and/ or the interpretation of such laws in state courts. ERA supporters argued that under a federal Equal Rights Amendment, there would be a uniform standard of protection for all Americans, regardless of the state in which they live. Under what is called the supremacy clause in Article VI of the US Constitution, federal laws are called the "supreme law of the land," taking priority over any conflicting laws at state and local levels.

ERA supporters also claimed the Equal Rights Amendment had nothing to do with abortion. "Putting the sexes on equal footing under the law would not abolish all abortion restrictions," declared the League of Women Voters. "This is not the purpose of the ERA" (League of Women Voters, 2020).

Supporters claimed that the ERA would unequivocally be a symbol of gender equity in a society where women are abused, assaulted, and harassed at rates higher than men. While the ERA could not prevent such acts, supporters said, it would stand as a symbol that under the Constitution, women are valued as full citizens under the law and should be protected from having to live in fear.

ERA supporters also addressed false assertions by ERA opponents that the Equal Rights Amendment would strike down existing laws that actually helped women, such as estate laws, social security regulations, and spousal and child support. Proponents of the amendment pointed out that these laws and programs had become gender neutral based on landmark cases in previous years that had been won at the US Supreme Court. Supporters added that the ERA would actually add a special protection for women: the safeguard against discrimination based on pregnancy.

Advocates of the Equal Rights Amendment declared that the STOP ERA movement was disproportionately composed of relatively prosperous upper- and middle-class white women who were supported by men. The ERA, supporters argued, was meant to protect untold numbers of working class women, minorities, women living in poverty, single mothers, abused women, and others who were in more precarious financial situations. Supporters also addressed concerns raised by some feminists that if the amendment passed it might instill a false sense of security that full equality had been reached for women. They agreed that gender inequities in America would not magically vanish if the ERA was passed, but having the Equal Rights Amendment in place, they said, would be an essential legal tool in addressing those inequities.

Further Reading

Castile, Eliza. 2017. "How to Argue for the Equal Rights Amendment." *Bustle*, March 22. Retrieved from https://www.bustle.com/p/how-to-argue-for-the-equal-rig hts-amendments-ratification-because-its-about-time-it-was-part-of-the-constitut ion-46194.

League of Women Voters. 2020. "Equal Rights Under the Law, What's Wrong with That?" Retrieved from https://www.lwv.org/blog/equal-rig hts-under-law-whats-wrong.

National Committee on Pay Equity. n.d. "Wage Gap over Time: In Real Dollars, Women See a Continuing Gap." Retrieved from https://www.pay-equity.org/info-time.html.

Separa, Matt. 2012. "Infographic: The Gender Pay Gap–See What Inequity in Earnings Costs Women and Their Families Each Year and over Their Lifetimes." *Center for American Progress*. Retrieved from https://www.americanprogress.org/issues/women/news/2012/04/16/11435/infographic the gender pay gap/#:~:text=In%202 010%20women%20made%20on,equal%20pay%20for%20equal%20work.

Vergun, David. 2020. "First Peacetime Draft Enacted Just before World War II." *DOD News, U.S. Department of Defense*. Retrieved from https://www.defense.gov/News/Feature-Stories/Story/Article/2140942/first-peacetime-draft-enacted-just-bef ore-world-war-ii/.

"Why We Need the Equal Rights Amendment." 2018. *ERA*. Retrieved from https://www.equalrightsamendment.org/why.

Q16: Why Did the Equal Rights Amendment Fail?

Answer: Historians and other scholars cite a variety of causes, but many believe the failure of the Equal Rights Amendment was primarily due to a well-organized opposition movement animated by conservative cultural, political, and religious values and belief systems. Opposition to the ERA was also based on the uneasiness of many Americans after the turmoil of the late 1960s. Some Americans perceived the feminist movement as another threat to the nation's already shaky social order. Some ERA supporters felt that the news media had a role in the amendment's failure by playing up the disagreements among women's rights advocates themselves and giving less attention to the points and perspectives that those leaders were making about the status of women in American society.

The Facts: In the 1970s, supporters of the Equal Rights Amendment were confident that the ERA would be passed. During that decade, women's rights advocates had grown active, pushing for the Equal Rights Amendment to be added to the US Constitution. In addition, "Presidents Eisenhower, Kennedy, Lyndon Johnson, and Nixon were on record as having endorsed an equal rights amendment" (Blakemore, 2019). In the early 1970s, "polls showed public opinion in favor of the ERA" (Granat, 1997).

During the 1970s, there was considerable activity from members of groups such as the National Organization of Women who vigorously promoted the ERA. Women organized large-scale demonstrations in favor of the amendment, such as the 1978 March for the Equal Rights Amendment in Washington, DC, attracting about 100,000 ERA supporters.

When both houses of the US Congress passed the Equal Rights Amendment in 1972, the ERA appeared to many to be on its way to becoming the 27th Amendment to the Constitution. However, there was also another sentiment brewing in America. In 1969, President Richard Nixon had made a speech about the Vietnam War. In it, he called on the "great silent majority" of the American people who did not take part in antiwar protest demonstrations to back his policies. That phrase—*the silent majority*—resonated with many Americans who had been shaken in the late 1960s and early 1970s by watching what they felt were their cultural, ethnic, patriotic, political, racial, and religious beliefs being under attack. Protest demonstrations were often seen as manifestations of civil disturbances that threatened the social order.

Amid speeches, newspaper columns, and television appearances by STOP ERA, a group that opposed the Equal Rights Amendment, official-looking letters began appearing in people's mailboxes. Conservative Senator Sam Ervin of North Carolina had given STOP ERA the privilege of franking, which is a benefit provided to government officials that is designed to mail information to constituents without paying postage. The anti-ERA correspondence was marked as Official Business in order "to send anti-ERA literature at the public expense" (Spruill, 2018). In addition, Ervin's Senate office "became a national clearinghouse for ERA opposition" (Diamond, 1996).

The tone and tenor of news coverage has also been identified by critics as playing a role in the eventual failure of the ERA. Reporters, who at the time were almost entirely male, "liked that the anti-ERAs had a clearly defined, easily accessible leader [in Phyllis Schlafly], always ready with a pithy quote" (Spruill, 2018) whom they could contact before deadline. She could always be counted on for a comment that could be transformed into a short "news bite." Schlafly made it easy for reporters to quickly produce stories with attention-getting quotes promoting the ERA's opposition.

On the other hand, it appeared to members of the news media that ERA supporters lacked unity. Many reporters sought out the articulate, photogenic Gloria Steinem, often irritating other women's rights advocates who felt that they were being ignored. Most members of the media did not perceive there to be a clear leader mobilizing the pro-ERA faction the way that Schlafly was doing for the opposition. Schlafly was not the only opponent speaking out against the ERA, but was considered by many to be the most effective.

Decades later, Steinem and Eleanor Smeal of the National Organization for Women added another factor that they felt the media tended to emphasize to the detriment of the ERA. Calling it the "Catfight Theory of American History" (Smeal & Steinem, 2020), they felt that during the struggle for the ERA, the male-dominated news media enjoyed the spectacle of women bickering among themselves, focusing on that angle rather than the issues.

Smeal and Steinem also maintained that STOP ERA forces were less crucial in defeating the Equal Rights Amendment than corporate interests. They claim that despite popular support, the ERA was opposed by corporate lobbyists representing industries that stood to lose millions of dollars if the Equal Rights Amendment forced them to cease practices such as "charging women more," adding that state legislators knew the ERA "was opposed by the insurance industry, chambers of commerce, the National Association of Manufacturers and other corporate lobbyists" (Smeal & Steinem, 2020), although no specific examples were provided.

Those who are skeptical of that theory argue that thirty-five states eventually ratified the ERA despite alleged corporate lobbying. Instead, many observers emphasize the effectiveness of STOP ERA in building a coalition of disparate groups coupled with Schlafly's persuasive communication skills as the major factors leading to the ERA's failure.

State legislators began to shy away from the Equal Rights Amendment after an early burst of approvals in thirty states. The ERA was turned from what was felt by some to be a guarantee of equal rights into a culture war of progressives versus traditionalists, "and spooked legislators in the process" (Blakemore, 2019).

Observers have noted that some of the most committed opponents of women's rights in American history have been female, such as those who were against women's suffrage. Regardless of other factors that may have been influential, such as the news media and corporate interests, one source specifically states, "the campaign that defeated the ERA … was led by a woman, Phyllis Schlafly" (Traister, 2018).

Further Reading

Blakemore, Erin. 2019. "Why the Fight over the Equal Rights Amendment Has Lasted Nearly a Century." *History*. Retrieved from https://www.history.com/news/equal-rig hts-amendment-fail-phyllis-schlafly.

Borstelmann, Thomas. 2013. *The 1970s: A New Global History from Civil Rights to Economic Inequality.* Princeton, NJ: Princeton University Press.

Diamond, Sara. 1996. *Roads to Dominion: Right-Wing Movements and Political Power in the United States.* New York: Guilford Press.

Granat, Jennifer. 1997. "The Failure of the Equal Rights Amendment." *Georgetown University Digital Georgetown.* Retrieved from https://repository.library.georgetown.edu/handle/10822/1051268.

Smeal, Eleanor & Steinem, Gloria. 2020. "Steinem and Smeal: Why 'Mrs. America' Is Bad for American Women." *Los Angeles Times.* Retrieved from https://www.latimes.com/entertainment-arts/tv/story/2020-07-30/steinem-and-smeal-why-mrs-america-is-bad-for-american-women.

Spruill, Marjorie. 2018. *Divided We Stand: The Battle over Women's Rights and Family Values That Polarized American Politics.* New York: Bloomsbury.

Traister, Rebecca. 2018. *Good and Mad: The Extraordinary Power of Women's Anger.* New York: Simon & Schuster.

Young, Neil J. 2016. "Sermonizing in Pearls: Phyllis Schlafly and the Women's History of the Religious Right." *Los Angeles Review of Books.* Retrieved from https://www.lareviewofbooks.org/article/sermonizing-pearls-phyllis-schlafly-womens-history-religious-right.

Q17: Did the Equal Rights Amendment Fail Permanently?

Answer: The original deadline to ratify the Equal Rights Amendment expired decades ago. However, ERA supporters claim that precedents "make clear that a time limit should not be the sole determining factor for ratification. Notably, the 27th Amendment to the U.S. Constitution [concerning congressional salaries] was ratified nearly 203 years after it was introduced in the first Congress" (Bleiweis, 2020).

Today, some observers believe that the US Congress could give the Equal Rights Amendment a fresh start, claiming that "Congress could simply pass a new measure to declare the ERA valid" (Levy, 2018).

By the 1979 deadline, the requisite number of states was not attained in order to ratify the proposed amendment. However, one source stated that 1979 was "an arbitrary deadline put in place by Congress but not required by the Constitution" ("Senate Vote on Resolution to Ratify Equal Rights Amendment Fails," 2023).

The Facts: In early 2023, there were renewed efforts to pass the Equal Rights Amendment in what one source called "ERA's surprising revival after a long period of dormancy" (Cohen & Codrington, 2023).

According to at least one pro-ERA group, those efforts emphasize greater diversity in the scope of the amendment than in the past. A group called Equality for All states on its website that while in the past the effort to pass the Equal Rights Amendment "was focused mainly on the work of white women … our renewed efforts are inclusive and diverse—centered on leadership in the Black, Native American/Alaska Native and Women of Color communities, including transgender women/girls, gender-expansive individuals, and those who are most vulnerable to systemic inequities" ("Equality for All," 2023).

On April 27, 2023, Senate Joint Resolution 4 titled "A Joint Resolution Removing the Deadline for the Ratification of the Equal Rights Amendment" was introduced in the US Senate. A simple majority of senators (51–47, with two not voting) voted in favor of recognizing the Equal Rights Amendment as "valid to all intents and purposes as part of the Constitution" ("Senate Vote on Resolution to Ratify Equal Rights Amendment Fails," 2023). However, a three-fifths majority, or a minimum of sixty votes in favor, was required to move the bill forward according to a Senate rule. The result was that the motion to proceed on the issue was rejected.

After that failure, ERA supporters vowed to continue the effort. According to a spokesperson from the group Equality Now, "The ERA is not dead and should be recognized as the 28th amendment as it has met all the requirements of Article 5 of the Constitution [pertaining to constitutional amendments]. This will not be the last word on the ERA" ("Senate Vote on Resolution to Ratify Equal Rights Amendment Fails," 2023). The source adds that after it failed to pass in early 2023, a motion to reconsider was introduced, so that the resolution could be presented again to Congress at a later time. As a study from the Brennan Center for Justice declared, "[when] a powerful social movement with deep popular support takes up the goal of constitutional change … history shows that this is a battle that can be won" (Cohen & Codrington, 2023).

However, opposition to the ERA remains fierce, and talk of a revived Equal Rights Amendment has been denounced by ERA opponents like the conservative Heritage Foundation: "First, the ERA that Congress proposed in 1972 cannot be ratified because its deadline expired. Second, proposing the original ERA again will fail because its risks far outweigh any potential benefits. Third, a radical new ERA, with a different concept of rights, has been introduced to promote an agenda that includes unrestricted abortion and LGBT+ policies" (Jipping, 2021).

Further Reading

Bleiweis, Robin. 2020. "The Equal Rights Amendment: What You Need to Know." *Center for American Progress*. Retrieved from https://www.americanprogress.org/issues/women/reports/2020/01/29/479917/equal-rights-amendment-need-know/.

Cohen, Alex & Codrington, Wilfred III. 2023. "The Equal Rights Amendment Explained," *Brennan Center for Justice*. Retrieved from https://www.brennancenter.org/our-work/research-reports/equal-rights-amendment-explained.

"Equality For All." 2023. *Fund for Women's Equality*. Retrieved from https://fundforwomensequality.org/communities-and-coalition-building/?gclid=CjwKCAjwx_eiBhBGEiwA15gLN19qNNXCYul9vXi8PbyTa-uE69PWSttRgKo57J1cUixNHe-4K32hcBoCv4gQAvD_BwE.

Jipping, Thomas. 2021. "Not Your Grandmother's ERA: Why Current Equal Rights Amendment Strategies Will Fail," *The Heritage Foundation*. Retrieved from https://www.heritage.org/civil-rights/report/not-your-grandmothers-era-why-current-equal-rights-amendment-strategies-will.

Levy, Gabrielle. 2018. "Equal Rights Amendment, Left for Dead in 1982, Gets New Life in the #MeToo Era." *U.S. News & World Report*. Retrieved from https://www.usnews.com/news/national-news/articles/2018-06-04/equal-rights-amendment-left-for-dead-in-1982-gets-new-life-in-the-metoo-era.

"Roll Call Vote 118th Congress—1st Session." 2023. *Senate.gov*. Retrieved from https://www.senate.gov/legislative/LIS/roll_call_votes/vote1181/vote_118_1_00099.htm.

"Senate Vote on Resolution to Ratify Equal Rights Amendment Fails." 2023. *Equality Now*. Retrieved from https://www.equalitynow.org/press_release/senate-vote-on-resolution-to-ratify-equal-rights-amendment-fails/.

4

The Third and Fourth Waves of the Women's Equality Movement in America

The third wave of the women's equality movement in America arrived in the early 1990s, reviving a cause that had seemingly lost steam after the Equal Rights Amendment fell short of passage and eight years of the conservative Reagan Administration. The onset of the fourth wave of feminism in America is typically identified as the early 2010s, when the movement expanded beyond long-standing concerns about economic and legal inequality for women to respond to basic safety and welfare issues such as sexual violence, rape culture, sexual harassment in the workplace, and toxic social attitudes that measure women by conventional notions of female attractiveness rather than their intellect, skill sets, or other qualities. Notable "fourth-wave" events include the emergence of the #MeToo Movement and the historic Women's March of 2017, which encompassed demonstrations in Washington, DC, across the United States, and around the world.

Q18: How Did the Third Wave Build on the First and Second Waves of the Women's Equality Movement?

Answer: The first wave in the women's equality movement was capped by women's suffrage, which became a vital tool of empowerment. The second wave was unable to realize its dream of adding the Equal Rights Amendment (ERA) to the Constitution, but it nonetheless was instrumental in generating public and legislative support for new laws and judicial rulings that addressed long-standing gender inequities in American society. Both the first and second waves were thus essential in laying a strong foundation for subsequent generations of activists and advocates for women's rights to build upon.

The Facts: After women's suffrage became a reality in 1920, many women's rights groups that had focused on that issue disbanded or merged with other organizations such as the League of Women Voters to educate women on the electoral process, so that they could effectively utilize their newly won franchise.

The second wave of the women's equality movement, running roughly from the 1960s to the 1980s, had a similar defining issue: the proposed Equal Rights Amendment (ERA). Following effective opposition from groups such as STOP ERA, the Equal Rights Amendment fell short of ratification. The defeat of the ERA was a severe blow to women's rights advocates, many of whom had worked on the issue for years. However, the second wave helped expand and strengthen women's rights in education, employment, and other sectors of American life. These victories created a foundation for the third wave when its adherents came of age as part of what is often called Generation X, which is loosely defined as consisting of individuals born between 1965 and 1980.

The third wave of the women's equality movement extended roughly from the early 1990s to around 2010 with a surge in female activism. Much of this activism focused on defending women from a backlash against the gains made by women in the 1960s and 1970s. This backlash manifested itself in a variety of ways, including "sustained violence against women, increasingly blatant objectification of women and girls, persistent attacks on women's bodily autonomy, and continued economic inequality" (Evans, 2015).

By the time third wavers came of age, trailblazing gains for women seemed commonplace. The world of the third wave included such entities as the Title IX program to provide equal access to educational programs, increased recognition of the extent to which girls and women are at risk of rape and other sexual abuse, greater access to contraception and reproductive services, codifying workplace sexual harassment policies, establishing shelters for abused women and children, expanding child care options, and launching women's studies courses. However, those gains were not always uniformly enforced and were subject to political intervention. As one scholar said, "What is private and social is political in its dynamics, and in one way or another, eventually supported or condemned by the state" (Zack, 2005).

During and after the second wave, there was effective opposition from conservative groups and provocative media figures who characterized women's rights advocates and self-proclaimed feminists as bitter, man-hating "feminazis." That image "would become canonical as the second wave began to lose its momentum, and it continues to haunt the way we talk about feminism today. It would also become foundational to the way the third wave would position itself as it emerged" (Grady, 2018).

When the third wave started to develop, its adherents were not merely the figurative or spiritual daughters of the second wave. Often, young women of the third wave were quite literally the offspring of second wavers, having been brought up as children amid the feminist rhetoric and gains of that time.

Some observers consider the third wave to have been driven by the young women of Generation X. However, others object to both the categorization of the women's equality movement into waves as well as compartmentalizing it according to age, stating that speaking of feminism in waves "polarizes its practitioners by demanding that they identify with members of 'their' generation" (Gillis, Howie, & Munford, 2007).

In fact, many scholars suggest that a hallmark of the third wave was spotlighting the concept of "intersectionality." The term was introduced in 1989 by legal scholar Kimberlé Crenshaw to describe how systems of oppression interconnect, creating distinct experiences for people with multiple identity categories such as class, gender, and race.

The intersectional ethos gained traction during the third wave, with a great deal of the activism of the time fostering the empowerment of women in general regardless of individual differences. Along with gender issues, third-wave intersectionality focused on class and racial discrimination across boundaries, including in matters such as child support, contraception, pregnancy care, reproductive concerns, sexual harassment, and the continued prevalence of violence against women—issues that millions of women grapple with, regardless of race, wealth, faith, sexual orientation, and other demographic categories.

Further Reading

Cohen, Alex & Codrington, Wilfred. 2020. "Equal Rights Amendment Explained." *Brennan Center for Justice*. Retrieved from https://www.brennancenter.org/our-work/research-reports/equal-rights-amendment-explained.

Evans, Elizabeth. 2015. *The Politics of Third Wave Feminisms: Neoliberalism, Intersectionality, and the State in Britain and the U.S.* New York: Palgrave Macmillan. Kindle edition.

Gillis, Stacy, Howie, Gillian, & Munford, Rebecca. 2007. *Third Wave Feminism: A Critical Exploration, 2nd Edition*. New York: Palgrave Macmillan, 8.

Grady, Constance. 2018. "The Waves of Feminism, and Why People Keep Fighting Over Them, Explained." *Vox*, March 20. Retrieved from https://www.vox.com/2018/3/20/16955588/feminism-waves-explained-first-second-third-fourth.

Zack, Naomi. 2005. *Inclusive Feminism: A Third Wave Theory of Women's Commonality*. Lanham, MD: Rowman & Littlefield, 17.

Q19: Was the Third Wave of the Women's Equality Movement Sparked by the Anita Hill Hearings?

Answer: The televised testimony of Dr. Anita Hill during the 1991 congressional hearings for nominee Clarence Thomas to sit on the US Supreme Court is often cited by scholars as a watershed event in the foundation of the third wave. The dismissive and sexist treatment she received from the all-male members of the Senate committee angered women across the country and galvanized new levels of political and social activism for women's rights.

The Facts: The dismissive treatment received by Anita Hill during her 1991 interrogation by an all-male Senate committee convened to consider the nomination of Clarence Thomas to the Supreme Court reverberated across American society long after the hearings concluded.

That year, a seat opened up on the US Supreme Court. The only woman on the court at that time was Sandra Day O'Connor, who in 1981 had become the nation's first female Supreme Court justice. Before O'Connor arrived, all nine seats on the Court had been filled by white males, with the exception of justice Thurgood Marshall, an African American who was appointed in 1967.

To fill a vacancy when Marshall retired, President George H. W. Bush nominated Black conservative Clarence Thomas, whose confirmation hearing before the Senate Judiciary Committee included explosive testimony by an African American law professor, Dr. Anita Hill, a former work colleague of the Supreme Court nominee.

After earning a law degree from Yale, Hill joined the federal Equal Employment Opportunity Commission (EEOC) in 1982. She worked for Thomas when he was chair of the commission. There, she claimed she was repeatedly subjected to sexual harassment from Thomas, who allegedly commented on her physical appearance, described his male anatomy in lewd terms, and performed other harassing acts. Hill said she found her situation at work became so intolerable that she left the EEOC in 1983. In 1989, after becoming a faculty member at the University of Oklahoma law college, she became the school's first tenured African American professor.

In 1990, President George H. W. Bush named Thomas to the US Court of Appeals for the District of Columbia Circuit. After serving in that role for sixteen months, Thomas was nominated by Bush in 1991 to fill the vacancy on the Supreme Court left by Marshall's retirement.

To determine if Supreme Court nominations are approved to be put forward for a vote in Congress, the mandate of the Senate Judiciary Committee is to hold confirmation hearings in which nominees for the Court provide testimony and respond to questions. Clarence Thomas had been an appeals court judge for sixteen months, which the Judiciary Committee felt was too short a period of time for them to adequately examine his judicial background during the confirmation hearings. Therefore, his character was presented as the primary qualification for Thomas to sit on the nation's highest court. During the process, the report of a private interview with Anita Hill by the FBI was leaked to the press, and Hill was called to publicly testify.

During the televised hearings conducted by the panel of white males on the Senate Judiciary Committee, Anita Hill was accused of lying in her testimony about Thomas's behavior. In addition, the senators raised doubts about her sanity. Hill later wrote that the men on the committee "shifted the hearing on whether Thomas was suitable to serve on the Court to a hearing on whether I could rebut their presumption that I was lying" (Hill, 1998).

Clarence Thomas denied Hill's allegations, which he described as the basis for a "high-tech lynching for uppity blacks" (Massie, 2016). Hill was not the only woman who accused Thomas of sexual harassment, but the other accusers were never called before the committee. Ultimately, Thomas was confirmed in the Senate by a 52–48 vote. As of 2023, he was still a member of the US Supreme Court.

The nationally televised confirmation hearings had a polarizing effect on many Americans, often along lines of race, gender, and political leanings. On one side, Anita Hill was called an attention seeker, an opportunist, and/or a "woman scorned." On the other, she was considered to have been victimized by Thomas when he was her boss as well as by the all-white male Senate committee members who treated her in a manner that was demeaning and sexist.

The galvanizing effect of the hearings led a number of women to enter politics. "Televised images of a committee composed exclusively of white males sharply questioning … Professor Anita Hill caused many to wonder where the women senators were" ("Year of the Woman," n.d.).

In 1991, when Anita Hill testified, there were two women in the US Senate out of 100 senators: Nancy Kassebaum of Kansas and Barbara Mikulski of Maryland. Neither of those women had been appointed to the Judiciary Committee. The year after Hill's testimony, some women ran for the Senate and won in the 1992 election, such as Patty Murray of Washington. In California, Barbara Boxer and Dianne Feinstein also won their Senate races that year, making California the first state in the nation's history to be represented by two female senators.

With the victory of Carol Moseley Braun from Illinois, a total of four women were elected to the Senate in a single election year, a history-making turn of events. Some newspapers dubbed 1992 as "The Year of the Woman."

Senator Barbara Mikulski responded: "Calling 1992 the Year of the Woman makes it sound like the Year of the Caribou or the Year of the Asparagus. We're not a fad, a fancy, or a year" ("Year of the Woman," n.d.).

In all, the number of females serving in the US Congress that year reached a total of six in the 100-seat Senate, along with 47 out of 435 in the House of Representatives, constituting a small fraction of both. According to some observers, the so-called Year of the Woman "turned out to be a blip, as the number of women entering national politics plateaued rapidly after 1992" (Grady, 2018).

Beyond a somewhat greater number of women being elected to political office afterward, the testimony by Anita Hill cast a spotlight on the issue of sexual harassment in the workplace. Until that time, such occurrences had basically been considered to be just the way things were, a common fact of life that always had been and always would be, with the disclaimer that "boys will be boys."

However, "Hill's testimony sparked an avalanche of sexual harassment complaints in much the same way as allegations in the 2000s were followed by a litany of sexual misconduct accusations against other powerful men" at the height of the #MeToo Movement in the late 2010s (Grady, 2018).

Following her appearance before the Senate judiciary committee at the 1991 Supreme Court hearings, Hill turned down requests for interviews. However, conservatives were determined to punish her for her testimony. Buffeted by public demands for her resignation, efforts in the state legislature to cut off funding for her endowed professorship, and the introduction of a bill that would have closed the entire University of Oklahoma law school, Hill decided she could not remain at the University of Oklahoma and resigned her position in 1996. She later became a professor at Brandeis University in Massachusetts, where apart from teaching and writing, she kept a relatively low profile.

However, Anita Hill was in the news again in 2010 when the wife of Clarence Thomas left a phone message for Hill asking her to apologize for her 1991 testimony about Thomas's alleged sexual harassment. The call was confirmed as genuine by Thomas's wife, a conservative activist. Hill subsequently "told *The New York Times* she had nothing to apologize for because she told the truth in 1991" (Totenberg, 2010).

Subsequent to Anita Hill's testimony, a number of women began running for political office through the 1990s on the state, local, and national levels. Around this time, the term "third wave" began to enter general usage.

The descriptor "third wave" is credited to Rebecca Walker, the daughter of Alice Walker, who was a second-wave feminist icon. Alice Walker had been the first African American woman to win the Pulitzer Prize in fiction (for her novel *The Color Purple*). Her daughter Rebecca Walker, also a writer, publicly declared her response to the Supreme Court appointment of Clarence Thomas in a 1992 essay for *Ms. Magazine* titled "Becoming the Third Wave."

In her essay, Rebecca Walker stated,

I write this as a plea to all women, especially women of my generation: Let Thomas' confirmation serve to remind you, as it did me, that the fight is far from over. Let this dismissal of a woman's experience move you to anger. Turn that outrage into political power. ... I am not a post-feminism feminist. I am the Third Wave. (Evans & Bobel, 2007)

Years later, Walker described the third wave as "a public reckoning of racism, classism, and sexism" ("The Missing Waves of Feminism," 2021). By naming and positioning the third wave as the next incarnation of the women's equality movement in America at the time, Walker was acknowledging that even after the triumphs of the first and second waves, there was still more work to be done to achieve the goal of gender equality in America.

Further Reading

Brayson, Johnny. 2016. "The Forgotten Accusers of Clarence Thomas." *Bustle*, April 15. Retrieved from https://www.bustle.com/articles/154816-did-other-women-accuse-clarence-thomas-after-anita-hills-testimony-hill-was-not-the-justices-only.

Evans, Meredith & Bobel, Chris. 2007. "I Am a Contradiction: Feminism and Feminist Identity in the Third Wave." *New England Journal of Public Policy*, March 21, vol. 22, no. 1, Article 17, 208. Retrieved from https://scholarworks.umb.edu/cgi/viewcont ent.cgi?article=1077&context=nejpp.

Grady, Constance. 2018. "The Waves of Feminism, and Why People Keep Fighting Over Them, Explained." *Vox*, March 20. Retrieved from https://www.vox.com/2018/3/20/16955588/feminism-waves-explained-first-second-third-fourth.

Hill, Anita. 1998. *Speaking Truth to Power*. New York: Anchor, 2.

Massie, Victoria. 2016. "How Racism and Sexism Shaped the Clarence Thomas/Anita Hill Hearing." *Vox*, April 16. Retrieved from https://www.vox.com/2016/4/16/11408576/anita-hill-clarence-thomas-confirmation.

"The Missing Waves of Feminism." 2021. *Clio, National Women's History Museum,* Winter, 2.

"October 11, 1991: Anita Hill Full Opening Statement (C-SPAN)." 1991. *YouTube.* Retrieved from https://www.youtube.com/watch?v=-QbVKSvm274.

Totenberg, Nina. 2010."Justice Thomas' Wife Asks Anita Hill to Apologize." *National Public Radio*, October 20. Retrieved from https://www.npr.org/templates/story/story.php?storyId=130688438.

"Year of the Woman." n.d. *United States Senate*. Retrieved from https://www.senate.gov/artandhistory/history/minute/year_of_the_woman.htm.

Q20: What Were the Defining Characteristics of the Third Wave?

Answer: Key issues tackled by third wavers include the empowerment of different forms of femininity and respect for the diverse ways in which individual womanhood is expressed. Intersectionality was a prominent concept among third wavers, who noted how previous efforts toward women's rights in the first and second waves often fell short in addressing the needs and experiences of racial minorities and women from lower socioeconomic classes. Third wavers were active in effectively utilizing the nascent social media of the day and were also characterized by elements such as the riot grrrls, who felt they embraced societal issues pertinent to all women, especially young women. Riot grrrls were considered to be part of a feminist, punk rock movement of the 1990s that delivered raucous anthems that expressed women's anger and celebrated their sexuality.

That rebellious subculture often aroused strong opposition to third-wave goals, which were felt by some—both inside and outside the women's equality movement—to be too radical.

The Facts: Some scholars have claimed that the "confusion surrounding what constitutes third-wave feminism is in some respects its defining feature" (Grady, 2018). With the perception of the first wave of the women's equality movement highlighted by seeking the right to vote and the second wave focusing on the passage of the Equal Rights Amendment, those two issues formed the most readily identifiable features for each of the two earlier phases of the women's rights movement.

If the third wave had a philosophical basis, it might be in the ways the first and second waves were judged and largely rejected by third-wave adherents. Third wavers were often critical of the first and second waves for what they saw as a lack of attention given to classism, racism, and sexism in American society. Third wavers also protested against pervasive and condescending patriarchal attitudes toward girls and women and their capabilities as well as the ways in which America's male-centered culture prioritizes physical appearance over any other qualities in its valuation of girls and women.

In seeking what they felt to be social justice, third wavers made intersectionality a significant theme, calling attention to what they called "layers of oppression, which tended to accumulate and intensify, particularly for poor people of color" ("Brief History of Third-Wave Feminism," 2022).

Members of the third wave also voiced their support of nonheterosexual women and those whose self-identified gender was not the one they were assigned at birth.

Reproductive rights were also a priority for third-wave activists. They sought greater accessibility for contraception, pregnancy care regardless of economic class, child support, and programs to help bring children out of the continuing spiral of poverty. Third wavers generally advocated maintaining the legal judgment known as *Roe v. Wade*, which legalized abortion across the country in 1973. The *Roe* decision provoked a strong negative reaction among social conservatives and triggered the development of a politically powerful pro-life movement in many parts of the country.

Sex itself was a keystone of third wavers, who claimed that it was a means of empowerment and self-expression. They believed women should have as much sexual freedom as men, without the imposition of the traditional "double standard" in which males had a wide socially acceptable latitude to pursue the kind of sexual behavior for which women were condemned. This point of view was increasingly represented in American popular culture in movies and television programs like *Sex and the City*, which ran on HBO from 1998 to 2004. Some third wavers felt *Sex and the City* was an indicator of updated values in American culture, while opponents denounced the popular show for what they considered immoral content.

In addition, a growing number of female performance artists tackled subject matter and onstage acts with a sexual focus that had previously not been undertaken in public, provoking condemnation by opponents who considered such subject matter to be offensive. For example, performance artist Karen Finley often took off her clothes at the end of the performance, smearing herself with chocolate or other substances. A play by Eve Ensler was titled *The Vagina Monologues*, shocking some not only for its title and direct language, but also its focus on that part of the female body.

Violence against women was another major area of concern. Noting a continuing pattern of domestic violence, rape, and sexual harassment suffered by women, third wavers sought greater awareness as well as more effective social and legal remedies. Some third-wave priorities were more controversial than others, such as reproductive rights.

Another criticism of the third wave by some observers was that it inadvertently added to gender oppression and stereotyping through its support of women's right to wear revealing attire. Third wavers generally claimed that a woman should be able to dress any way she wants and that efforts to blame sexual assaults and harassment on their wardrobe choices amounted to blaming the victim. This topic had ramifications for many women who reported being raped or otherwise subjected to sexual violence and abuse to legal authorities. Studies in the 1990s examined the relationship of a rape victim's clothing to the perception of the offense, such as might be the case for a judge and/or jury. They generally found that research participants viewing a photo of the victim in provocative clothing "were more likely to believe she was responsible for the behavior of her assailant, more likely to view the assailant's behavior as justified, and less likely to recognize rape" (Patrick, 2022). As part of the third-wave agenda, advocates generally embraced multiple facets of economics, ethnic elements, gender differentiation, life experiences, race, sexual identity, and social class. They tended to support the diversity and individualism of all women, aiming to redefine what it meant to be a female and/or a feminist.

However, there were disagreements that arose among third wavers themselves. Some questioned whether the concept of feminism could be sustainable by casting such a wide net. Some individuals who self-identified as feminists felt that concerns such as transgender issues did not have a place in the women's equality movement.

While some third wavers considered the embrace of female diversity in all its forms to be a positive thing, others felt that the multiple issues voiced by members of the third wave diluted its message. "As such, its greatest strength, multivocality, was attacked by some as its greatest weakness" ("Brief History of Third-Wave Feminism," 2022).

Third wavers often responded that "the creation of a unified agenda or philosophy … was a goal that was not only unrealistic but undesirable" ("Brief History of Third-Wave Feminism," 2022). They claimed that trying to force the movement into one prototype would not only defeat the purpose of being inclusive to all women, but also contribute to the kind of racism and elitism that they felt had tainted the first and second waves.

According to some scholars, "most third-wavers refuse to identify as 'feminists' and reject the word that they find limiting and exclusionary" (Rampton, 2015), adding that "third wave feminism breaks boundaries" (Rampton, 2015).

Some critics felt that third wavers broke *too many* boundaries, while others believed they merely opened the door toward greater inclusion for more adherents of women's rights.

Further Reading

"Brief History of Third-Wave Feminism." 2022. *MasterClass.* Retrieved from https://www.masterclass.com/articles/third-wave-feminism#a-brief-history-of-thirdwave-feminism.

Grady, Constance. 2018. "The Waves of Feminism, and Why People Keep Fighting Over Them, Explained." *Vox*, March 20. Retrieved from https://www.vox.com/2018/3/20/16955588/feminism-waves-explained-first-second-third-fourth.

Heywood, Leslie. 2005. *The Women's Movement Today: An Encyclopedia of Third-Wave Feminism.* Westport, CT: Greenwood Press.

Heywood, Leslie & Drake, Jennifer. 1997. *Third Wave Agenda: Being Feminist, Doing Feminism.* Minneapolis: University of Minnesota Press.

Lewis, Cora. 2010. "Steinem Headlines Talk about Feminism." *Yale Daily News*, February 1. Retrieved from https://yaledailynews.com/blog/2010/02/01/steinem-headlines-talk-about-feminism/.

Patrick, Wendy. 2022. "Was She 'Asking for It'?: The Perils of Provocative Clothing." *Psychology Today*, August 16. Retrieved from https://www.psychologytoday.com/us/blog/why-bad-looks-good/202208/was-she-asking-it-the-perils-provocative-clothing.

Rampton, Martha. 2015. "Four Waves of Feminism." *Pacific University Oregon.* Retrieved from https://www.pacificu.edu/magazine/four-waves-feminism.

Q21: Was the Riot Grrrls' Subculture
Characteristic of the Third Wave?

Answer: Some critics perceived the third wave as radical, possibly undermining the women's equality movement in general by alienating public perception. At the same time, others argued that the third wave was an appropriate response to the changing times by expressing new freedoms, promoting greater inclusion of all women, and displaying new ways of female self-expression. This dichotomy can be seen through the lens of the riot grrrl movement which many considered to be a significant feature of the third wave. To its supporters, the riot grrrl subculture was seen as a source of pride due to its tendency to break traditional taboos. For critics, the self-proclaimed riot grrrls were a potential source of damage to the women's equality movement as a whole for their perceived outrageousness.

The Facts: In the early 1990s, the riot grrrl trend emerged after a group of young women in Olympia, Washington, gathered to discuss what they considered to be the sexism of the punk rock music scene. Expanding their vision, "the women decided they wanted to start a 'girl riot' against modern society, which they felt offered no validation of women's experiences" (Feliciano, 2013).

They believed in producing a specific culture for females by creating their own music along with written materials such as "fanzines" that shunned the conventions of corporate-controlled mainstream music magazines. Bands who identified themselves as riot grrrls used their music to express their own viewpoints, emphasizing feminist and racial issues.

Some observers consider the riot grrrls not only as one of several features of the women's equality movement in the 2000s but also more actively as a "catalyst for the third-wave feminist movement" ("Brief History of Third-Wave Feminism," 2022).

From its birthplace in Olympia, Washington, the riot grrrl subculture spread throughout the western United States in the 1990s before expanding nationally and around the world.

The words "girl" and "grrrl" themselves are a point of differentiation between the second wave and the third wave. Many second wavers of the 1970s and 1980s wanted to be known as women rather than girls, which they felt recognized their dignity as adult human beings. They did not want to be treated like children and instead demanded that they be accorded respect. For example, many second wavers found it demeaning for a male boss to say something to a colleague, such as "My girl will get the information to your girl," regardless of the age or rank of the female employees in question.

Not only did third wavers have absolutely no problem with the word "girl," but they also sought to add a new dimension of power to it. Third wavers "liked being girls. They embraced the word; they wanted to make it empowering, even threatening—hence grrrl" (Grady, 2018). Through a kind of primal growl, grrrls were young women who sought to be regarded as independent, confident, and strong.

The riot grrrl subculture of the third wave is usually said to combine feminism, politics, and punk music. The idea was for women to be able to express themselves through the arts, especially music, in the same boundary-breaking ways that males always had. Some observers describe the riot grrrls in terms of "a noisy message of female empowerment voiced by several punk musicians and a few of their friends" (Marcus, 2010).

Some of the musical groups in the United States that are considered to be part of the riot grrrl scene in the 1990s include Bikini Kill, a band from Olympia, Washington. Bikini Kill is generally credited with pioneering the riot grrrl movement through their feminist lyrics and raucous performances. Another band from Olympia, called Heavens to Betsy, stunned listeners with what was considered to be the sound of primal female rage.

Some of the top examples of riot grrrl music include the songs "Rebel Girl" by Bikini Kill, "Love Thing" by Bratmobile, "Get Loud" by Kitten Forever, and "A Living Human Girl" by The Regrettes.

According to one source, "the 'grrrls' of the third wave stepped onto the stage as strong and empowered, eschewing victimization and defining feminine beauty for themselves as subjects, not as objects of a sexist patriarchy. They developed a rhetoric of mimicry, which appropriated derogatory terms like 'slut' and 'bitch' in order to subvert sexist culture and deprive it of verbal weapons" (Rampton, 2015). By the late 1990s, however, " 'girl power,' a slogan that began in the pages of Riot Grrrl 'zines, started being appropriated by pop sensations like the Spice Girls. Some claim this to be the end of the movement" (Feliciano, 2013).

Further Reading

"Brief History of Third-Wave Feminism." 2022. *MasterClass*. Retrieved from https:// www.masterclass.com/articles/third-wave-feminism#a-brief-history-of-thirdwave-feminism.

Feliciano, Stevie. 2013. "The Riot Grrrl Movement." *New York Public Library*. Retrieved from https://www.nypl.org/blog/2013/06/19/riot-grrrl-movement.

Grady, Constance. 2018. "The Waves of Feminism, and Why People Keep Fighting Over Them, Explained." *Vox*, March 20. Retrieved from https://www.vox.com/2018/3/20/16955588/feminism-waves-explained-first-second-third-fourth.

Heywood, Leslie. 2005. *The Women's Movement Today: An Encyclopedia of Third-Wave Feminism*. Westport, CT: Greenwood Press.

Marcus, Sara. 2010. *Girls to the Front: The True Story of the Riot Grrrl Revolution*. New York: Harper Perennial, 14.

Rampton, Martha. 2015. "Four Waves of Feminism." *Pacific University Oregon*. Retrieved from https://www.pacificu.edu/magazine/four-waves-feminism.

Q22: What Were the Most Significant Achievements of the Third Wave?

Answer: The third wave was characterized by its inclusiveness toward people of various ethnicities, gender identities, life experiences, races, and socioeconomic classes. Observers consider this inclusion, along with the emphasis on intersectionality, to be the third wave's most significant legacy. The third wave also supported the rights of nonheterosexual people and transsexuals. Other third-wave elements include the demand for greater availability of gender studies in academic settings and accessibility of online forums for the widespread exchange of information. In addition, a number of strong female figures were represented during the third wave via cultural markers such as movies and television. However, some third-wave rhetoric and policies were criticized by more conservative supporters of women's rights as divisive and counterproductive.

The Facts: Some critics felt that beyond such underpinnings as the riot grrrls, there was little substance to the third wave, if, in fact it was a distinct wave in its own right. One observer said, "The third wave was a diffuse movement without a central goal, and as such, there's no single piece of legislation or major social change that belongs to the third wave the way the 19th Amendment belongs to the first wave or *Roe v. Wade* belongs to the second" (Grady, 2018).

Other observers strongly disagree with that assessment, pointing to important federal legislation that became law during the third wave, such as the Family and Medical Leave Act (FMLA) of 1993. Passage of the FMLA was a significant development for women, since it covered job-protected time away from work for childbirth, tending to a newborn child, and caregiving for an immediate family member with a serious health condition, situations often handled by women.

The following year, in 1994, the provisions of the Violence Against Women Act (VAWA) included establishing the federal Office on Violence Against Women (OVW), designed to provide assistance to communities "to help them create programs, policies, and practices to end sexual assault, domestic violence, dating violence, and stalking" ("About the Office on Violence Against Women," 2016).

Some scholars consider programs such as the FMLA and VAWA to be a third-wave legacy. However, others declare that those programs evolved naturally as a sign of the times and would have come to pass with or without third-wave activism.

There was conservative criticism of the third wave that often pertained to what many considered the outrageousness of the riot grrrls as well as feminist authors, playwrights, and performance artists whom they considered to be overly radical and/or vulgar.

Some who self-identified as conservatives questioned whether there was a place for them in the third wave along with wondering whether there actually was such a thing as "conservative feminism." There were those who argued that conservative feminism indeed had a place in the third wave and could play a significant role. Organizations considered to be conservative in outlook include the Independent Women's Forum, which describes itself as "dedicated to developing and advancing policies that aren't just well intended, but actually enhance freedom, opportunities, and well-being" ("Independent Women's Forum," 2020).

Some sources argue that conservative feminism can be viewed as "equity" feminism, "grounded in free market principles that favor equality of opportunity over equality of outcome" (Ianello, 2010). This concept took hold among some younger conservative women who felt "alienated from feminist-based programs and organizations, such as women's centers on their college campuses" (Ianello, 2010). Feminist activists of the third wave were also sometimes accused of hypocrisy by conservatives. "Feminists accuse the religious right of trying to dictate what a woman should be and how she should think about a vast array of complicated problems," noted Elizabeth Fox-Genovese, a leading voice in the conservative women's movement. "Feminist diversity [in the third wave] does not embrace women who oppose abortion … (or) prefer to stay at home with children" (Fox-Genovese, 1996).

In 2004, the March for Women's Lives took place in Washington, DC. Estimates run from 500,000 to about a million participants. While it was said to be a march for women's rights in general and support for women's reproductive health, the demonstrators "particularly marched in support of abortion rights" (Bonney,

2022). The impetus of the march was to protest rollbacks in the availability of abortion through federal laws such as what was called the Partial-Birth Abortion Ban Act of 2003, which prohibited late termination of pregnancy. While the demonstrators did not attain their goal of repealing that 2003 legislation, "they were successful in showing how strong the support [was] for women's health and reproductive rights" (Bonney, 2022).

Further Reading

"About the Office on Violence against Women." 2016. *U.S. Department of Justice.* Retrieved from https://www.justice.gov/file/29836/download.

Bonney, Shannon. 2022. "March for Women's Lives – Apr 25 2004." Retrieved from https://socialmovements.trinity.duke.edu/actions/march-women%E2%80%99s-lives.

"Family and Medical Leave (FMLA)." n.d. *U.S. Department of Labor.* Retrieved from https://www.dol.gov/general/topic/benefits-leave/fmla#:~:text=The%20Family%20 and%20Medical%20Leave,be%20maintained%20during%20the%20leave.

Fox-Genovese, Elizabeth. 1996. *Feminism Is Not the Story of My Life: How Today's Feminist Elite Has Lost Touch with the Real Concerns of Women.* New York: Doubleday, 30.

Grady, Constance. 2018. "The Waves of Feminism, and Why People Keep Fighting over Them, Explained." *Vox*, March 20. Retrieved from https://www.vox.com/2018/3/20/16955588/feminism-waves-explained-first-second-third-fourth.

Greer, Germaine. 1999. *The Whole Woman.* New York: Knopf.

Heywood, Leslie. 2005. *The Women's Movement Today: An Encyclopedia of Third-Wave Feminism.* Westport, CT: Greenwood Press.

Heywood, Leslie & Drake, Jennifer. 1997. *Third Wave Agenda: Being Feminist, Doing Feminism.* Minneapolis: University of Minnesota Press.

Ianello, Kathleen. 2010. "Women's Leadership and Third-Wave Feminism." *The Cupola.* Retrieved from https://cupola.gettysburg.edu/cgi/viewcontent.cgi?article=1017&context=poliscifac.

"Independent Women's Forum." 2020. *Independent Women's Forum.* Retrieved from https://www.iwf.org/.

Q23: Did the Third Wave Have a Cultural Impact on American Society?

Answer: Along with such legislation as the Family and Medical Leave Act (FMLA) and the Violence Against Women Act (VAWA), a number of observers feel that some of the most significant touchstones of the third wave could be found in its cultural legacy. Several books that were published during the third wave led many people to view women's issues in new ways. Events emerged such as "Take Our Daughters to Work Day" to show girls that they had a place in the workforce (although it was later changed to "Take Our Daughters and Sons to Work Day" after there were objections that it excluded boys). The most wide-ranging cultural impact of the third-wave movement, however, may have been in the world of popular entertainment, as movies and television increasingly presented portraits of strong, powerful girls and women for mass audiences.

The Facts: Like a number of third-wave elements, the riot grrrl trend was a brash response to the anti-feminism that sprang up against the second wave. In the 1970s and 1980s, there had been both males and females who characterized second-wave supporters of women's rights as "shrill, hairy, and unfeminine and no man would ever want them" (Grady, 2018).

Partially in response, some third wavers embraced "girliness," arguing that wearing lipstick did not diminish their commitment to female empowerment. Rather than censuring women for wearing things that brought them pleasure, in the third wave, there was a "growing belief that effective feminism had to recognize both the dangers and the pleasures of the patriarchal structures that create the beauty standard" (Grady, 2018).

Some observers felt that "third-wave feminism had an entirely different way of talking and thinking than the second wave did—but it also lacked the strong cultural momentum that was behind the grand achievements of the second wave" (Grady, 2018). However, others saw significant signposts in American culture that both reflected and reinforced the spirit of the third wave.

One cultural milestone of the third wave was the publication of *The Beauty Myth* by Naomi Wolf. The book was released in 1991, the same year as the Anita Hill hearings, and remained popular throughout the third-wave era. Wolf's bestseller proclaimed that for all their gains into the 1990s, women continued to be trapped in the unrealistic demands of a male-dominated society. She maintained that the quest to be beautiful at all costs spawned self-hatred among females who had been led to believe from an early age that they are unattractive and it is only through buying expensive beauty products that they might be helped.

Wolf claimed that the demand for female attractiveness served financial purposes for the male-dominated beauty industry through profits for manufacturers, advertising dollars for marketers, and revenue for media. In addition, she declared that the societal demand for females to always be attractive also served a political end: "The stronger women were becoming politically, the heavier the ideals of beauty would bear down upon them, mostly in order to distract their energy and undermine their progress" (Wolf, 2002).

Another book cited as a third-wave cultural landmark was Susan Faludi's *Backlash: The Undeclared War Against American Women*, also published in 1991 and popular throughout the third-wave era. Faludi asked why women accounted for two out of three poor Americans. She also asked, "Why are they still far more likely than men to live in poor housing, receive no health insurance, and twice as likely to draw no pension? … Why are almost half of all homeless women … refugees from domestic violence?" (Faludi, 2006).

In 1995, Rebecca Walker, who had coined the term "third wave," published *To Be Real: Telling the Truth and Changing the Face of Feminism*. The book is an early voice for the concept of intersectionality in American society, with Walker stating her assertion that "to be black and female generally placed one outside the power structure" (Walker, 1995).

In an attempt to combat certain perceptions and realities of being female in America's workforce during the third wave, "Take Our Daughters to Work Day" was initiated in 1993. It began as an effort to build confidence in girls and encourage them to explore any career they wished, including ones traditionally dominated by men. However, after objections were raised that the program did not include boys, it was renamed "Take Our Daughters and Sons to Work Day." Some observers felt that changing the event to include boys defeated its purpose, transforming it into a kind of general "Career Day." Some supporters of the original plan felt that by adding boys, it became "very different from the female empowerment program it was initially intended to be … as a way to inspire confidence in young women" (Moses, 2015).

Another kind of cultural milestone that stimulated a strong third-wave reaction was the 1991 movie *Thelma & Louise*, with an Academy Award–winning script written by Callie Khouri. The movie was embraced by many women as a film about both female empowerment and institutionalized gender inequality in America.

Thelma & Louise "took all those feelings of alienation and anger … and turned them into something rebellious, transgressive, iconic, punk rock and mainstream … [the film] dramatized how it felt to be pushed around or underestimated or otherwise relegated to the sidelines" (Chocano, 2011).

One group of third-wave women who fought against being relegated to the sidelines became known as the Guerrilla Girls. Their cultural battlefield was the art world, and their arsenal included what they said were "disruptive headlines, outrageous visuals, and killer statistics to expose gender and ethnic bias and corruption in art, film, politics and pop culture" ("Guerrilla Girls," 2002). In order to remain anonymous, these arts activists (or "guerrillas") wore gorilla masks because they said they wanted to focus on the issues, not on their own artwork, determining that the issues at stake mattered more than individual identities.

Throughout the third wave, the Guerrilla Girls confronted "the idea of a mainstream narrative by revealing the understory, the subtext, the overlooked, and the downright unfair" ("Guerrilla Girls," 2002). They did so through art projects, banners, posters, and videos along with "interventions and exhibitions at art museums, blasting them on their own walls for their bad behavior and discriminatory practices" ("Guerrilla Girls," 2002). One popular poster proclaimed that less than 5 percent of the artists in the Modern Arts section of the Metropolitan Museum of Art in New York were female but 85 percent of the nude artworks depicted women, adding the tagline, "Do women have to be naked to get into the Met Museum?"

Some third wavers commented on the mushrooming of so-called "reality romance" programs on television. In 2003, noting the shows in which female competitors vied for the affections of a male, comedian Wanda Sykes asked, "Are all the feminists in a coma?" (Johnson, 2007, 1). Some saw this type of programming in the 1990s and 2000s as retrograde and sexist "because it represents stereotypes of conniving gold-diggers and because it deploys the motifs of romance—red roses, special meals, lingering gazes, unexpected gifts—in the service of a conservative backlash against women's independence" (Johnson, 2007, 13). Others responded to the remark by Sykes, stating, "All the feminists are not in a coma, but our alertness does not predispose us to a particular stance on reality romance or anything else on television" (Johnson, 2007, 13).

During the third wave, some observers felt that popular culture reflected the ethos of third wavers by being more inclusive of women of various races and ethnicities. Third wavers rejected stereotyped images of females as passive and weak as well as women being portrayed as demanding, domineering, and emasculating. They also rejected the notion that women were sluttish for engaging in sexual activity.

Third wavers preferred to redefine women as assertive, powerful, and in charge of their own sexuality. Icons of the era included entertainers such as Madonna and Queen Latifah, among others. The era also saw a rise in television shows with strong female leads such as *Buffy the Vampire Slayer*, which ran from 1997 to 2003;

Sex and the City (1998–2004); and *Girlfriends* (2000–8). TV characters for younger people included the adventurous *Dora the Explorer* (1999–2006) and the teenage Carly of *iCarly* (2007–12). At PBS, *Sesame Street* featured its first female lead, Abby Cadabby, on the children's educational program in 2006. Popular animated films included those from the Disney production company with a diverse array of strong heroines such as Mulan (*Mulan*, 1998), a Chinese girl, and Tiana (*The Princess and the Frog*, 2009), the Disney studio's first African American princess. "Girl Power" merchandise found its way to stores across the nation.

The March for Women's Lives protest demonstration held on April 25, 2004, at the National Mall in Washington, DC, was seen by some as a watershed third-wave event, with estimates that more than a million people demonstrated across the country. However, others claim that the third wave had settled into a quiet phase by that time, at least as far as the media and general public were concerned. That would change with the onset of what was called the fourth wave of the women's equality movement in the 2010s.

Further Reading

Chocano, Carina. 2011. "Thelma, Louise and All the Pretty Women." *New York Times*, April 24. Retrieved from https://www.nytimes.com/2011/04/24/magazine/mag-24R iff-t.html.

Dow Jones Newswires staff. 2000. "CBS Agrees to Pay $8 Million to Settle Sex-Bias Lawsuit." *Wall Street Journal*, October 25. Retrieved from https://www.wsj.com/artic les/SB972503778606216326.

Faludi, Susan. 2006. *Backlash: The Undeclared War against American Women*. Unabridged anniversary edition. New York: Crown.

Grady, Constance. 2018. "The Waves of Feminism, and Why People Keep Fighting over Them, Explained." *Vox*, March 20. Retrieved from https://www.vox. com/2018/3/20/16955588/feminism-waves-explained-first-second-third-fourth.

"Guerrilla Girls: Reinventing The 'F' Word: Feminism." 2002. *Guerrilla Girls*. Retrieved from https://www.guerrillagirls.com/our-story.

Johnson, Merri Lisa. 2007. *Third Wave Feminism and Television: Jane Puts It in a Box*. New York: I.B. Tauris.

Moses, Michele. 2015. "Erasing Feminism from Take Our Daughters to Work Day." *The New Yorker*, May 13. Retrieved from https://www.newyorker.com/business/curre ncy/erasing-feminism-from-take-our-daughters-to-work-day.

"Thelma & Louise." n.d. *Internet Movie Database*. Retrieved from https://www.imdb. com/title/tt0103074/.

Walker, Rebecca. 1995. *To Be Real: Telling the Truth and Changing the Face of Feminism.* New York: Anchor Books.

Waxman, Olivia. 2017. "The Inside Story of Why Take Your Daughter to Work Day Exists." *Time*, April 26. Retrieved from https://time.com/4753128/take-your-our-daughters-to-work-day-history/.

Wolf, Naomi. 2002. *The Beauty Myth: How Images of Beauty Are Used against Women.* Reprint edition. New York: Harper Perennial.

Q24: Was the Fourth Wave the Same Thing as the #MeToo Movement?

Answer: For much of the general public, the fourth wave of feminism centered on the widespread attention surrounding the #MeToo movement. #MeToo had been launched in the United States in 2006 to focus attention on predatory sexual behavior by men in positions of power against women The fourth wave is also known for encompassing #TimesUp, which was officially founded in 2018 to confront sexual misconduct and harassment in the workplace. Other defining characteristics of the fourth wave included extensive use of social media in stimulating new types of widespread activism, identifying and addressing layers of oppression and discrimination experienced by women, and encouraging solidarity among girls and women of different ages, ethnicities, gender identities, and races.

One landmark event in the history of the fourth wave was the Women's March of January 21, 2017, an international protest event held the day after the inauguration of Donald Trump, who had issued numerous misogynistic statements during his election campaign the previous year. The Women's March brought together millions of participants around the world and attracted an estimated 470,000 participants in Washington, DC. The gathering, which was three times the size of the crowd that attended Trump's inauguration, was the largest single-day protest in US history (Wallace, 2017).

The Facts: Activist Tarana Burke (1973–), founder of the MeToo Movement, was a director of a youth camp when one of the girls at the camp privately disclosed that she had been the victim of sexual abuse. As a survivor of sexual abuse herself, Burke did not feel she responded the way she really wanted to, which was to say, "Me too." This moment became "the foundation for the 'Me Too' movement she created … using the phrase 'me too' to promote the idea of 'empowerment through empathy'" (Alexander, 2020).

Burke developed the concept through the mid-2000s, a period coinciding with the advent of internet social media platforms such as Facebook (2004), YouTube (2005), and Twitter (2006). With Google rising to become the dominant search engine in the 2000s, information could easily be located online and shared. Burke's #MeToo advocacy campaign became widely known during this period. In 2017, the #MeToo hashtag went viral, spreading like wildfire on social media after a series of explosive revelations about powerful men who used their positions in politics, business, and entertainment to harass and assault women. The first such scandal involved Hollywood producer Harvey Weinstein, who was accused of using his power to sexually exploit women for more than thirty years. In the wake of almost a hundred women coming forward to accuse Weinstein, millions of people around the world, both in person and on social media, publicly shared their own individual experiences with sexual assault and harassment.

The Weinstein scandal was a turning point in part because it became clear that the producer's predations on women were well-known in the entertainment industry. At the 2013 presentation of the Academy Awards, comedian Seth MacFarlane read the names of the five women who were nominated for Best Supporting Actress adding, "Congratulations, you five ladies no longer have to pretend to be attracted to Harvey Weinstein" (Harris, 2017). The quip, which MacFarlane later said came from "a place of anger," was followed by sustained, knowing laughter from the audience.

One year after that, in 2014, popular entertainer Bill Cosby was accused of having been a long-time sexual predator, allegedly responsible for using his power in the entertainment industry to drug and assault a number of women. His 2017 trial ended in a mistrial. At retrial in 2018, he was found guilty of aggravated indecent assault and was sentenced to three to ten years in state prison. However, in 2021, the Pennsylvania Supreme Court released him based on a ruling that the prosecutor who brought the case to trial was bound by a previous district attorney's agreement not to charge Cosby—even though there was no evidence that the agreement was put in writing.

In random attacks in 2014, six students at the University of California in Santa Barbara were murdered and fourteen others injured—both male and female—by a killer who had posted an online video about punishing women for rejecting him as well as attacking sexually active men because he envied them. In an internet "manifesto," he expressed his hatred of women, a desire to seek retribution for not having a girlfriend, and contempt for couples, particularly those who were interracial.

As a response, the #YesAllWomen public education campaign was launched on social media to share examples of violence against women and to rally support for laws and policies to combat these crimes.

Also in 2014, a scandal that came to be known as GamerGate had "toxic fans harassing the creators of feminist computer games that decreased the violence against women" (Frankel, 2019). In a harassment campaign against women who objected to female stereotypes and gender violence in video games, the women were inundated with death threats and threats of rape and other sexual violence. GamerGate was said to be a manifestation of what was called the men's rights movement, which "itself became a hallmark of the new fourth wave. 'Toxic masculinity' and 'rape culture' became buzzwords for a new era" (Frankel, 2019).

In the aftermath of the Weinstein scandal, about 700,000 primarily Hispanic women represented by the Alianza Nacional de Campesinas (National Alliance of Women Farmworkers) from across the country wrote an open letter supporting those who became known as the "Silence Breakers" in Hollywood. These often-unheard female farmworkers shared personal experiences similar to those who came forward against Weinstein: "As you cope with scrutiny and criticism because you have bravely chosen to speak out against the harrowing acts that were committed against you, please know that you're not alone. We believe and stand with you" (Alianza Nacional de Campesinas, 2017).

Others had a different viewpoint. Author Germaine Greer commented on the #MeToo movement by stating that if a woman submitted to a powerful man "because he said, 'Be nice to me and I'll give you a job in a movie,' then I'm afraid that's tantamount to consent, and it's too late now to start whining about that" (Thomas, 2018).

Along with massive exposure on social media, women's anger and frustration with continued gender-based social inequities were given voice in several significant books of the fourth wave. One author, Rebecca Solnit in *Men Explain Things to Me* (2015), wrote about her contention that women were still subjected to marginalizing and patriarchal attitudes and actions from men. She maintained that these realities have "trampled down many women … this is the same power that silences and erases and annihilates women" (Solnit, 2015).

In 2012, conservative US congressman Todd Akin made a public statement that there was no need to permit abortion for the termination of pregnancy due to rape, "because if it's a legitimate rape, the female body has ways to try to shut the whole thing down" (Associated Press, 2021). When medical and scientific experts strongly refuted his statement as patently false, Akin apologized for having "misspoken" but later retracted the apology. Some fourth-wave writers, such as Jessica Valenti in 2017's *Sex Object*, expressed incredulousness that such attitudes continued to exist, stating, "We still have no name for what happens to women living in a culture that hates them" (Valenti, 2017).

One of the landmark events of the fourth wave was the Women's March in Washington, DC on January 21, 2017, the day after the inauguration of US President Donald Trump, who had made inflammatory comments about women, especially those who had accused him of sexual misconduct toward them. The march was characterized by historians as the largest single-day demonstration in US history. Outside Washington, more than 650 individual protest marches took place across the country, with a total average estimate of about 4 million people participating. Similar events were held in many nations around the world as well.

The following year, in 2018, Brett Kavanaugh was nominated by Trump to fill the vacancy on the US Supreme Court left by the retirement of Anthony Kennedy. After a woman, Christine Blasey Ford, testified before the Senate Judiciary Committee and alleged past sexual misconduct by Kavanaugh, which he denied, the Republican-controlled committee voted 11–10 along party lines to report Kavanaugh's nomination to the full Senate. Observers noted that all of the four women (all Democrats) on the twenty-one-person Judiciary Committee voted against his nomination. In the Senate, Kavanaugh was narrowly confirmed to a lifetime seat on the Supreme Court by a vote of 50–48.

By that time, many observers shared the opinion that a full-fledged fourth wave of the women's equality movement was already in force, with its own distinct characteristics. Most young women did not know a time when the internet was not a dominant fact of life. Therefore, among the distinguishing characteristics of the fourth wave, many sources would place the internet and its attendant social media platforms as the most significant.

Not only could fourth wavers share information and organize global campaigns online, but the internet allowed new means of organization and activism. It was possible to publicly accuse powerful figures for alleged sexual misconduct, which many felt was a way for traditionally disempowered women to have their voices heard. Therefore, through the use of the internet, the fourth wave has been known for its ability to shine a light on cases of alleged predatory sexual behavior by powerful men. In the past, such incidents were often kept in the dark, generally going unknown by the vast majority.

Another distinguishing characteristic of the fourth wave has been its emphasis on expanding the concept of intersectionality. The theory of intersectionality had been a cornerstone of the third wave and became a continuing theme of the fourth. Along with what intersectionality adherents called various modes of oppression such as class, race, and sexual identity, the fourth wave probed the connection between layers of oppression and the prevalence of violence against women in situations where they coexist.

Some sources also include solidarity as a facet of the fourth wave. Its adherents often tend to see themselves as partners across lines of age, ethnicity, nationality, race, and gender identities. As one scholar put it, a strength of the fourth wave is because "the millennials' articulation of themselves as 'feminists' is their own: not a hand-me-down from grandma. The beauty of the fourth wave is that there is a place in it for all—together" (Rampton, 2015).

However, there was also criticism of the fourth wave. Writing in *The American Conservative*, one critic argues that "women—specifically feminists—are now in positions of power across the whole of society" (Williams, 2018). That writer said that when women believe the odds are stacked against them in a patriarchal society, they look to the government and the legal system for help, abandoning other efforts instead of competing with men as equals, adding, "Women's disadvantage thus becomes a self-fulfilling prophecy" (Williams, 2018).

Others expressed concerns that the efforts of the fourth wave were concentrated on those who have access to the internet, can afford digital devices, and are able to use the system effectively, especially in regions of the world where free communication is restricted and efforts toward social justice are repressed. These critics allege that activists need to do more to reach and represent poor women without access to these resources.

Some observers, including women's rights advocates, have expressed frustration:

> "Slacktivists [who] wait for others to make the change that we so desperately need … as if they don't have time to volunteer or be an integral part of the movement, [and just] continue on with their day, 'liking' other posts or re-tweeting" (Guardado, 2015). Other critics had issues with the increasingly contentious atmosphere of the internet itself as it pertained to the women's equality movement. One self-described feminist called it "time to question the hypocritical, petty *Mean Girls* atmosphere of fourth-wave feminism today. … Feminism is supposed to be inclusive, not alienating." (Simpkins, 2014)

In what became a national news story, Katie Way, a twenty-two-year-old *Babe. net* reporter, slammed television journalist Ashleigh Banfield as "someone who I am certain nobody under the age of 45 has ever heard of … [and] a burgundy-lipstick, bad-highlights, second-wave-feminist has-been" (Tani, 2018). Banfield, a former war correspondent, replied that insulting a woman's age, hair, and so on was "the last thing you should do. … That is not the way we have this conversation as women or men" (Hassan, 2018).

Fourth-wave scholarship has emphasized attempts to spotlight women who have been traditionally erased from history and the arts, such as seventeenth-century Italian painter Artemisia Gentileschi, whose works have either been ignored or attributed to males in major museums for centuries. Other artists whose work has been championed by the fourth wave include nineteenth-century sculptor Edmonia Lewis, who had been kidnapped, beaten, and left to die by a white mob but went on to become "the first sculptor of African American and Native American descent to achieve international recognition" ("American Women Artists," n.d.).

In the film industry, some women took action during the fourth wave, including filing official complaints of discrimination with the Equal Employment Opportunity Commission (EEOC).

However, some film scholars have seen a degree of progress for women during the fourth wave. This came via the depiction of women's roles in major motion pictures compared to those of the past, so that contemporary women "could be strong without being campy, ludicrous, or underdressed" (Frankel, 2019).

Fourth-wave film scholars also unearthed females who were important contributors to the movie industry in the past but who have generally been forgotten. One was early-twentieth-century filmmaker Alice Guy-Blaché, who made a short comedy about gender role reversal in 1906 that gained an entirely new cadre of fans in the fourth wave. *The Consequences of Feminism* presents a fictional world in which men are subservient, acting as housekeepers and caretakers for children. The women sexually harass and abuse the males, leading to the men rebelling. That uprising by the males is followed by the patriarchal order of society being restored to men. It was a significant link between the first wave of the women's equality movement and the fourth more than a century later. One contemporary film scholar states that "to accept the ending is to admit that half the world's population is currently subject to a raw deal" (Malone, 2022).

During the fourth wave, two national museums dedicated to contributions by women were publicly announced as being in the works. Plans for the privately funded National Women's History Museum (NWHM) originated in 1996 to fundamentally change the way women and girls see their potential and power. In addition to the online NWHM, a physical version exists at the Martin Luther King branch of the Washington, DC Library system. It will be merged with the Smithsonian at some point in the future, though a target date has not been specified by either group.

Also in the nation's capital, the Smithsonian Institution announced plans to build the American Women's History Museum (AWHM) to recognize women's accomplishments and history. In 2020, Congress enacted legislation to create the museum, although Smithsonian officials estimate it "will be at least ten years before physical buildings are open" ("Smithsonian American Women's History Museum," n.d.).

Both museum initiatives currently provide online programming and classroom packets, which they intend to do even after permanent buildings are constructed. In that way, they feel that women's history and significance can be accessed worldwide. Many fourth-wave observers applaud these developments in their attempt to illuminate the contributions of women, many of which have often been erased in the past.

Further Reading

"About the National Women's History Museum." n.d. *National Women's History Museum.* Retrieved from https://www.womenshistory.org/about-national-womens-history-museum.

Alexander, Kerri Lee. 2020. "Tarana Burke." *National Women's History Museum.* Retrieved from https://www.womenshistory.org/education-resources/biographies/tarana-burke.

Alianza Nacional de Campesinas. 2017. "700,000 Female Farmworkers Say They Stand With Hollywood Actors Against Sexual Assault." *Alianza Nacional de Campesinas.* Retrieved from https://www.alianzanacionaldecampesinas.org/news?offset=156183 4596648.

"American Women Artists." n.d. *Smithsonian.* Retrieved from https://www.si.edu/spotli ght/women-artists.

Associated Press. 2021. "Ex-U.S. Rep. Todd Akin, Sunk by 'Legitimate Rape' Remark, Dies." *Politico*, October 4. Retrieved from https://www.politico.com/news/2021/10/04/todd-akin-dies-514988.

Chenoweth, Erica & Pressman, Jeremy. 2017. "This Is What We Learned by Counting the Women's Marches." *Washington Post*, February 7. Retrieved from https://www.washingtonpost.com/news/monkey-cage/wp/2017/02/07/this-is-what-we-lear ned-by-counting-the-womens-marches/.

"'Consequences of Feminism' (1906)—Alice Guy Blaché." 2012. *YouTube.* Retrieved from https://www.youtube.com/watch?v=dQ-oB6HHttU.

"Feminism: The Fourth Wave." 2021. *National Women's History Museum*. Retrieved from https://www.womenshistory.org/exhibits/feminism-fourth-wave.

"Fourth-Wave Feminism Explained." 2022. *MasterClass*. Retrieved from https://www.masterclass.com/articles/fourth-wave-feminism.

Frankel, Valerie. 2019. *Fourth Wave Feminism in Science Fiction and Fantasy: Volume 1. Essays on Film Representations, 2012–2019*. Jefferson, NC: McFarland. Kindle edition.

Guardado, Alex. 2015. "Hashtag Activism: The Benefits and Limitations of #Activism." *New University, University of California, Irvine*, March 3. Retrieved from https://newuniversity.org/2015/03/03/hashtag-activism-the-benefits-and-limitations-of-activism.

Harris, Hunter. 2017. "Seth MacFarlane Explains His Weinstein Joke at the Oscars." *Vulture*, October 11. https://www.vulture.com/2017/10/seth-macfarlane-harvey-weinstein-joke-at-the-oscars.html.

Hassan, Mohamed. 2018. "Reporter behind Ansari Story Slams HLN Host's Looks in Scathing Email." *New York Post*, January 17. Retrieved from https://nypost.com/2018/01/17/reporter-behind-ansari-story-criticizes-hln-hosts-looks-in-scathing-email/.

Malone, Alicia. 2022. *The Female Gaze: Essential Movies Made by Women*. Coral Gables, FL: Mango Publishing. Kindle edition.

"Nomination of Brett Kavanaugh to the U.S. Supreme Court." n.d. *Ballotpedia*. Retrieved from https://ballotpedia.org/Nomination_of_Brett_Kavanaugh_to_the_U.S._Supreme_Court.

Rampton, Martha. 2015. "Four Waves of Feminism." *Pacific University Oregon*. Retrieved from https://www.pacificu.edu/magazine/four-waves-feminism.

Simpkins, Jennifer. 2014. "'You Can't Sit with Us!'—How Fourth-Wave Feminism Became 'Mean Girls.'" *Huffington Post*, January 19. Retrieved from https://www.huffingtonpost.co.uk/jennifer-simpkins/feminism-fourth-wave-became-mean-girls_b_4616597.html.

"Smithsonian American Women's History Museum." n.d. *Smithsonian*. Retrieved from https://www.si.edu/unit/american-womens-history-museum.

Solnit, Rebecca. 2015. *Men Explain Things to Me*. Chicago, IL: Haymarket Books. Kindle edition.

Tani, Maxwell. 2018. "Read the Email the Writer behind the Aziz Ansari Sexual Misconduct Story Wrote Slamming an HLN Anchor Who Criticized Her." *Business Insider*, January 17. Retrieved from https://www.businessinsider.com/aziz-ansari-writer-email-to-hln-ashleigh-banfield-2018-1.

Thomas, Holly. 2018. "Germaine Greer's Dangerous Ideas about Rape." *CNN*, June 2. Retrieved from https://www.cnn.com/2018/06/02/opinions/germaine-greer-comments-on-rape-thomas/index.html.

Valenti, Jessica. 2017. *Sex Object: A Memoir*. New York: Dey Street Books.

Ventresca, Rachel. 2018. "Here's How the Senate Judiciary Committee Voted." *CNN*, September 28. Retrieved from https://www.cnn.com/2018/09/28/politics/kavana ugh-judiciary-committee-votes/index.html.

Wallace, Tim, and Alicia Parlapiano. 2017. "Crowd Scientists Say Women's March in Washington Had Three Times as Many People as Trump's Inauguration." *New York Times*. March 13.

Williams, Joanna. 2018. "Fourth Wave Feminism: Why No One Escapes." *The American Conservative*, September 4. Retrieved from https://www.theamericanconservative. com/articles/fourth-wave-feminismwhy-no-one-escapes/.

5

Women's Equality and Intersectionality

The term "intersectionality" was coined in 1989 by Dr. Kimberlé Crenshaw (1959–), a professor of law at Columbia University and UCLA. Crenshaw presented the theory in the *University of Chicago Legal Forum*, an academic journal, to describe the ways in which class, race, gender, and other characteristics of an individual overlap and impact one another. Scholars note, however, that the basic concept of intersectionality was actually voiced in the 1800s with advocates of equality such as Sojourner Truth, who was both a woman and of African descent.

In her academic paper, Crenshaw construed the theory of intersectionality as a legal term. It remained in relative obscurity outside academic and judicial circles until the early 2000s, when the concept began to attract increased attention. The term "intersectionality" first appeared in the *Oxford English Dictionary* in 2015, where it was described as the "interconnected nature of social categorizations such as race, class, and gender, regarded as creating overlapping and interdependent systems of discrimination or disadvantage; a theoretical approach based on such a premise."

In its most basic terms, intersectionality defines the way in which the life experiences of a Black woman, for example, will differ from those of a Black man or a white woman. Those who oppose the concept agree that people from different backgrounds may encounter the world in different ways. Today, discussions of intersectionality tend to encompass three issues: what Crenshaw intended by the term, how the theory is interpreted, and why there are concerns about its uses and implications.

Q25: Is Intersectionality a New Concept?

Answer: Primarily due to the massive reach of the internet, the word and the concept of intersectionality have become better known to the general public since Kimberlé Crenshaw's foundational 1989 piece. However, some historians assert that while the word itself is new, the concept is not. Some point to the *Combahee River Collective Statement* of 1977, which addressed "interlocking oppressions." Some trace the concept even further back in American history, noting the 1851 "Ain't I a Woman" speech by Sojourner Truth, which is often cited as one of the earliest known explorations of the conjunction of race and gender. The efforts of Harriet Tubman, Matilda Joslyn Gage, and Ida B. Wells-Barnett in the 1800s and early 1900s are also seen as precursors to the contemporary concept of intersectionality.

The Facts: As coined by Kimberlé Crenshaw in 1989, intersectionality is basically defined as an individual dealing not only with one form of oppression but with several forms, "which link together TO make a double, triple, multiple, many layered blanket of oppression" (National Conference for Community and Justice, 2022). Activists such as Audre Lorde (1934–1992) have pointed to intersectionality as vital to understanding the complex lives of women: "There is no such thing as a single-issue struggle, because we do not live single-issue lives" (Springate, 2016).

Crenshaw's groundbreaking study, "Demarginalizing the Intersection of Race and Sex: A Black Feminist Critique of Antidiscrimination Doctrine, Feminist Theory and Antiracist Politics," begins with observations on the life experience of African American women: "Because the intersectional experience is greater than the sum of racism and sexism, any analysis that does not take intersectionality into account cannot sufficiently address the particular manner in which Black women are subordinated" (Crenshaw, 2016, 140). Since the article was in a legal journal, Crenshaw expressed her thesis in the context of the law, stating that in judicial matters, "the entire framework that has been used as a basis for translating 'women's experience' or 'the Black experience' into concrete policy demands must be rethought and recast" (Crenshaw, 2016, 140).

Therefore, according to Crenshaw, both the word and the concept of intersectionality attempt to illustrate how the various aspects of a person combine to create different layers of discrimination and/or privilege. Under the umbrella of the theory of intersectionality, some of the multiple factors that determine a person's relative advantage and disadvantage include appearance, citizenship, disability, ethnicity, gender, height, weight, race, religion, sexuality, and socioeconomic class. The way they intersect and overlap often determines a person's life experience by either being empowering or oppressive, or perhaps varying degrees of both. Many observers have criticized the first and second waves of the women's equality movement for their focus on women who were white, heterosexual, and middle to upper class. Defenders of first- and second-wave activists, however, often claim that this focus was based on pragmatism, claiming that the only way advocates of women's rights felt they could achieve their goal was to avoid antagonizing the all-male white lawmakers. Others believe that the *Declaration of Sentiments* at the Seneca Falls Convention of 1848, which included a demand for female suffrage, ironically would not have passed if it had not been for the eloquent speech of an African American, Frederick Douglass, "the only man there who knew what it was to be disenfranchised" (DuBois, 2020).

According to some scholars, suffragists Susan B. Anthony and Elizabeth Cady Stanton first pursued the abolitionist goal of equality for all, with voting rights for Black men and all American women. However, in 1867, a pair of referenda in Kansas, one for Black suffrage and another for female suffrage, were both defeated. After that, Stanton and Anthony excluded African American women from their efforts, narrowing their focus to mainstream whites "as they desperately sought some way to win the vote. ... [In doing so] the coalition across race and gender lines was shattered" (Dudden, 2014).

The concept of intersectionality, however, was actually being discussed more than a century before Crenshaw's study. In 1832, Maria W. Stewart (1803–1879) became the first known African American woman to make public speeches about the intersection of female equality as the issue pertained to women of color. "It was extremely rare for women to give public addresses in the early 19th century, especially in front of a 'promiscuous audience'—one that contained both men and women. Many people considered it improper and even immoral" ("Maria W. Stewart," 2021).

The mid-nineteenth century was an era when it was precarious for Black women to voice such beliefs, although there were some small, tenuous steps toward inclusion and intersectionality, if only for the sake of expedience. In 1854, when a group of white female students at Ohio's Oberlin College met to discuss women's rights, "given the strength of men's commitment to maintaining their political monopoly ... [the white women] were so afraid of official intervention that they met in a Black woman's home on the outskirts of town" (DuBois, 1999).

Before becoming known for her work freeing enslaved people via the Underground Railroad, Harriet Tubman (ca. 1820–1913) also supported women's voting rights, giving speeches on abolitionism and women's suffrage in the 1850s. The original text of her intersectional speeches is often difficult to determine due to her need to speak under false names for fear of being captured and sold into bondage under the Fugitive Slave Act. That very fact would tend to suggest she sought her rights to be protected both as a female and as a Black person.

After the Civil War, other intersectional voices were heard. Anna Julia Haywood Cooper (1859–1964), sometimes called the Mother of Black Feminism, had been born into slavery but became an influential author and scholar. A century before the term intersectionality rose to the forefront of academic inquiry, Cooper stated that Black women faced both "a woman question and a race problem, and as a result they were unknown or unacknowledged in both" (Carey, 2021).

Frances Ellen Watkins Harper (1870–1911) invoked the reality of the status of African American women through her poems and essays. In her pursuit of equal rights, employment opportunities, and especially education for Black women, Harper was focused on women's suffrage as those issues interconnected with race. She had a unique perspective, having been born in 1825 to free Black parents in Maryland. As a young woman, though, Maryland passed highly restrictive laws targeting free Blacks. Harper spent many years in the late 1800s and early 1900s delivering lectures and writing about the condition of Black women in the United States.

During the same era, Ida B. Wells-Barnett (1862–1931) fought both racism and sexism. As a suffrage leader who was African American, she encountered such slights as Black women being told to march at the back of the 1913 Suffrage Parade in Washington. Wells-Barnett saw the two issues of feminism and racism as inextricable. The murder of a friend led her to become an activist fighting the widespread practice of lynching. Over time, she spearheaded a national campaign to pass anti-lynching laws. Drawing on her background in social work, Wells-Barnett considered multiple points of oppression—including those erected by other women. As one scholar observed, "white female Temperance organizers used stereotypes of Black drunkenness and violence. Wells called out the impact this had not only on Black men but Black women who were otherwise involved in the movement" (Russell, 2021).

Historical efforts in the 1800s and early 1900s regarding what later came to be known as intersectionality pertained to other groups as well. Matilda Joslyn Gage (1826–1898) was a longtime advocate of women's suffrage, abolitionism, and the struggles of Native American women. In 1886, Gage became known nationwide for leading a protest at the unveiling of the Statue of Liberty in New York Harbor. She denounced the hypocrisy of portraying Liberty as a woman when real-life American women were denied their rights.

Gage credited the influence of Haudenosaunee (Iroquois) women in the formation of American democracy by the Founding Fathers, although basic rights were denied to Native people. Gage also stirred controversy for her direct way of confronting power, such as criticizing organized Christianity for its role in oppressing women. After America erupted into civil war in 1861, Gage declared there would be no "permanent peace in this country until there is absolute equality for every group, rich and poor, men and women, native born, immigrant." As one scholar observed, Cage was essentially "naming intersectionality in 1862" (Rios, 2021).

Gage's insistence on inclusion and intersectionality did not endear her to white women contemporaries in the women's rights movement, particularly in what was later published as the official documentation of the history of the suffrage campaign by Susan B. Anthony and Elizabeth Cady Stanton. Because of her activism in espousing equality for all, "Matilda Joslyn Gage was a suffrage leader who was erased from history by her own compatriots" (Rios, 2021).

Still, Gage is recognized today for her efforts to illuminate the achievements of women. In 2013, American scientist Margaret Rossiter coined a phrase, "the Matilda Effect," in honor of Gage, whose work "was overlooked by historians, and who also wrote about the way women scientists, in particular, had been erased by history" (Dominus, 2019).

The concept of intersectionality was championed in the mid-twentieth century by civil rights attorney Pauli Murray (1910–1985), an African American woman who felt that "differences of culture, appearance, nationality, religion, or any other human circumstance were sources of enrichment, not barriers to human intercourse" (Murray, 2018). When Murray began her legal studies at Howard University, a historically Black institution, she was the only woman in her law school class. On the first day, a professor remarked that he did not know why women went to law school, infuriating her. In response, Murray coined the phrase "Jane Crow," a gendered allusion to the racial discrimination against Blacks under the Jim Crow system in the South. Murray later angered many in the 1960s by publicly criticizing the sexism of the civil rights movement.

During the 1970s, when the second wave was evolving, the Combahee River Collective in Boston was an organization of Black feminist lesbians. The Collective, which was active from 1974 to 1980, argued that neither mainstream feminism nor the civil rights movement were addressing their particular needs since they encountered racism, sexism, and homophobia. The group's name reflected an early fighter for Black women, Harriet Tubman, by commemorating an 1863 action at the Combahee River in South Carolina. Although it is little known in comparison to other Civil War battles, it was planned and led by Tubman, "the only woman known to have led a military operation during the American Civil War" (Leichner, 2012). More than seven hundred enslaved people were freed, including one hundred Black men who subsequently joined the Union Army.

Over a century later, the members of the Combahee River Collective are best known for issuing the *Combahee River Collective Statement* of 1977. It notes the individual's "specific social location within interlocking webs of power and privilege. … Different strands of injustice—racism, sexism, heterosexism, classism, xenophobia, trans-hatred, ageism and others—are completely interwoven" (Jones, Eubanks, & Smith, 2014). Today's concept of intersectionality is often said to have found its contemporary origins in the *Combahee River Collective Statement* with its denunciation of "interlocking oppressions."

The intersectionality concept gained widespread attention during the Women's March of 2017. At that time, the event's organizers particularly emphasized what they considered to be women's intersecting identities and how they factor into various human rights and social justice issues. For their part, conservative critics such as scholar Sumantra Maitra have condemned intersectionality as "the latest fad" and attacked it for "peddling pseudoscientific gibberish" (Maitra, 2017).

Further Reading

Carey, Mia L. 2021. "Dr. Anna Julia Cooper." In *Exploring the Meaning of Black Womanhood Series: Hidden Figures in NPS Places*. National Park Service. Retrieved from https://www.nps.gov/people/dr-anna-julia-cooper-1859-1964.htm.

Coaston, Jane. 2019. "The Intersectionality Wars." *Vox*, May 20. Retrieved from https://www.vox.com/the-highlight/2019/5/20/18542843/intersectionality-conservat ism-law-race-gender-discrimination.

Crenshaw, Kimberlé. 1989. "Demarginalizing the Intersection of Race and Sex: A Black Feminist Critique of Antidiscrimination Doctrine, Feminist Theory and Antiracist Politics." *University of Chicago Legal Forum*, vol. 1, no. 8: 139–67. Retrieved from https://chicagounbound.uchicago.edu/cgi/viewcontent.cgi?article=1052&cont ext=uclf.

Dominus, Susan. 2019. "Women Scientists Were Written Out of History. It's Margaret Rossiter's Lifelong Mission to Fix That." *Smithsonian*, October. Retrieved from https://www.smithsonianmag.com/science-nature/unheralded-women-scientists-finally-getting-their-due-.

DuBois, Ellen Carol. 2020. *Suffrage: Women's Long Battle for the Vote.* New York: Simon & Schuster.

DuBois, Ellen Carol. 1999. *Feminism and Suffrage: The Emergence of an Independent Women's Movement in America, 1848–1869.* Ithaca, NY: Cornell University Press.

Dudden, Faye. 2014. *Fighting Chance: The Struggle over Woman Suffrage and Black Suffrage in Reconstruction America.* New York: Oxford University Press.

"Frances Ellen Watkins Harper." 2021. *National Park Service.* Retrieved from https://www.nps.gov/places/frances-ellen-watkins-harper-house.htm.

National Conference for Community and Justice, "Intersectionality." 2022. Retrieved from https://www.nccj.org/intersectionality.

Jones, Alethia, Eubanks, Virginia, & Smith, Barbara. 2014. *Ain't Gonna Let Nobody Turn Me Around: Forty Years of Movement Building with Barbara Smith.* Albany: State University of New York Press.

"Kimberlé W. Crenshaw." 2022. *Columbia Law School.* Retrieved from https://www.law.columbia.edu/faculty/kimberle-w-crenshaw.

Leichner, Helen, 2012. "Combahee River Raid (June 2, 1863)." *BlackPast.org.* Retrieved from https://www.blackpast.org/african-american-history/combahee-river-raid-june-2-1863/.

Maitra, Sumantra. 2017. "Intersectionality and Popper's Paradox." *Quillette.* Retrieved from https://quillette.com/2017/11/06/intersectionality-poppers-paradox/.

"Maria W. Stewart." 2021. *National Park Service.* Retrieved from https://www.nps.gov/people/maria-w-stewart.htm#:~:text=It%20was%20extremely%20rare%20for,called%20for%20in%20her%20speeches.

Murray. Pauli. 2018. *Song in a Weary Throat: Memoir of an American Pilgrimage.* New York: Liveright.

Rios, Carmen. 2021. "A Courageous Retelling: Rooting Feminist History in Intersectionality." *A Different Point of View, National Women's History Museum,* Winter, 6–11.

Rosenberg, Rosalind. 2017. *Jane Crow: The Life of Pauli Murray.* New York: Oxford University Press.

Russell, Alison. 2021. "Learning with Ida B. Wells Barnett." *National Park Service.* Retrieved from https://www.nps.gov/articles/000/learning-with-ida-b-wells-barnett.htm.

Springate, Megan. 2016. "A Note about Intersectionality." *National Park Service.* Retrieved from https://www.nps.gov/articles/lgbtqtheme-intersectionality.htm.

Wanger, Sally Roesch. 2019. *The Women's Suffrage Movement.* New York: Penguin Classics.

Waters, Kristin. 2021. *Maria W. Stewart and the Roots of Black Political Thought.* Jackson: University Press of Mississippi.

Q26: How Did Intersectionality Impact the Suffrage Movement?

Answer: In 1920, American women were granted the right to vote through the 19th Amendment to the US Constitution. This amendment stated that discrimination in voting rights on the basis of gender was prohibited. In practice, however, it did not eliminate discrimination and barriers to suffrage that many American women faced—especially if they were African American, Asian American, Hispanic, and Native American. Confronted with racially discriminatory policies, laws, and attitudes, these women faced a far more difficult path to exercising their voting rights than many of their white counterparts.

The Facts: The 19th Amendment to the US Constitution reads, "*The right of citizens of the United States to vote shall not be denied or abridged by the United States or by any State on account of sex.*" On the surface, the text would seem to be straightforward. However, the reality was more complex for millions of American women of color burdened by laws that explicitly discriminated on the basis of race.

When the 19th Amendment was enacted in 1920, there were approximately 26 million women in the United States, about half the country's population. Some Native Americans were not considered to be citizens of the United States in 1920, thus barring them from the opportunity to vote. The notorious Dawes Act of 1887 divided certain Indian reservations into small individual allotments for the residents, selling the remaining land to white settlers. The act "provided an avenue for citizenship, but only for those Indians who accepted allotments and completely abandoned their tribe and adopted Anglo culture" (McCool, Olson, & Robinson, 2007).

Scholars note that a few early white suffragists, including Matilda Joslyn Gage, studied indigenous societies such as the Haudenosaunee (Iroquois) as an example of a democratic system in which all community members, both male and female, enjoyed equality. That model is said to have influenced the creation of the US government after America won its independence from England. In those Native societies, women were considered equal to males.

However, democracy—as it was established in early America by the Founding Fathers—did not enfranchise women or grant females the same rights as males. Most of the overwhelmingly white first-wave suffragists did not include Native American women in the quest for the vote.

Native American women: From the earliest days of the nation, Native American activists continued to press for their right to citizenship and the attendant right to vote. The Snyder Act in 1924 granted citizenship to Native Americans born in the United States, theoretically enabling them to vote. However, some states denied voting rights to Native Americans through the use of loopholes, such as claiming that tribal affiliations barred them from full citizenship. In 1948, this practice was struck down among most states, although as late as 1962, individual states often found grounds to deny the vote to Native Americans by such means as claiming that people who lived on a reservation were not residents of that state. In addition, "American Indians, like African Americans and other minorities, faced barriers to voting such as poll taxes, literacy tests and intimidation" (Johnson, 2020).

Asian American women: Many Asian Americans faced a situation that was similar to that of indigenous people in their inability to become citizens, which meant that they could not vote. A series of federal laws dating back to the 1800s such as the Page Act of 1875 and the Chinese Exclusion Act of 1882 denied them a path to citizenship.

When women's suffrage was enacted as part of the US Constitution in 1920, Mabel Ping-Hua Lee (1896–1966) was already known as a supporter of the rights of women and an advocate for Chinese people in America. Although Lee was a popular public speaker on the subject of female suffrage, she herself was unable to become an American citizen due to discriminatory laws and therefore could not vote. Her speeches emphasized that "Chinese women in the United States suffered under the burden of not only sexism, but also racial prejudice" (Cahill, 2020), which was an early reference to what today is considered to be intersectionality. Like other Chinese suffragists, she hoped that by illuminating both sexism and racism, it might help change American policies.

However, instead of helping their situation, Congress passed the 1924 Immigration Act, a law that not only excluded all classes of Chinese immigration, but also restricted immigration from other Asian countries. Although some of the restrictions were gradually lifted, many Asian American women were barred from voting until 1952. That year, the Immigration and Nationality Act generally afforded them a path to earn citizenship and the opportunity to vote, more than three decades after the 19th Amendment passed.

Hispanic American women: The ability of Hispanic women to vote after the passage of the 19th Amendment was often based on the state in which they lived. For example, "the demographics of New Mexico gave Spanish-speakers a political advantage they did not have in other states" (Cahill, 2021). New

Mexico was home to many longtime residents who came from entrenched Hispanic families with a tradition of relative political power. Much of the female Hispanic American population of New Mexico advocated woman's suffrage. The state legislature's vote to ratify the 19th Amendment was encouraged by its Hispanic women, many of whom were able to exert a degree of political influence.

However, it was a different situation for Mexican Americans who lived in Texas. They did not have the same level of influence in Texas as their neighbors in New Mexico since "most of them were poor sharecroppers who were disenfranchised by Jim Crow laws, like the poll tax as well as extra-legal threats of violence" (Cahill, 2021).

Other Hispanic American women had different kinds of experiences in their attempt to vote after the passage of the 19th Amendment. In the US territory of Puerto Rico, for example, suffragists worked to secure women's voting rights. At first, the vote was awarded in 1929 to Puerto Rican women who were considered literate. Then, in 1935, the franchise was theoretically extended to all women in Puerto Rico. However, even after that time, stringent literacy tests remained in effect in some places, often barring many Hispanics and others from voting for decades. In 1975, the extension of the Voting Rights Act prohibited discrimination against women whose primary language was other than English.

African American women: The struggle for suffrage by African American women was ongoing from the time of the nation's beginnings and continued well past the enactment of the 19th Amendment in 1920. Black activists in the twentieth century, such as Fannie Lou Hamer (1917–1977), helped win the passage of the Voting Rights Act of 1965, although voter suppression tactics continued to be used against African American women and men.

Under the theory of intersectionality, Black women historically had to contend with opposition both because of their race and their gender. That hostility came not only from the outside world, but also from within their own community. Suffragist stirrings in the early 1800s saw African American women such as Maria W. Stewart making speeches advocating voting rights for both Black men and women. However, in 1827, an African American newspaper, *Freedom's Journal*, proclaimed, "A man, in his furious passion, is terrible to his enemies; but a woman, in a passion, is disgusting to her friends, she loses all respect due to her sex, and she has not the masculine strength and courage to enforce any other kind of respect" (Jones, 2021, 15).

Stewart and others continued their quest for universal suffrage, recognizing the intersection of both gender and race before intersectionality was articulated. In a few cases, they were successful. With the passage of the 19th Amendment in 1920, some African American women in certain parts of the country such as California, Illinois, and New York were able to cast their vote.

However, in other places, the same kinds of suppression that kept African American men from voting after the 15th Amendment granted them that right in 1870 also kept Black women from casting a ballot after the 19th Amendment was enacted in 1920. Constitutional quizzes, "grandfather" clauses, literacy tests, poll taxes, and stringent identification requirements along with intimidation, threats, and violence were all roadblocks to the right to vote for African Americans.

Through the years, Black women faced the intersection of race and gender, such as the case of activist Fannie Lou Hamer. After she attempted to register to vote, Hamer was "beaten and sexually assaulted by law enforcement in 1963 in a Winona, Mississippi, jail, [and was] left with permanent kidney and eye damage, as well as a limp" (Jordan-Heint, 2018).

A critical moment for the intersectionality of race and gender came in 1913 with the women's voting rights march on Washington, DC. By that time, suffragist leaders such as Alice Paul of the National American Woman Suffrage Association (NAWSA) were frustrated with the lack of success as a result of the kinds of understated tactics that the women's movement had used since Seneca Falls in 1848. In the past, they had relied on such 'ladylike' approaches as writing articles and attempting to politely persuade lawmakers to grant them the vote.

By 1913, they were ready to confront the issue in a highly visual public display. On the eve of Woodrow Wilson's presidential inauguration, suffragists converged on Washington, DC. There, they organized a massive protest parade that would become such a striking visual image that it earned a nationwide media spotlight as well as a place in history books.

Alice Paul and other suffrage leaders may have been adopting new strategies, but they kept the long-running undercurrent of racism in the women's movement intact. As Black suffragists traveled to Washington, the word went out that they would not necessarily be excluded from the protest, but neither would they be welcomed.

Black women were ordered to march at the back of the parade. However, a few African American women, such as Ida B. Wells-Barnett, resolutely took their places among thousands of white marchers. Suffragists may have "stepped into a new phase of the suffrage movement, but they failed to leave racism behind" (Jones, 2020).

Among the Black women marching that day were prominent figures, including Mary Church Terrell (1863–1954). Along with Ida B. Wells-Barnett, Terrell was a leader of the National Association of Colored Women (NACW) founded in 1896. That group was a keystone in campaigns for the voting rights of Black women. Terrell's activism had been sparked in 1892, when an old friend "was lynched in Memphis by whites because his business competed with theirs" (Michals, 2017). Joining Wells-Barnett in anti-lynching campaigns, Terrell's work also advocated the idea of racial uplift, believing that Blacks would help end racial discrimination by advancing themselves through education, work, and community activism.

Terrell's philosophy was that through those efforts, the entire Black race, both male and female, would be elevated. She summed up her activism with the words "Lifting as We Climb," which became the motto of the National Association of Colored Women (NACW), the group she helped create. In 1909, Mary Church Terrell was also among the founders of the National Association for the Advancement of Colored People (NAACP).

Terrell believed that voting was only one piece of a much larger system that impacted Black women on a daily basis. She fought for both female suffrage and civil rights concurrently, feeling that she belonged to "the only group in this country that has two such huge obstacles to surmount ... both sex and race" (Michals, 2017). To contemporary observers, this would appear to be an early manifestation of intersectionality.

Terrell also believed that for women of color, there were "myriad issues that Black women had to overcome as they fought to secure voting rights that included lynching, sexual violence, segregation, and being ignored or abandoned by white suffragists" (Dionne, 2022). Along with earning the vote, Terrell felt that political rights included holding public office and serving on juries, opportunities that were denied to people of her race and gender. "African Americans did not write the laws that governed their lives. They had little say about how their taxes were allocated, and struggled in courts to protect their property and persons" (Jones, 2021, 18).

She also felt that once civil rights such as voting had been earned, they were not necessarily guaranteed forever. Laws granting rights could be overturned at any time. Therefore, Terrell's efforts to attain political equality by addressing the intersection of race and gender did not diminish with time.

Terrell, who had been born during the Civil War and lived through the Second World War, may have recalled the mood of the nation in 1920. At that time, on the surface, it seemed to many suffragists that women, who had contributed a great deal to America's victory in the First World War, could not continue to be denied the vote. However, despite their optimism, the era following the First World War did not look like a promising time for either women's rights or racial equality, much less both of them at once.

The First World War may have officially ended in 1918, but by 1920, America was still reeling in many ways from its aftermath as well as from societal upheavals. The carnage and losses of the war continued to affect many grieving American families. Some mourned the death of loved ones taken by the flu epidemic, which had begun in 1918, spread throughout the war, and was still claiming lives in 1920. There was unrest in America due to anarchist bombings and violence from gangsters. Prohibition, which banned the manufacture and sale of alcohol, had been imposed on the nation, contributing to an atmosphere of lawlessness among some Americans who found illegal ways to drink. There were raids and mass arrests of immigrants under assistant attorney general J. Edgar Hoover, "who'd begun keeping secret files on anyone who questioned or criticized the government" (Weiss, 2019) in order to monitor their activities. FBI files would later include suffragist leader Carrie Chapman Catt.

A presidential election was coming up in 1920. One of the candidates, Warren Harding, espoused a "return to normalcy." The other candidate, James Cox, remained neutral on issues such as women's suffrage. There was little discussion of racial equality by either candidate. Some historians have sought to explain, if not to justify, the suffragists' abandonment of nonwhite women in their battle for the vote. Suffrage leaders such as Catt believed that whoever won the presidency, it would mean "a retreat from progressive ideals and a slide back to comfortable, conservative policies … If the [19th] Amendment didn't pass before the election, before the nation swung into an isolationist, reactionary frame of mind, it might never pass at all" (Weiss, 2019).

Some scholars believe it was in large part a sense of expedience as well as desperation that caused suffragists to ignore the intersectionality of women who faced discrimination, both due to their gender and due to their race. After the 19th Amendment passed, Black women still faced a struggle for suffrage that ran into the 1960s and beyond. Even after the Voting Rights Acts of 1965 and 1968 were in place, when Black women in some parts of the country tried to register to vote, officials attacked them with dogs and sprayed them with high-power fire hoses. Some women suffered physical violence and sexual assault. "Voter suppression persisted in the form of fear long after formal barriers had been lifted" (Jones, 2021, 274).

Apart from the racial matters that were prevalent in other parts of the country, women in Utah experienced intersectionality in a way that had to do with religion. In 1870, women in the Territory of Utah received the right to vote. However, the US Congress was mounting efforts against polygamy, the practice of having more than one wife. This custom was acceptable in Utah's predominant religion, the Church of Jesus Christ of Latter-Day Saints. Subsequent to females receiving the vote in Utah, after a few elections, federal officials noted that women did not seem to be voting for candidates who were opposed to polygamy. Therefore, Congress redoubled its efforts against polygamists. The Edmunds–Tucker Act was passed in 1887 as a law that "stripped all Utah women of their right to vote 17 years after it was first granted" (Jacobs, 2020).

According to Kimberlé Crenshaw, the originator of the term, "intersectionality is a lens through which you can see where power comes and collides, where it interlocks and intersects. It's not simply that there's a race problem here, a gender problem here, and a class or LBGTQ problem there. Many times that framework erases what happens to people who are subject to all of these things" ("Kimberlé Crenshaw on Intersectionality, More than Two Decades Later," 2017).

Further Reading

Block, Melissa. 2020. "Yes, Women Could Vote after the 19th Amendment—But Not All Women. Or Men." *National Public Radio*, August 26. Retrieved from https://www.npr.org/2020/08/26/904730251/yes-women-could-vote-after-the-19th-amendment-but-not-all-women-or-men.

Cahill, Cathleen D. 2020. "Mabel Ping-Hua Lee: How Chinese-American Women Helped Shape the Suffrage Movement." *National Park Service*. Retrieved from https://www.nps.gov/articles/000/mabel-ping-hua-lee-how-chinese-american-women-helped-shape-the-suffrage-movement.htm.

Cahill, Cathleen D. 2021. "Suffrage in Spanish: Hispanic Women and the Fight for the 19th Amendment in New Mexico." *National Park Service*. Retrieved from https://www.nps.gov/articles/000/suffrage-in-spanish-hispanic-women-and-the-fight-for-the-19th-amendment-in-new-mexico.htm.

Dionne, Evette. 2022. *Lifting as We Climb: Black Women's Battle for the Ballot Box*. New York: Viking.

"Exclusion." n.d. *Immigration and Relocation in U.S. History, Library of Congress*. Retrieved from https://www.loc.gov/classroom-materials/immigration/chinese/exclusion/.

Jacobs, Becky. 2020. "Polygamy, Statehood and the First Woman to Vote." *American Experience*. Retrieved from https://www.pbs.org/wgbh/americanexperience/features/vote-polygamy-statehood-and-first-woman-vote/.

Johnson, Risa. 2020. "Overcoming Barriers for Native American Voters." *American Experience*. Retrieved from https://www.pbs.org/wgbh/americanexperience/features/vote-overcoming-barriers-for-native-american-voters/.

Jones, Martha S. 2020. "Black Women's 200 Year Fight for the Vote." *American Experience*. Retrieved from https://www.pbs.org/wgbh/americanexperience/features/vote-black-women-200-year-fight-for-vote/.

Jones, Martha S. 2021. *Vanguard: How Black Women Broke Barriers, Won the Vote, and Insisted on Equality for All*. Reprint edition. New York: Basic Books.

Jordan-Heint, Sara. 2018. "Remembering Fannie Lou." *Times Republican* (*Marshalltown, Iowa*), March 25. Retrieved from https://www.timesrepublican.com/opinion/2018/03/remembering-fannie-lou/.

Kendall, Mikki. 2019. *Amazons, Abolitionists, and Activists: A Graphic History of Women's Fight for Their Rights*. New York: Ten Speed Press.

"Kimberlé Crenshaw on Intersectionality, More Than Two Decades Later." 2017. *Columbia Law School*. Retrieved from https://www.law.columbia.edu/news/archive/kimberle-crenshaw-intersectionality-more-two-decades-later.

McCool, Daniel, Olson, Susan, & Robinson, Jennifer L. 2007. *Native Vote: American Indians, the Voting Rights Act, and the Right to Vote*. New York: Cambridge University Press.

Michals, Debra. 2017. "Mary Church Terrell." *National Women's History Museum*. Retrieved from https://www.womenshistory.org/education-resources/biographies/mary-church-terrell.

"Not All Women Gained the Vote in 1920." 2020. *American Experience*. Retrieved from https://www.pbs.org/wgbh/americanexperience/features/vote-not-all-women-gained-right-to-vote-in-1920/.

Rios, Carmen. 2021. "A Courageous Retelling: Rooting Feminist History in Intersectionality." *A Different Point of View, National Women's History Museum*, Winter, 6–11.

Weiss, Elaine. 2019. *The Woman's Hour: The Great Fight to Win the Vote*. Reprint edition. New York: Penguin.

Q27: Does Intersectionality Carry Socioeconomic Implications?

Answer: Legal scholar Kimberlé Crenshaw has stated that when she presented the theory she called intersectionality in an academic journal, her intent was to identify a gap in antidiscrimination law, which recognized categories such as racial discrimination and gender discrimination, but which did not consider situations in which two or more categories overlapped. Rather than pose the concept as merely a theoretical construct that would exist only in law books, Crenshaw intended for it to be used in real-world situations where there were significant socioeconomic implications. Her hypothesis led to developing a methodology that could address such situations when they found their way to the courts, with decisions impacting the lives of the individuals involved. Looking at specific courtroom cases that demonstrated overlapping racial discrimination and gender discrimination at the same time, Crenshaw sought to address what she felt the courts were not considering: intersectional elements that carried direct socioeconomic ramifications.

The Facts: The theory of intersectionality maintains that people can be disadvantaged by multiple sources of oppression, including class, gender, race, religion, and sexual orientation. Crenshaw's concept asserts that identity markers such as "Black" and "female" do not and cannot exist independently of each other. Each one, she states, is intertwined with the others, often leading to a complex convergence resulting in a web of oppression with real-world consequences.

The concept of intersectionality came into being "to help people think that discrimination can happen on the basis of several different factors at the same time, and they are colliding in their lives in ways we don't anticipate or understand" ("Kimberlé Crenshaw Discusses 'Intersectional Feminism,'" 2015). It evolved as the result of several court cases in which legal scholar Kimberlé Crenshaw felt that the judges failed to consider a "double bind" faced by the plaintiffs. The judges' rulings were based on case law and precedent, involving either racial discrimination or gender bias but not the overlapping effect of both. Crenshaw felt there was no legal means at the time of addressing such cases and set out to construct a framework in order to meet that need. She especially studied three cases with direct socioeconomic implications: *DeGraffenreid v. General Motors* (1976), *Moore v. Hughes Helicopter* (1980), and *Payne v. Travenol Labs* (1972).

DeGraffenreid v. General Motors was a 1976 discrimination case in which five African American women sued their employer, General Motors Assembly Division, over policies that discriminated specifically against Black women. In one allegation concerning the company's seniority policy, Black women had not been hired before 1964, so when there were seniority-based layoffs in the 1970s, Black women were laid off first because other employees had been there longer. In another aspect of the *DeGraffenreid* suit, General Motors argued that they hired African Americans and they also hired women, so there was no discrimination. Ms. DeGraffenreid and the other plaintiffs, who were Black females, contended that the company's African American employees were males who were typically hired for factory work. The women further alleged that females hired by the company were white women who were given jobs as secretaries or receptionists. The African American women claimed that because of compound discrimination, they were excluded from employment opportunities such as front office jobs.

The court ruled against the Black women, dismissing the case after finding that Black female workers could not prove gender discrimination by their employer because not all women were being discriminated against, nor could they prove racial discrimination because not all Black people were being discriminated against.

Crenshaw believed the women in the *DeGraffenreid* suit had faced a double form of discrimination based on both their gender *and* their race. She felt that the court needed to be able to interpret and apply the law in terms of how the employer's policies left Black women outside typical hiring patterns by facing compound discrimination.

In *Moore v. Hughes Helicopter* (1980) and *Payne v. Travenol Labs* (1972), similar situations existed in which Black women charged that discrimination existed due to the companies' selection of employees for supervisory and upper-level positions—jobs that were not offered to nonwhite women. The plaintiffs alleged that there had been discrimination, which they felt was based on both their gender *and* their race. Neither case was decided in favor of the plaintiffs.

It is not only in industrialized settings that alleged socioeconomic consequences of intersectionality can be seen. A study by Dr. Stacy L. Smith of the University of Southern California looked at more than 1,100 Hollywood movies made over ten years. Smith's results showed that "only six of all those filmmakers over ten years were women of color" (Malone, 2017, 160). Out of the 1,100 movie productions, two of the six were Asian, one was Latina, and three were African American. "Each of these women has to work even harder than white women do to get a spot behind the lens, with the double bind of dealing with bias against their gender *and* their race" (Malone, 2017, 161).

Adherents to the theory of intersectionality see the double bind in this situation as having a major socioeconomic impact not only on filmmakers' immediate careers but also on their futures. Most movie directors making films for larger studios belong to the Directors Guild of America, which operates on a points system. Members must earn a certain number of points to qualify for health insurance and a pension plan. Since the way to earn those points is to work, Smith's study indicates that "by not being given equal employment, these women were also losing their ability to look after themselves in their old age" (Malone, 2017, 135).

Kimberlé Crenshaw does not believe that the basic concept of intersectionality is new. She cites the work of people such as Anna Julia Cooper and Maria W. Stewart in the nineteenth century, adding that in each generation "there have been African American women who have articulated the need to think and talk about race through a lens that looks at gender, or think and talk about feminism through a lens that looks at race" (Adewunmi, 2014). In 1893, Anna Cooper spoke about the status of Black women at the World Congress of Representative Women, stating that "the white woman could at least plead for her own emancipation; Black women, doubly enslaved, could but suffer and struggle and be silent" (hooks, 2014, 2).

Within the historical perspective, some observers state that many African American women "emphasized the 'female' aspect of their being, which caused their lot to be different than that of the Black male, a fact that was made evident when white men supported giving Black men the vote while leaving all women disenfranchised" (hooks, 2014, 3).

In 2014 women's rights advocate bell hooks commented on the relatively small number of women of color in the feminist movement. She claimed many Black women did not believe that they had much to gain in the feminist cause: "They fear losing what little they have. They are afraid to openly confront white feminists with their racism or Black males with their sexism, not to mention confronting white men with their racism and sexism" (hooks, 2014, 195).

Crenshaw states that from a legal point of view, when women of color experienced compound or overlapping discrimination, "the law initially just was not there to come to their defense" (Adewunmi, 2014). She sees the 1991 confirmation hearings for Supreme Court nominee Clarence Thomas as a watershed moment for the theory of intersectionality. During that hearing, law school professor Anita Hill testified that Thomas had sexually harassed her when she worked for him. Thomas, an African American like Hill denied the allegation, calling it a "high tech lynching."

Crenshaw, who had already coined the concept of intersectionality by that time, served on the legal team representing Hill. Crenshaw says that the "lynching" comment made by Thomas "communicated to many African Americans this was a race issue ... Lynching is representative of the quintessential moment of racism, and that in turn centers African American male experiences," even though Black women were also lynched. Crenshaw claims that Anita Hill's situation reinforced the idea that it was an issue of race versus gender, while "African American women feminists were trying to say, 'You cannot talk about this just in gender terms—you have to be intersectional'" (Adewunmi, 2014).

Some studies have shown significant implications of intersectionality in terms of socioeconomic factors. A writer for *YW Boston* stated, "a Black man and a white woman make $0.74 and $0.78 to a white man's dollar, respectively. Black women, faced with multiple forms of oppression, only make $0.64" ("What Is Intersectionality, and What Does It Have to Do with Me?" 2017). For those who are Hispanic, one source indicates that "Latina women make 54 cents for every male dollar" ("Women's Voices, Women's Votes, Women's Rights," 2022).

As Crenshaw notes, intersectionality encompasses more dimensions than only the overlap of gender and race. For example, activist bell hooks sought to include women from lower socioeconomic classes in the quest for equality, several years before Crenshaw's 1989 article appeared. Many of those women felt that the cause of women's rights did not include them or recognize their struggles—until hooks's 1981 *Ain't I a Woman: Black Women and Feminism* "helped Black and working-class women gain footing in the feminist movement" ("The Legacy of bell hooks," 2022).

Beyond economics, discussions of intersectionality often result in conversations involving a societal dimension that is summed up in the contemporary expression "Check Your Privilege." In its most basic terms, the phrase suggests walking in another person's shoes, since "we may, unknowingly, have certain advantages over others. And this is only because there are aspects of our identity that society values over others" (Finch, 2015). Furthermore, laws and other institutional constructs can sometimes reflect this bias unintentionally, resulting in different people experiencing different relative advantages and disadvantages, depending on their intersecting societal positions.

Some scholars see intersectionality as an important component of the women's equality movement, not only as a theoretical hypothesis but also as a means of looking differently at the larger picture of socioeconomic implications. One source utilizes an interesting metaphor, stating that in the pursuit of social justice for all women and for people in general, "we stop treating it like we're all competing for a slice of the pie and look around and realize that we're fighting in a room full of apples and pie crusts. We could just make some more pies" (Rios, 2021, 11).

Further Reading

Adewunmi, Bim. 2014. "Kimberlé Crenshaw on Intersectionality: 'I Wanted to Come Up with an Everyday Metaphor that Anyone Could Use.'" *The New Statesman*,

April 2. Retrieved from https://www.newstatesman.com/politics/welfare/2014/04/
kimberl-crenshaw-intersectionality-i-wanted-come-everyday-metaphor-any
one-could.

Crenshaw, Kimberlé. 2016. "The Urgency of Intersectionality." *TED Women*. Retrieved
from https://www.ted.com/talks/kimberle_crenshaw_the_urgency_of_intersectional
ity?language=en.

"DeGraffenreid v. General Motors Assembly Div, etc., 413 F. Supp. 142 (E.D. Mo. 1976)."
2022. *Justia*. Retrieved from https://law.justia.com/cases/federal/district-courts/
FSupp/413/142/1660699/.

Finch, Sam Dylan. 2015. "Ever Been Told to 'Check Your Privilege'? Here's What That
Really Means." *Everyday Feminism*, July 27. Retrieved from https://everydayfemin
ism.com/2015/07/what-checking-privilege-means/.

hooks, bell. 2014. *Ain't I a Woman: Black Women and Feminism*. 2nd ed.
New York: Routledge.

"Kimberlé Crenshaw Discusses 'Intersectional Feminism.'" 2015. *YouTube*. Retrieved
from https://www.youtube.com/watch?v=ROwquxC_Gxc.

"Kimberlé Crenshaw on Intersectionality, More Than Two Decades Later." 2017.
Columbia Law School. Retrieved from https://www.law.columbia.edu/news/archive/
kimberle-crenshaw-intersectionality-more-two-decades-later.

"The Legacy of bell hooks." 2022. *People*, January 5, 22.

Malone, Alicia. 2017. *Backwards & in Heels: The Past, Present and Future of Women
Working in Film*. Coral Gables, FL: Mango Publishing.

"Moore v. Hughes Helicopters, Inc." 2021. *CaseText*. Retrieved from https://casetext.
com/case/moore-v-hughes-helicopters-inc-a-div-of-summa-corp.

"Payne v. Travenol Laboratories, Inc., 416 F. Supp. 248 (N.D. Miss. 1976)." 2022.
Justia. Retrieved from https://law.justia.com/cases/federal/district-courts/
FSupp/416/248/1500534/.

Rios, Carmen. 2021. "A Courageous Retelling: Rooting Feminist History in
Intersectionality." *A Different Point of View, National Women's History Museum*,
Winter, 6–11.

"What is Intersectionality, and What Does It Have to Do with Me?" 2017. *YW Boston*,
March 29, Retrieved from https://www.ywboston.org/2017/03/what-is-intersecti
onality-and-what-does-it-have-to-do-with-me/#:~:text=Intersectionality%20recogni
zes%20that%20identity%20markers,a%20White%20man's%20dollar%2C%20respe
ctively.

"Women's Voices, Women's Votes, Women's Rights." 2022. *Clinton Foundation*.
Retrieved from https://www.clintonfoundation.org/womensvoices/?emci=1e4db
3b4-8d71-ed11-819c-000d3a9eb474&emdi=0216a250-4372-ed11-819c-000d3a9eb
474&ceid=354383&utm_source=20221202womenvoices_tuneinreminder&utm_c
ampaign=2022wv&utm_medium=email.

Q28: What Are the Arguments For and Against Intersectionality?

Answer: When the theory of intersectionality was introduced in 1989 by Dr. Kimberlé Crenshaw, her thesis was to suggest the ways in which class, gender, race, and other characteristics can overlap and intersect to form webs of oppression. At that time, Crenshaw posed the concept of intersectionality as a legal framework that she felt would be useful in the judicial system for cases that involved, for example, a Black woman who experienced potential discrimination not only through her race as an African American but also through her gender as a female. As the idea became better known, it attracted opponents with concerns that it could disrupt the existing social order, particularly the status of white males. However, Crenshaw has stated that those concerns are based on false assumptions outside the scope of the intersectionality theory itself.

The Facts: According to political commentator Jane Coaston, "there may not be a word in American conservatism more hated right now than 'intersectionality.' On the right, intersectionality is seen as 'the new caste system' placing non-white, non-heterosexual people on top" (Coaston, 2019).

Kimberlé Crenshaw has stated that her theory does not seek to build a new hierarchy with certain groups such as women of color at the top, adding that she would prefer to demolish such societal hierarchies altogether. She has also claimed that criticisms of intersectionality—through possible misinterpretation or mischaracterization of the theory—are the result of what happens to an idea when it moves "beyond the context and the content" (Coaston, 2019).

Some opponents of the theory allude to a sense of what emerged in the 1970s when allegations of "reverse discrimination" arose. Reverse discrimination or reverse racism were terms that gained traction in the 1970s to designate bias against members of a dominant group, such as white males, in favor of members of a minority or historically disadvantaged group. Initiatives such as affirmative action were considered by some to be reverse discrimination, in which people are categorized in terms of ethnicity, gender, nationality, race, religion, sex, or sexual orientation, and felt by opponents to be given an unfair advantage.

One of the most well-known cases of alleged reverse discrimination in the 1970s involved a white male student, Allan Bakke, who was passed over in his effort to attend medical school, although the admissions board of the medical college maintained that there were factors apart from his race and gender that caused them to deny his application. By setting aside sixteen places for minority students in a class of one hundred, Bakke maintained that it discriminated against him as a white male. With massive media coverage of a 1978 US Supreme Court decision in *Regents of the University of California v. Bakke*, generally called the *Bakke Case*, "the public was inundated with terms such as 'preferential treatment,' 'affirmative action,' and 'reverse discrimination'" (Ball, 2000). The case had so many controversial elements that the nine Supreme Court justices issued six opinions. Allan Bakke was ordered by the Court to be admitted to the medical school at the University of California at Davis.

The word "intersectionality" was not in popular usage until Crenshaw's 1989 article, but there were those who saw the *Bakke* decision in 1978 in terms that were analogous to its usage today. The focus at the time was on affirmative action, which was often manifested in the intersection of race and gender. Civil rights leader Julian Bond said the *Bakke* decision reinforced "the 200-year old racial and sexual quota system" (Bennett & Eastland, 1978). National Organization for Women spokesperson Gene Boyer responded to the ruling by saying, "Employers and universities who choose to interpret *Bakke* as a license to remain male and pale are in for a rude awakening" (Bennett & Eastland, 1978). Liberal politician Eleanor Holmes Norton, the first woman to chair the Equal Employment Opportunity Commission, stated, "we are not compelled to do anything differently from the way we've done things in the past [via affirmative action], and we are not going to" (Bennett & Eastland, 1978).

Today, some opponents do not necessarily object to the idea of intersectionality itself but rather how it is applied, believing that "it could be (or is being) used against them, making them the victims, in a sense, of a new form of overlapping oppression" (Coaston, 2019). Some critics even assert that intersectionality "excludes or even vilifies straight white men and other people who don't suffer from multiple oppressions" (Young, 2019).

For her part, Crenshaw has responded to these detractors and critics by noting that from the beginnings of the civil rights movement in the 1960s, there have been those who "denounced the creation of equality rights on the grounds that it takes something away from them" (Coaston, 2019).

Some sources note that it is difficult to find a term that is both as descriptive and recognizable as intersectionality. Yet, "many scholars will not regard intersectionality as a neutral term, for it immediately suggests a particular theoretical paradigm based in identity categories" (McCall, 2005).

Further Reading

Ball, Howard. 2000. *The Bakke Case: Race, Education, and Affirmative Action.* Lawrence: University Press of Kansas.

Bennett, William & Eastland, Terry. 1978. "Why Bakke Won't End Reverse Discrimination, *Commentary*. Retrieved from https://www.commentary.org/articles/william-bennett/why-bakke-wont-end-reverse-discrimination-1/.

Coaston, Jane. 2019. "The Intersectionality Wars." *Vox*, May 28. Retrieved from https://www.vox.com/the-highlight/2019/5/20/18542843/intersectionality-conservatism-law-race-gender-discrimination.

Friedersdorf, Conor. 2018. "Intersectionality Is Not the Problem." *The Atlantic*. March 8. Retrieved from https://www.theatlantic.com/politics/archive/2018/03/intersectionality-is-not-the-enemy-of-free-speech/555014/.

McCall, Leslie. 2005. "The Complexity of Intersectionality." *Signs*. University of Chicago Press, vol. 30, no. 3, Spring, 1771–1800. Retrieved from https://lsa.umich.edu/content/dam/ncid-assets/ncid-documents/Ten%20Diversity%20Scholarship%20Resources/McCall%20(2005)%20The%20Complex%20of%20Intersectionality%20.pdf.

Rios, Carmen. 2021. "A Courageous Retelling: Rooting Feminist History in Intersectionality." *A Different Point of View*, National Women's History Museum, Winter 2021, 6–11.

Young, Cathy. 2019. "What They Talk about When They Talk about Intersectionality." *Tablet Magazine*, January 29. Retrieved from https://www.tabletmag.com/sections/news/articles/what-they-talk-about-when-they-talk-about-intersectionality.

6

Women's Equality in Present-Day America

The *Declaration of Sentiments*, a document that was issued at the Seneca Falls women's rights conference in 1848, aimed at the goal of women being equal to men in such areas as education, employment, and property rights. After heated debate, the document also asked that American women be permitted to vote, just like men. The inclusion of female voting rights was considered so radical that two-thirds of the one hundred conference attendees—both males and females who were presumably supporters of women's rights—refused to sign the document. At that time, the press generally treated the matter of women's rights, particularly voting rights, as ludicrous at best and dangerous at worst, heralding the upheaval of the social structure.

As subsequent women's rights conferences were held annually through the nineteenth and early twentieth centuries, a counter-movement grew in response to continued demands for women's equality. Opponents claimed women's rights advocates posed a dangerous threat to the established social order by challenging traditional gender roles set down by God.

In current times, a men's rights movement has emerged that maintains women already have enough rights and that gender discrimination is no longer a serious issue. Some even contend that in present-day America, women have taken rights and opportunities away from men, resulting in "reverse gender discrimination." In reality, though, government reports and scholarly studies that assess a broad range of socioeconomic data agree that gender discrimination is a fact of life that millions of women face every day in American workplaces and other institutions.

Q29: Have American Women Attained Socioeconomic Equality with Men?

Answer: Some people argue American women have achieved parity with men by having the right to vote, gaining admission to higher education, and having greater opportunities in employment. They point to the larger number of women who are business executives and government officials in today's world as well as more strong female characters in movies and on television. They declare that average female wages have risen to the point where any gender-based pay gap no longer exists and that gender discrimination in the workplace is not the problem it is made out to be.

In reality, however, numerous studies have found that while some gender gaps and disparities in American economic life have at least improved, others have not. That is especially true for women with children, as a 2023 Century Foundation study documented that whereas 68 percent of American fathers have retirement savings, only 50 percent of American mothers do:

> Mothers face significant financial precarity heading into retirement when compared to fathers and men and women without children. Together, gender pay gaps, occupational segregation, and care responsibilities all negatively impact women's financial health and their ability to prepare for retirement. Not only are women more likely to work in low-wage jobs or work part-time, these jobs are less likely to have benefits, including retirement accounts. For women that do have access to retirement plans, gender pay gaps mean they often also have less to contribute to retirement plans. Furthermore, care responsibilities, by impacting whether and how much women work, result in less access to employee-sponsored retirement accounts, and lower earnings, which translates into lower savings. (Gutierrez, 2023)

The Facts: One of the arguments by those who believe American women have achieved equality is in the area of relative wages in the pay scale among men and women. Historically, this gap in compensation between men and women, often referred to as the "gender gap" or "income inequity," has been evident even when women and men have equivalent qualifications and work experiences. Supporters of the theory that women have reached, or have almost reached, equality with males in this area point to women's wages increasing in recent years. To illustrate what they feel is steady growth, they cite studies such as one from the US Bureau of Labor Statistics in 2021 showing that in 1979, which was the first year when comparable earnings data were available, women's earnings were 62 percent of men's. In the 1980s, women's earnings relative to men's grew to 70 percent, followed by the 1990s when the ratio rose to 77 percent. In the 2000s, the women's-to-men's earnings ratio increased to the 80 percent range. "In 2020, women who were full-time wage and salary workers had median usual weekly earnings that were 82% of those of male full-time wage and salary workers" ("Highlights of Women's Earnings in 2020," 2021).

Another argument used by those who believe women have almost attained equality with males is that in cases where women are confined to lower-paying jobs, receive less of a salary, and are passed over for promotion, it is only because women choose family over career and/or simply do not ask for more money.

The matter of perceived gender-based pay inequity was studied by the Pew Research Center in Washington, DC, an institution that calls itself a nonpartisan fact-based research entity. The report from the Pew Center determined that in the United States, the gender gap in pay has remained about the same over the past twenty years, with women earning around 82 percent of what men earned for the same type of job in an analysis of median hourly earnings of both full- and part-time workers. This represents a 2 percent rise from 2002, when women earned 80 percent as much as men (Aragão, 2023).

The Pew Research study determined that motherhood can indeed lead to interruptions in women's career paths and thus have an impact on long-term earnings. Some women leave the workforce for years in order to raise their children and often have to rejoin the job market in entry-level positions with lower salaries.

Insofar as the belief that women have achieved equality with males as business executives and as government officials, the Pew Research study reported that in the past twenty years or so, more women are indeed present in higher-paying jobs that have traditionally been dominated by men, such as managerial positions and in professional careers as doctors or attorneys. However, women generally continue to be overrepresented in lower-paying occupations.

The same holds true in politics, even though there has also been a relative rise in the number of women serving in government. In 2021, Kamala Harris became the first woman to hold the office of vice president of the United States. In addition, at the federal level after the 2022 midterm elections, there were twenty-five women in the US Senate, or 25 percent of the one hundred senatorial seats. In the House of Representatives, there were 125 women, or 28.7 percent of 435 seats. Although the percentages may appear low since women comprise about 50 percent of the US population, many see this as progress compared to the 234-year history of the US Congress where overall, "3.2% of all members of Congress to date have been women" ("Women in the U.S. Congress 2022," 2022).

Similarly, those who assert that women have achieved equality with men often point to the increasing number of female leading characters on television programs and in Hollywood movies. In one report studying the top films of 2021, women represented 35 percent of major characters. That figure represents a drop compared to "38% of major characters in 2020, and 37% in 2019" (Women and Hollywood staff, 2022).

While female characters are more prominent in the entertainment industry than in the past, women in the acting profession are not paid as much as males. In 2018, when the movie *All the Money in the World* required reshooting certain scenes, male actor Mark Wahlberg received $1.5 million for the extra time (on top of his salary of $5 million). For the same amount of work, his costar Michelle Williams, whose screen time was roughly equivalent to that of Wahlberg, received $80 per diem for less than $1,000 (in addition to her base salary of $625,000) (Wittmer, 2018). A 2022 *Forbes* report indicates that across the board, actresses earned only about 35 cents on the dollar compared to their male counterparts in the entertainment industry (Friedman, Hollander, & Ulubay, 2022).

Researchers also point to economic factors like the so-called "pink tax." Studies find that women pay more for common household items such as shampoo and deodorant aimed at female buyers than men do for equivalent products aimed at males. Similarly, female entrepreneurs receive less investment support for their businesses than male counterparts. At home, employed women are said to bear more of the household burden (often called the "second shift") and have less leisure time than their male partners (Friedman, Hollander, & Ulabay, 2022).

Other examples of gender disadvantage abound. Women are more likely to be injured in car crashes because safety features were designed for men. In the area of medical care, they state that women's health issues are not taken as seriously as they are for males, with female patients often being told their problems are all in their head. Women are said to be charged more for health care and health insurance because they are considered higher risks by the insurance industry and to experience more side effects to medications because drugs are typically tested by and designed for male bodies. Toys marketed to girls (pink teddy bears, for example) are more expensive than the same product (in blue) aimed at boys. Women are also often charged more for senior home health care products, "meaning they pay more for common items from the beginning to the end of their lives" (Friedman, Hollander, & Ulubay, 2022). The cumulative impact of these gender-based disparities is often significant, as evidenced by the fact that retired women are twice as likely as retired men to live in poverty (Friedman, Hollander, & Ulabay, 2022). A 2023 study conducted by the Century Foundation, meanwhile, found that whereas two-thirds of men have retirement savings, only half of women do.

Further Reading

Aragão, Carolina. 2023. "Gender Pay Gap in U.S. Hasn't Changed Much in Two Decades," *Pew Research Center*. Retrieved from https://www.pewresearch.org/short-reads/2023/03/01/gender-pay-gap-facts/.

Friedman, Megan, Hollander, Jenny & Ulabay, Gabrielle. 2022. "30 Ways Women Still Aren't Equal to Men," *Marie Claire*, March 8. Retrieved from https://www.mariecla ire.com/politics/news/a15652/gender-inequality-stats/.

Geiger, A.W. & Parker, Kim. 2018. "For Women's History Month, a Look at Gender Gains – and Gaps – in the U.S." *Pew Research Center*. Retrieved from https://www.pewresearch.org/fact-tank/2018/03/15/for-womens-history-month-a-look-at-gen der-gains-and-gaps-in-the-u-s/.

Gutierrez, Laura Valle. 2023. "New Data Demonstrates Mothers' Retirement Insecurity." *The Century Foundation*. https://tcf.org/content/report/new-data-demonstrates-mothers-retirement-insecurity/ Accessed May 15, 2023.

"Highlights of Women's Earnings in 2020." 2021. *U.S. Bureau of Labor Statistics*. Retrieved from https://www.bls.gov/opub/reports/womens-earnings/2020/home.htm.

Hochschild, Arlie & Machung, Anne. 2012. *The Second Shift: Working Families and the Revolution at Home*. New York: Penguin Books.

"How a Massive Pay Gap Occurred in the 'All the Money In The World' Reshoot." 2018. *NPR*. Retrieved from https://www.npr.org/2018/01/10/577163183/how-a-mass ive-pay-gap-occurred-in-the-all-the-money-in-the-world-reshoot.

O'Neill, Brendan. 2017. "What Happened to 'Innocent Until Proven Guilty'?" *Chicago Tribune*, November 28. Retrieved from https://www.chicagotribune.com/opinion/commentary/ct-perspec-innocense-presumption-guilty-metoo-sexual-miscond uct-1128-20171127-story.html.

Sharkey-Steenson, Sinead. 2017. "7 Gender Equality Myths Debunked." *Generation Women*. Retrieved from https://genwomen.global/10-gender-equality-myths-debunked/.

Wittmer, Carrie. 2018. "4-time Oscar Nominee Michelle Williams was Reportedly Paid 8 times Less than Mark Wahlberg for 'All the Money in the World'– with Comparable Screen Time," *Business Insider*. Retrieved from https://www.businessinsi der.com/michelle-williams-paid-nearly-ten-times-less-than-mark-wahlberg-all-th e-money-in-the-world-2018-1.

Women and Hollywood staff. 2022. "Study: Women Made Up 34% of Speaking Roles in 2021's Top Films, Majority of Those Characters Were White."

Women and Hollywood. Retrieved from https://womenandhollywood.com/study-women-made-up-34-of-speaking-roles-in-2021s-top-films-majority-of-those-characters-were-white/#:~:text=In%202021's%20top%20films%2C%20females,and%2034%20percent%20in%202019.

"Women in the U.S. Congress 2022." 2022. *Center for American Women and Politics.* Retrieved from https://cawp.rutgers.edu/facts/levels-office/congress/women-us-congress-2022.

Q30: Does Women's Equality Damage American Families?

Answer: Some critics have seen the expansion of women's rights as destructive to the traditional family and the American social structure, reflected in such developments as the easing of divorce laws, increased numbers of single mothers, and harmful effects on young people being raised in single-parent homes, including higher rates of alcoholism, drugs, depression, and obesity.

The Facts: Feminist movements and women's rights advocates have opened career opportunities for American women in industries and professions that were once explicitly hostile to earlier generations of women. Many sources credit the women's equality movement with advances in areas such as greater opportunities for women's employment, with more females being admitted into previously all-male careers, including such professions as medicine and law.

However, there are also those who believe that while those advances became available primarily to relatively affluent women, the reality is different for lower socioeconomic groups. In addition to women performing the majority of traditionally "pink collar" jobs such as waitressing, health care aides, or clerical work, there are also obstacles for certain classes of women due to phenomena popularly known as the "glass ceiling" and the "sticky floor."

The "glass ceiling" refers to invisible gender barriers that bar women from promotion to the top of industries, corporations, and professions, while the "sticky floor" keeps them at the bottom. While there is a popular perception that the women's equality movement has allowed more females to advance in employment opportunities by being admitted into previously all-male careers, the reality often paints a different picture. According to observers, males in the workplace are not generally subjected to ill effects due to the kind of "glass ceiling" and "sticky floor" that are experienced by equivalent female employees who remain in positions with poor pay and/or little opportunity for advancement.

Opponents of the women's equality movement blamed feminists for what newspapers in the 1970s were calling the "divorce revolution" (White, 2022, 76). In reality, however, the steady rise in the American divorce rate in the last decades of the twentieth century and the opening decades of the new century is directly attributable to to the loosening of stringent divorce laws across the nation—itself a phenomenon driven by a host of complex social and economic factors in addition to the women's equality movement.

Throughout most of American history, divorce was generally granted only on very limited grounds such as documented adultery. Moreover, for females, it was historically accessible only to those women who were relatively affluent since the average woman had few financial resources of her own, nor ways to earn a living in order to support herself and her children if she was no longer married. Even hiring an attorney or a detective to secure documentation of a husband's adultery would have been beyond the grasp of most women.

Prior to the 1960s and 1970s, there was generally a strong societal pressure against divorce by the clergy as well as from the "political and judicial classes" (White, 2022, 68), who were typically all males. Divorce was seen as a dire threat to the American family, which in turn was seen as foundational to the nation's prosperity and moral standing. In 1905, speaking against the dissolution of marriages, President Theodore Roosevelt referred to "the stakes in the divorce debate [as] a struggle for 'our own national soul'" (White, 2022, 68). As the twentieth century progressed, however, attitudes changed. Starting in the late 1960s, "no-fault" divorces were approved at the state level all across the country by individual states, being signed into law by governors, including California's Ronald Reagan, who himself was divorced. Cultural conservatives such as Mona Charen have decried these trends, stating that "feminists greeted unwed parenthood and easy divorce as steps on the ladder of liberation … but the price has been steep" (Charen, 2018).

In some cases, the cost can be a literal one. "In 2017, the poverty rate for woman-headed families with children was 36.5%, compared with … 7.5% for families headed by a married couple" (Charen, 2018).

In addition to the routine expenses of raising a family, there is also the cost of child care while the single parent, usually a mother, is at work. As US Senator Elizabeth Warren (D-MA) observed, "the cost of child care has gone up so much that it's now more expensive than in-state college tuition in most states" ("Glass Ceiling: What Are the Biggest Problems Women Face Today?" 2019).

Some sources contend that there are also indirect results of the women's movement through the negative impact on the traditional family unit of a mother and a father, and therefore on society. This outcome, they feel, is due to the trend toward greater female freedom—and a corresponding loss of family unity and cohesion. According to conservative writer Mona Charen, "the traditional family remains the gold standard. ... Diseases of despair—alcoholism, overdoses, suicide—have been rising among white, working-class Americans, the very population that has witnessed a steep decline in family stability over the past several decades" (Charen, 2018). Studies have identified a greater degree of obesity in Americans over the past few decades, especially in children, in homes with working mothers. A study in the journal *Child Development* "found that for every five months a mother worked, a child could gain a pound more than normally expected" (Martin, 2011).

The same study found that sixth graders whose mothers were employed outside the home were several times more likely to be overweight than those children whose mothers did not work outside the home. Contributing factors include the working single-parent challenges of preparing nutritious and healthy meals all week, the ubiquity of prepared or fast foods in the American food system, and food budget limitations in single-mother families that encourage the purchase of inexpensive but fattening food products. In addition, children in these households are more likely to lead sedentary daily lives heavy on "screen time"—video games, cell phones, television, and the like—which makes them more vulnerable to weight gain.

Some critics of feminism assert that the increase in women's rights and opportunities, especially due to women taking outside jobs instead of staying at home to raise their children, can lead to the destabilization of the traditional family unit as well as America's societal foundations. Journalist Jill Brooke wrote that women would be better off to wait until they are at least twenty-five or older to get married and have children. By doing so, a woman would be better able to use her younger years for the benefit of herself and her future children through getting an education and job experience because economic independence provides "more protections if she doesn't marry or if her husband dies or divorces her" (Brooke, 2011). Economic data indicate, for example, that 50 percent of women with children report having "no retirement savings at all compared to 32 percent of fathers" (Gutierrez, 2023).

Further Reading

Brooke, Jill. 2011. "Did Feminism Cause Divorce?" *Huffington Post*, March 25. Retrieved from https://www.huffpost.com/entry/did-feminism-cause-many-d_b_836327.

Charen, Mona. 2018. "Feminism Has Destabilized the American Family." *New York Post*, July 7. Retrieved from https://nypost.com/2018/07/07/feminism-has-destabili zed-the-american-family/.

"Glass Ceiling: What Are the Biggest Problems Women Face Today?" 2019. *Politico*, March 8. Retrieved from https://www.politico.com/magazine/story/2019/03/08/ women-biggest-problems-international-womens-day-225698/.

Gutierrez, Laura Valle. 2023. "New Data Demonstrates Mothers' Retirement Insecurity." *The Century Foundation*. https://tcf.org/content/report/new-data-demonstrates- mothers-retirement-insecurity/ Accessed May 15, 2023.

Martin, Michel. 2011. "Study Finds Link Between Working Moms, Overweight Kids." *National Public Radio*, February 15. Retrieved from https://www.npr. org/2011/02/15/133777158/Study-Finds-Link-Between-Working-Moms-Overwei ght-Kids.

Miller, Claire Cain. 2014. "The Divorce Surge Is Over, But the Myth Lives On." *New York Times*, December 2. Retrieved from https://www.nytimes.com/2014/12/02/ upshot/the-divorce-surge-is-over-but-the-myth-lives-on.html.

Noble, Barbara Presley. 1992. "At Work; And Now the 'Sticky Floor.'" *New York Times*, November 22. Retrieved from https://www.nytimes.com/1992/11/22/business/ at-work-and-now-the-sticky-floor.html.

Schlafly, Phyllis. 1972. "What's Wrong with 'Equal Rights' for Women? *Iowa State University Archives of Women's Political Communication*. Retrieved from https://awpc. cattcenter.iastate.edu/2016/02/02/whats-wrong-with-equal-rights-for-women-1972//

White, April. 2022. "Escape from the Gilded Cage." *Smithsonian*, June, 68, 76.

Q31: Did the Men's Rights Movement Develop in Response to Growing Gender Equality in the United States?

Answer: There are those who feel that advances in women's equality have brought about a decline in men's rights. This, they believe, has occurred due to laws, judicial decisions, shifting trends, and other societal developments that adversely affect or blatantly discriminate against boys and men. Some of the common grievances by those who espouse men's rights include concerns such as alimony, child support, custodial issues, distribution of marital property, domestic violence against men, educational matters, health policies, military service, reproductive rights, and social programs that they feel favor women. Some supporters of men's rights claim that the increase in the number of women in the workplace has meant a decrease in the availability of jobs for men. In terms of both employment prospects and educational opportunities, men's rights supporters claim that "reverse discrimination" has taken place by rejecting males in favor of females. Some observers describe the men's rights movement as a backlash against the rise in feminism. However, others point out that it is not a recent development prompted by the contemporary women's equality movement, since the term "men's rights" is documented as having been used in America at least as early as 1856.

The Facts: With the rise of the women's equality movement in the 1970s, there arose a widespread discussion about how an increase in women's rights might affect men. At the time, there were a number of articles, books, and speeches on the topic, which made many modern-day people think that the subject of men's rights was a recent development as a response to the second wave of feminism.

However, the term "men's rights" was not a product of the 1970s. Its first documented usage in America was more than a century before that. In 1856, an article appeared in *Putnam's Monthly Magazine of American Literature, Science and Art*. The article was called "A Word for Men's Rights," written by Ernest Belfort Bax, who claimed that what he considered to be the sexist laws of his day—the 1850s—benefited women and oppressed men. One of his main arguments was a condemnation of what he considered to be frivolous lawsuits by a woman against a man for alleged breach of promise of marriage or an implied promise. He also had concerns about what happened after marriage if a man grew tired of his wife: "American beauty fades ... Thus, in fact, we are worse off than the Chinaman. He, if not suited with one wife, can take another, and so on, till he is suited" ("A Word for Men's Rights," 2015).

Bax later returned to the topic when feminist ideas were gaining popularity in the 1890s by writing *The Legal Subjection of Men* in 1896. Its arguments might sound similar to those voiced by critics of the #MeToo movement in the 2000s: "A woman has only to complain against a man, and the tribunal is already convinced of the justice of her claim" (Bax, 2020). In *The Legal Subjection of Men*, he condemned the women's rights movement of his era as "farcical," challenging women, whom he called the "privileged sex," to prove they were oppressed.

In Bax's time, women were barred from most colleges and workplaces. From his view of females in the 1890s as the "privileged sex," he might have been interested in a phrase that became well known in the 1970s: "reverse discrimination." According to the *Merriam-Webster Dictionary*, the term is defined as discrimination against whites and/or males, usually in employment or education. The term gained national attention in 1978 when a medical school applicant, Allan Bakke, filed a lawsuit because he felt he had been passed over for admission because he was a white male.

Some observers at the time countered that there is no such thing as "reverse discrimination"—there is simply "discrimination."

During the rise of the second wave of the women's equality movement in the 1970s, a number of popular books were published that focused on gender-related issues. Some of the most-discussed mainstream books include *The Female Eunuch* by Germaine Greer, *The Liberation of Black Women* by Pauli Murray, *Sexual Politics* by Kate Millett, and *Sisterhood Is Powerful* by Robin Morgan, all in 1970. The landmark *Our Bodies, Ourselves* by the Boston Women's Health Book Collective was published in 1973, and *The Women's Room* by Marilyn French was a bestseller in 1977. Much of the subject matter of those books concerned women's relationship to men in negative terms, becoming topics for heated debate. This was especially true of *The Women's Room*, which was considered even by some feminists to be divisive in its slant that "declares men the enemy" (Loudermilk, 2004, 11).

Coming from a different perspective around the same time, one of the most talked-about books during the second-wave era was *The Liberated Man—Beyond Masculinity: Freeing Men and Their Relationships with Women* by Warren Farrell (1974). Some people pointed to *The Liberated Man* as a harbinger that heralded the growth of a full-scale men's rights movement in a backlash against increased demands for women's rights. In the book, Farrell centers on the male gender role as leader, protector, and provider. He also stated that men had as much to gain from feminism as women did if men's voices were heard and if their rights were taken seriously.

In 1993, Farrell followed up with *The Myth of Male Power: Why Men Are the Disposable Sex*. By that time, Farrell was widely known as "the intellectual father of the focus on men's issues" (Dastagir, 2018), with *The Myth of Male Power* considered "the bible of the men's rights movement" (Dastagir, 2018). Farrell became the voice of "American men who feel their culture demonizing masculinity [and] are flocking to the men's rights movement" (Dastagir, 2018).

Farrell and his adherents have argued that men are not oppressors, but are instead the victims of gender discrimination "who are now suffering more than their female counterparts" (Dastagir, 2018). He claims that the perception of men being at the top of the hierarchy through economic and societal dominance is false, because male power is overstated and men are disadvantaged in many ways, being the victims in American society rather than women.

He argues that society forces men into harm's way through hazardous jobs and military service, where they risk their lives "so that everyone else might benefit economically while men died prematurely" (Farrell, 2017). As another example, he cites the damage to young men's brains from concussions in football. Further, he states, "When slaves gave up their seats to whites, we called it subservience; when men give up their seats to women, we call it politeness. ... These symbols of deference and subservience are common with slaves to masters and men to women" (Farrell, 2017).

Another author, David Benatar, stirred debate in 2012 with his book, *The Second Sexism: Discrimination Against Men and Boys.* Some of his opinions include his contention that "most victims of violent crime are male and men are often (although not always) specially targeted for mass killing," adding that "although males are less often victims of sexual assault than females, the sexual assault of males is typically taken less seriously" (Benatar, 2012, 2). Reflecting a common concern by men's rights advocates, he states that "fathers are less likely than mothers to win custody of their children in the event of divorce" (Benatar, 2012). He also says that "laws permitting corporal punishment of boys but not of girls amounts to wrongful discrimination" (Benatar, 2012, 4).

Considered a watershed book when it was originally published in 1990, Robert Bly's *Iron John: A Book about Men* stirred heated conversations over the nature of manhood. Bly, better known as a poet, summoned his vision of the archetypal male in relation to modern society with such statements as, "When a contemporary man looks down into his psyche, he may, if conditions are right, find ... an ancient, hairy man" (Bly, 2015). Some found it to be profound and insightful, while others saw it as a denunciation of the ways women were felt to be guilty of emasculating men.

In 2019, Bettina Arndt countered America's #MeToo culture in which powerful men were being accused of predatory acts. In Arndt's book, *#MenToo,* she claimed that "#MeToo is simply the latest salvo in the long crusade by feminists to crush male sexuality" (Arndt, 2019). She cited issues with women's clothing: "Everywhere you look, women are stepping out dressed provocatively but bristling if the wrong man shows he enjoys the display," also targeting "SlutWalks, where scantily dressed women took to the streets, proudly proclaiming their right to dress as they wish" (Arndt, 2019).

In recent years, there has been growing discussion of men's rights activism, which is "essentially a movement based on the belief that men are losing power and status because of feminism" (Bote, 2020). One of the largest advocacy groups for men's rights activists is called MensGroup, which argues that presumably due to the greater degree of women's rights, "society has become biased and sexist against men" (Cox, 2022) and that "men face discrimination from the media, government, and Supreme Court for being male" (Cox, 2022).

MensGroup cites the "red pill," a metaphor signifying "the realization that the world is an illusion that supports the myth of male power. ... Until the red pill enlightens you, your world is nothing but lies and shadows [and] any man who is not a member of men's rights groups is a member of the matriarchy" (Galla, 2022). Some critics of feminism attacked it as "a political strategy to take power and an individual lifestyle that despised and denigrated men" (Bote, 2022).

While there are differences in priorities, one of the most common grievances of men's rights advocates is in the area of child support and custody issues. They feel that women have an unfair advantage over men by being given a preference in custody determinations. Some men's rights activists claim that women seek custody of the children "both for revenge and to get more money" (Bote, 2022).

According to some observers, much of men's rights activism is centered on the perception that "as women and minority groups gain rights, men—primarily white men—begin to lose theirs [and] arguments steeped in legitimate concerns curdle into something based on hate" (Bote, 2022).

Some point to the extremities of some men's rights activists, resulting in domestic violence by angry males against women, although others claim it only appears that way because there has been more public attention on domestic abuse in contemporary times. One argument goes that as recently as the 1990s, "sharing experiences of gender-based violence was taboo." As women gained more rights, though, they also spoke up more about domestic violence in their lives. "Sexual harassment claims went up ... [and increased] public attention of sexual violence and spousal abuse put pressure on law enforcement to bring more rape and domestic violence charges" (Hill, 2021). Other observers speculated that feminism sparked particular conflict in relationships with traditional gender roles "because women felt less pressure to simply put up with bad behavior or an unfair division of labor" (Brooke, 2011).

One of the most pervasive criticisms of the women's equality movement by men's rights adherents concerns females taking jobs away from males due to "reverse discrimination." Some sources disagree, stating that certain low-paying jobs are typically assigned to females because they are considered "women's work—jobs typically filled by women—[which] is valued less and rewarded less because it is done by women, not primarily because of market forces or the law of supply and demand" (Noble, 1992).

The term "glass ceiling," an invisible barrier that is said to keep women from rising to more senior positions, is fairly well known in contemporary usage. Another theory, called the "sticky floor," maintains that there are "obstacles for women preventing them from advancing to first level management positions" (Johnson, Long, & Faught, 2014). According to the sticky floor theory, women cannot even move into first-level management positions because their qualifications are overlooked. Therefore, opportunities for further advancement are limited. "The issue of gender diversity in organizations supports the sticky floor effect more strongly than the glass ceiling effect in that managers in higher level positions are more likely to be diversified than entry level positions" (Johnson, Long, & Faught, 2014). Without women advancing as far as the first level, the sticky floor keeps them in nonmanagement positions before they can even begin to approach the glass ceiling.

Along with traditional pink collar fields such as waitressing and clerical work, the type of low-wage jobs usually assigned to women in the workplace includes caregiving for such groups as children, the elderly, and the mentally ill. In addition, women can often be found in low-wage jobs interacting with the public in high-stress frontline positions at agencies such as the Department of Motor Vehicles, where there are often few male coworkers beneath the supervisory level. "We don't recognize or compensate for the grief [female] workers take from the public: angry citizens in line or on the phone ... [although the women] are relatively powerless to do what the citizen wants them to do" (Noble, 1992).

Apart from economic issues such as perceived reverse discrimination, the men's rights movement in the age of increased women's rights has also focused on societal issues faced by males, which they feel puts men at a disadvantage. Some sources state that when men are pressured by cultural norms to not show sadness or fear, and provide "financially and not emotionally ... we contribute to a culture that harms both men and women" (Friedman, Hollander, & Ulubay, 2022).

Calling it "toxic masculinity," there are some observers who state that "the stereotypical sense of masculinity is at war with everything we know about what it means to be human. ... It's muted suffering. It's filthy jokes, flaunting sexual conquests and insecurity disguised as bravado. It's being taught that power is dominating others. ... For this, men pay a steep price. So do women" (Dastagir, 2018).

Some men blame their discomfort with the changing societal landscape on the rise of the women's equality movement. They see more females arriving in places that had been exclusively male domains, such as the armed forces, government, and top-level management. As women gained more opportunity and greater power, many men felt threatened by the possible loss of things "they were taught made them 'real men,' [making some] feeling powerless and a lot of men angry" (Dastagir, 2018).

Researchers speculate that some male hostility toward females has less to do with the rise in women's equality than with their sense of being compelled to adhere to traditional masculine stereotypes while trying to navigate ever-changing societal norms. "Men don't live as long. They have a harder time making and maintaining fulfilling friendships. They commit suicide more often" (Dastagir, 2018).

Advocates for women's equality, though, point out that men have no business laying those problems at the doorsteps of feminists. "Feminists envisioned a world in which neither sex would be automatically dependent and both might be breadwinners," wrote social critic Barbara Ehrenreich. "Perhaps men may live longer in America when women carry more of the burden of the battle with the world, instead of being a burden themselves. … [if men supported women's equality, they would have] nothing to lose but their coronaries" (Ehrenreich, 2020).

Further Reading

Arndt, Bettina. 2019. #*MenToo*. Melbourne: Wilkinson Publishing. Kindle edition.

Bax, E. Belfort. 2020. *The Legal Subjection of Men*. Kindle edition.

Benatar, David. 2012. *The Second Sexism: Discrimination against Men and Boys*. Malden, MA: Wiley.

Bly, Robert. 2015. *Iron John: A Book about Men, 25th Anniversary Edition*. Boston: Da Capo Press.

Bote, Joshua. 2020. "Shooting Suspect Roy Den Hollander was a Men's Rights Activist. What Does That Mean?" *USA Today*, July 22. Retrieved from https://www.usato day.com/story/news/nation/2020/07/21/roy-den-hollander-what-mens-rights-activ ism-how-did-start/5481054002/.

Brooke, Jill. 2011. "Did Feminism Cause Divorce?" *Huffington Post*, March 25. Retrieved from https://www.huffpost.com/entry/did-feminism-cause-many-d_b _836327.

Cox, Hannah. 2022. "A Woman's Take on the Men's Rights Movement." *Foundation for Economic Education (FEE)*, April 5. Retrieved from https://fee.org/articles/a-wom ans-take-on-the-mens-rights-movement/.

Dastagir, Alia. 2018. "Men Pay a Steep Price When it Comes to Masculinity." *USA Today*, April 26. Retrieved from https://www.usatoday.com/story/news/2017/03/31/ masculinity-traditional-toxic-trump-mens-rights/99830694/.

Ehrenreich, Barbara. 2020. *Had I But Known: Collected Essays*. New York: Hatchette Book Group.

Farrell, Warren. 1974. *The Liberated Man: Beyond Masculinity: Freeing Men and Their Relationships with Women*. New York: Random House.

Farrell, Warren. 2017. *The Myth of Male Power: Why Men Are the Disposable Sex*. Anniversary Edition. Kindle Edition.

Friedman, Megan, Hollander, Jenny & Ulubay, Gabrielle. 2022. "30 Ways Women Still Aren't Equal to Men." *Marie Claire*, March 8. Retrieved from https://www.mariecla ire.com/politics/news/a15652/gender-inequality-stats/.

Galla, Sean. 2022. "Men's Rights Groups: Everything You Need to Know." *MensGroup. com*. Retrieved from https://mensgroup.com/mens-rights-groups/#What_Do_Mens_Rights_Groups_Believe.

Hill, Anita. 2021. *Believing: Our Thirty-Year Journey to End Gender Violence*. New York: Viking.

Johnson, Cooper, Long, Jamye, & Faught, Sam. 2014. "The Need to Practice What We Teach: The Sticky Floor Effect in Colleges of Business in Southern U.S. Universities," *Journal of Academic Administration in Higher Education*. Retrieved from https://files.eric.ed.gov/fulltext/EJ1140893.pdf.

Loudermilk, Kim. 2004. *Fictional Feminism: How American Bestsellers Affect the Movement for Women's Equality*. New York: Routledge.

Noble, Barbara Presley. 1992. "At Work: And Now the 'Sticky Floor.'" *New York Times*, November 22. Retrieved from https://www.nytimes.com/1992/11/22/business/at-work-and-now-the-sticky-floor.html.

"A Word for Men's Rights (1856)." 2015. *Gynocentrism*, December 19. [Originally published in *Putnam's Monthly*, Volume II, February 1856.] Retrieved from https://gynocentrism.com/2015/12/19/a-word-for-mens-rights-1856.

Q32: What Is the Current Financial Status of Women Compared to Men?

Answer: From the beginning of the women's equality movement in America, one of the major goals has been to establish parity between the genders in terms of their financial status. By the early 2020s, the financial gap between men and women has closed, but significant disparities remain. Women are frequently limited to lower-paying jobs, receive a smaller salary for doing the same work as males, commonly shoulder the majority of family care obligations, and do not attain the kind of promotions that generally go to men despite women's proven success on the job. These disadvantages often accumulate over the life course, leaving American fathers much more financially secure in retirement than American mothers (Gutierrez, 2023).

The Facts: The Pew Research Center of Washington, DC, has regularly compared gender-based wage issues over the years and found there to be an inequity that has not dramatically improved for women as time has passed. In an analysis that was based on median hourly earnings of both full- and part-time workers, the Pew Center found that in 2022, women earned an average of 82 percent of what men earned. "These results are similar to where the pay gap stood in 2002, when women earned 80% as much as men" (Aragão, 2023).

To put it another way, according to the 2020 Pew study, "women in the U.S. would have to work an additional 42 days to pull in the same amount of money as men did. That gap remained unchanged from a year earlier" (Gonzalez, 2021).

The US Census Bureau has also analyzed pay-related issues reflecting gender, although its study looks only at full-time workers, omitting part-timers. This segmentation slightly raises the 82 percent gap cited by the Pew Center for all female workers. Census research determined that "in 2021, full-time, year-round working women earned 84% of what their male counterparts earned on average, according to the Census Bureau's most recent analysis" (Aragão, 2023).

Some researchers sought to discover any differences between men and women in their viewpoint regarding what might cause a gender wage gap. According to the Pew study, "women are much more likely than men (61% vs. 37%) to say a major reason for the gap is that employers treat women differently. And while 45% of women say a major factor is that women make different choices about how to balance work and family, men are slightly less likely to hold that view (40% say this)" (Aragão, 2023).

The discussion often centers on the belief that the gender gap is the result of women favoring their family over their job, thus being perceived as taking their careers less seriously than men do. To cite the Pew study, 48 percent of employed women—almost half—report feeling a great deal of pressure to focus on their responsibilities at home, compared with 35 percent of employed males.

Due to the necessity of providing childcare and/or caregiving for other family members, women often take time out of the workforce, causing a disruption in a woman's career path that impacts her long-term earnings. When a woman has to leave the workforce to care for her children, often for years at a time, she may be forced to rejoin the job market in an entry-level position that carries a lower salary—that is, if she is hired at all, since some employers feel she probably lacks the requisite state-of-the-art job skills, not having kept up with technological advances.

There are other reasons that can play a part in a gender pay gap. According to the Pew study, some elements include measurable factors such as educational attainment, occupational segregation (i.e., "pink collar jobs"), and relevant work experience. The narrowing of the gap over the long term can often be attributed to gains that women have made in those areas.

That is good news for advocates of women's equality according to studies that indicate that although the gender pay gap has not changed greatly, there have been encouraging signs that the gap is indeed slowly being narrowed. "The estimated 18-cent gender pay gap among all workers in 2022 was down from 35 cents in 1982. And the 8-cent gap among workers ages 25 to 34 in 2022 was down from a 26-cent gap four decades earlier" (Aragão, 2023).

According to some, there still remains the issue of the "glass ceiling," which refers to the inability of women to break through invisible barriers that keep them from top-level positions. At the other end of the spectrum, the "sticky floor" keeps them stuck at the bottom in low-paying jobs. Male employees are generally not affected by the glass ceiling or sticky floor like their equivalent female coworkers are. Those women tend to remain for years in positions with poor pay and/or little opportunity for advancement.

Another factor in climbing the corporate ladder has been labeled the "broken rung" (Margolis, 2023), usually at the very first step upward. Many women relate having trained the males who then become their bosses, with men leapfrogging over the "broken rung" into management positions for which the women trained them.

Additionally, female employees often find themselves trapped in what might be called non-promotable tasks. "This invisible labor includes things such as training new hires, planning team celebrations, leading low-revenue and low-visibility projects, or taking notes in meetings" (Margolis, 2023). Utilizing their time on non-promotable tasks depletes the energy that women could spend on projects that would make them more promotable.

Sometimes, the pay inequity begins even before a woman's first day on the job when potential employers ask their salary history without revealing the wage scale for the position under consideration. Economists have long noted that "past pay inequality [determines] how much a person makes at their next job." They also note that "women who take time off paid work to care for kids are paid nearly 40% less than those who don't" (Molla, 2022).

Another factor is occupational segregation that erects barriers to keep women and people of color in low-paying service jobs.

In terms of women who do receive promotions, *LeanIn.org's* annual *Women in the Workplace* study indicates that "women make up 40% of managers, the report found, and the proportion gets more rarified the higher women progress" (Molla, 2022, "Women in Leadership …"). However, many women who did receive promotions to leadership positions "said they were much more likely to be burnt out than their male colleagues (43% of women versus 31% of men)" (Molla, "Women in Leadership …"). Part of the reason given by many, apart from having responsibilities at home as well as in the workplace, is being more likely to have male colleagues get credit for their work.

When women burn out and leave their management positions, it has a large impact because there were so few to begin with. It also becomes a self-fulfilling prophecy in the perception that women are not management material.

This becomes an issue of inequity that follows females for their entire lives. Using data collected by the RAND Corporation's American Life Panel, women tend to live longer than men, have shorter work lives, earn less pay, and accumulate lower levels of pensions or retirement benefits. "These factors put women at higher risk than men of having financial problems … and of approaching retirement with insufficient savings" (Fonseca, Mullen, Zamarro, & Zissimopoulos, 2011).

Research by the Financial Health Network found that women are more likely to be financially vulnerable than men (24 percent versus 17 percent), "meaning they struggle in nearly all areas of their financial lives" (Warren, McKay, & Greene, 2022). Further, "only 11% of Black women and 7% of Latina women are financially healthy" (Warren, McKay, & Greene, 2022).

According to Warren, McKay, and Greene, "research has shown that the U.S. economy loses billions of dollars due to imbalances in labor force participation and gender wage gaps." Those observers believe that the nation has the opportunity to "build a more sustainable economy that invests in and reaps the benefits of a financially healthy populace. Investing in women would benefit us all" (Warren, McKay, & Greene, 2022).

Further Reading

Aragão, Carolina. 2023. "Gender Pay Gap in U.S. Hasn't Changed Much in Two Decades," *Pew Research Center*. Retrieved from https://www.pewresearch.org/short-reads/2023/03/01/gender-pay-gap-facts/.

Casselman, Ben. 2021. "For Women in Economics, the Hostility Is Out in the Open," *New York Times*. Retrieved from https://www.nytimes.com/2021/02/23/business/economy/economics-women-gender-bias.html.

Fonseca, Raquel, Mullen, Kathleen, Zamarro, Gema, & Zissimopoulos, Julie. 2011 "What Explains the Gender Gap in Financial Literacy? The Role of Household Decision Making," *National Library of Medicine*. Retrieved from https://www.ncbi.nlm.nih.gov/pmc/articles/PMC3462438/.

Gonzalez, Carolina. 2021. "U.S. Women Had to Work 42 More Days to Earn What Men Did in 2020," *Bloomberg News*. Retrieved from https://news.bloomberglaw.com/daily-labor-report/u-s-women-had-to-work-42-more-days-to-earn-what-men-did-in-2020.

Gutierrez, Laura Valle. 2023. "New Data Demonstrates Mothers' Retirement Insecurity." *The Century Foundation*. https://tcf.org/content/report/new-data-demonstrates-mothers-retirement-insecurity/.

Lowrey, Annie. 2022. "Harassment in Economics Doesn't Stay in Economics," *The Atlantic*. Retrieved from https://www.theatlantic.com/ideas/archive/2022/11/economics-sexual-harrassment-women-sexism/672239/.

Margolis, Jaclyn. 2023. "Overlooked Reasons Why Women Don't Get Promoted," *Psychology Today*. Retrieved from https://www.psychologytoday.com/us/blog/shifting-workplace-dynamics/202304/overlooked-reasons-why-women-dont-get-promoted.

Molla, Rani. 2022. "Companies Are Being Forced to Reveal What a Job Pays. It's a Start," *Vox*. Retrieved from https://www.vox.com/recode/2022/10/17/23404953/pay-transparency-laws-salary-wage-gap.

Molla, Rani. 2022. "Women in Leadership are Leaning Out," *Vox*. Retrieved from https://www.vox.com/recode/2022/10/18/23409042/women-leadership-leaving-mckinsey-leanin-report-companies.

Noble, Barbara Presley. 1992. "At Work; And Now the 'Sticky Floor.'" *New York Times*, November 22. Retrieved from https://www.nytimes.com/1992/11/22/business/at-work-and-now-the-sticky-floor.html.

Warren, Andrew, McKay, Jess, & Greene, Meghan. 2022. "The Gender Gap in Financial Health," *Financial Health Network*. Retrieved from https://finhealthnetwork.org/research/gender-gap-in-financial-health/.

Q33: Have Women Reached Gender Equality in Political, Educational, Professional, and STEM Fields?

Answer: In 2023, women comprise slightly more than a quarter of all members of the US Congress, the highest percentage in American history. However, despite accounting for slightly more than half of the US population, women are underrepresented in positions of power, not only in politics but also in education, law, science, engineering, and other STEM fields. In addition, advocates for women's equality claim that the level of misogyny directed against women in those fields has long been problematic.

The Facts: When former South Carolina Governor Nikki Haley declared her intention to run for the office of US president in 2024, CNN news anchor Don Lemon stated on air that Haley was not "in her prime." Haley, at age fifty-one, was six years younger than Lemon. Similar examples of sexist commentary in American life and culture are not hard to find. According to one writer, "whether it's cracks about their clothes, face, body, or even parenting, sexist comments are pretty much a rite of passage for any woman in American politics today. ... Political commentators routinely focus on women's age or appearance instead of their policies, their positions, and their effectiveness" (North, 2023).

By 2023, women had attained historic firsts—the highest percentage in US history—both on the state and national levels of political office. The first woman was holding the office of vice president of the United States. In the Senate, there were twenty-five women among the one hundred seats, or 25 percent. With the record number of 125 women in the US House of Representatives, females held 28.7 percent of 435 seats.

On the state level, twelve females were serving as governors, a record high for women in that office. There were twenty-two women as lieutenant governors and sixty-three in other statewide elective offices such as attorney general, state treasurer, secretary of state, and so on, all of which showed an increase. There were 2,414 female state legislators, comprising 32.7 percent of 7,383 seats.

Those figures represent "the highest percentage in U.S. history and a considerable increase from where things stood even a decade ago" (Leppert & DeSilver, 2023). The numbers are especially encouraging when compared to 1973 when the percentage of women in the US Congress topped out at 3 percent and female state office holders were equally sparse. Although women are about 50 percent of the US population, many see today's numbers as progress compared to the 234-year history of the US Congress where overall, "3.2% of all members of Congress to date have been women" ("Women in the U.S. Congress 2022," 2022).

However, despite their increased presence in most governmental positions, many women in elective office at both the state and national levels find themselves subjected to "the same kind of undermining rhetoric that the very first women candidates experienced more than a century ago. ... Women are still subject to enormous amounts of misogyny from commentators, voters, and their fellow elected officials" (North, 2023).

In another field, some studies are indicating what is being called a "serious gender gap in higher education" (Bryant, 2022), but not the same kind of gender gap as income inequality, for example, where women are lagging behind. According to findings from the Pew Research Center, "women increasingly outpace men in college graduation and enrollment rates, [accounting] for nearly 60% of all college students by the end of the 2021–2022 academic year" (Bryant, 2022).

That source reports that the number of women pursuing higher education has increased steadily over the last forty years, outpacing men in both college enrollment and graduation. Since the 1990s, women have earned college degrees at higher rates than men, and the gender gap in college completion has widened as "men are more likely to drop out and avoid enrollment altogether … [yet] despite this, women are still underrepresented in high-paying jobs" (Bryant, 2022).

Beyond graduation, women currently account for 50.7 percent or more than half of the college-educated labor force in the United States, according to a Pew Research Center analysis of government data, a change that "occurred in the fourth quarter of 2019 and remains the case today. … In contrast, men and most other educational groups now have lower rates of labor force participation than they did in the second quarter of 2019" (Fry, 2022).

One of the fields that has shown a dramatic rise in female participation, both in their rate of higher education and in the job market, is the legal profession. Reports have noted that beginning in 2016, for the first time, there are more women than men in law school. According to 2021 data, enrollment in law school is comprised of about 55.3 percent female and 44.4 percent male. "The majority of law schools (82.91%) had more female attendees than male attendees last year" (Zaretsky, 2022).

However, it must be noted that "although women are enrolling in law school in droves, the vast majority of those are lower-ranked institutions" (Zaretsky, 2022), not the iconic law schools of the Ivy League and other top-tier institutions.

Law schools themselves reflect an interesting phenomenon regarding females in the profession. Studies have shown that women who are employed at law schools are more than twice as likely as men to have what are considered to be lower-status positions, such as adjuncts, lecturers, and librarians rather than being full professors. In addition, rather than being named deans of law schools, "women are two times as likely as men to work as interim deans" (Ward, 2022) but not being awarded the permanent position.

In addition, when female law students graduate and go out into the job market, a study has determined that "female lawyers' median weekly pay is 26.5% less than male lawyers, and the gap is larger for partners. … This is something that cannot be explained just by differences in roles, [sounding like a joke] that men choose high-paying careers like lawyer and women choose lower paying roles like *female lawyer*" (Hendrickson, 2022).

In STEM fields (science, technology, engineering, and mathematics), a similar situation exists, with the difference being that there are fewer women in those fields to begin with. According to a study by the American Association of University Women (AAUW), it starts long before women enter the job market. "Girls and women are systematically tracked away from science and math throughout their education, limiting their access, preparation and opportunities to go into these fields as adults" ("The STEM Gap: Women and Girls in Science, Technology, Engineering and Mathematics," n.d.).

The AAUW report found that females make up only 28 percent of the workforce in the STEM fields of science, technology, engineering, and math, and men vastly outnumber women majoring in most STEM fields in college. "The gender gaps are particularly high in some of the fastest-growing and highest-paid jobs of the future, like computer science and engineering—two of the most lucrative STEM fields—[and] remain heavily male dominated. Only 21% of engineering majors and 19% of computer science majors are women" ("The STEM Gap: Women and Girls in Science, Technology, Engineering and Mathematics," n.d.).

According to the AAUW study,

38% of women who major in computers work in computer fields, and only 24% of those who majored in engineering work in the engineering field. Men in STEM annual salaries are nearly $15,000 higher per year than women ($85,000 compared to $60,828). And Latina and Black women in STEM earn around $33,000 less (at an average of around $52,000 a year). ("The STEM Gap: Women and Girls in Science, Technology, Engineering and Mathematics")

One source reports that "while the percentage of women employed across job sectors in the U.S. has reached 47%, representation at the five tech giants is only 34.4%" (Corbo, 2022). The five firms cited—Amazon, Apple, Facebook, Google, and Microsoft—are generally considered the companies that are the most desirable to work for.

Some might find it to be a self-fulling prophecy the longer that women continue to be underrepresented in STEM. "Gender discrimination and gender bias reinforce cultural stereotypes about women and their ability to perform in male-dominated STEM fields" (Kong, Carroll, Lundberg, Omura, & Lepe, 2020).

The relatively few women who find jobs in STEM fields such as computer technology sometimes find a toxic "bro culture," which is a term used to describe "a culture dominated by over-confident, arrogant, obnoxious men. ... In Silicon Valley, 'bro culture' is very much alive" (Doyle, 2020). One source reports that "72% of women in tech say they've worked at a company where bro culture is pervasive" (Corbo, 2022).

Summing up, it appears that the gender pay gap in earnings between men and women has been narrowing, but women working full time still earn less than men. According to one source, "Even when we compare men and women in the same or similar occupations who appear nearly identical in background and experience, a gap of about 10% typically remains. As such, we cannot rule out that gender-related impediments hold back women, including outright discrimination, attitudes that reduce women's success in the workplace, and an absence of mentors" (Yellen, 2020).

This source goes on to state, "One recent study estimates that increasing the female participation rate to that of men would raise our gross domestic product by 5%." The source, economist Janet Yellen, is in a unique position to know. She served as the US Secretary of the Treasury since 2021 and formerly served as chair of the Federal Reserve.

Further Reading

Bryant, Jessica. 2022. "Women Continue to Outnumber Men in College Completion," *Best Colleges*. Retrieved from https://www.bestcolleges.com/news/analy sis/2021/11/19/women-complete-college-more-than-men/.

Corbo, Giuliana. 2022. "Leadership in Tech: How Can We Get More Women to the Top?" *Forbes*. Retrieved from https://www.forbes.com/sites/ forbestechcouncil/2022/03/04/leadership-in-tech-how-can-we-get-mor e-women-to-the-top/?sh=32e1b2ba2808.

Doyle, Rob. 2020. "Sexism in Tech: An Inconvenient Truth," *Medium*. Retrieved from https://medium.com/swlh/sexism-in-tech-an-inconvenient-truth-26df 0329e39.

Fry, Richard. 2022. "Women Now Outnumber Men in the U.S. College-Educated Labor Force," *Pew Research Center*. Retrieved from https://www.pewresearch.org/

short-reads/2022/09/26/women-now-outnumber-men-in-the-u-s-college-educa
ted-labor-force/.

Hendrickson, Christine. 2022. "Huge Pay Gap for Women Lawyers: What Firms Can
Do," *Bloomberg Law*. Retrieved from https://news.bloomberglaw.com/business-and-
practice/huge-pay-gap-for-women-lawyers-what-firms-can-do.

Hewlett, Sylvia Ann. 2022. "Executive Women and the Myth of Having It All,"
Harvard Business Review. Retrieved from https://hbr.org/2002/04/execut
ive-women-and-the-myth-of-having-it-all.

Kong, Stephanie, Carroll, Katherine, Lundberg, Daniel, Omura, Paige, & Lepe, Bianca.
2020. "Reducing Gender Bias in STEM," *MIT Science Policy Review*. Retrieved from
https://sciencepolicyreview.org/2020/08/reducing-gender-bias-in-stem/.

Leppert, Rebecca & DeSilver, Drew. 2023. "118th Congress Has a Record Number
of Women," *Pew Research Center*. Retrieved from https://www.pewresearch.org/
short-reads/2023/01/03/118th-congress-has-a-record-number-of-women/.

North, Anna. 2023. "The Stubborn Sexism of American Politics." *Vox*. Retrieved from
https://www.vox.com/culture/23671498/don-lemon-nikki-haley-sexism-polit
ics-women.

Stebbins, Samuel & Frohlich, Thomas. 2018. "Employment Trends: 20 Jobs That Are
Now Dominated by Women," *USA Today*. Retrieved from https://www.usatoday.
com/story/money/careers/employment-trends/2018/08/08/20-jobs-that-have-bec
ome-dominated-by-women/37330779/.

"The STEM Gap: Women and Girls in Science, Technology, Engineering and
Mathematics." n.d. *American Association of University Women*. Retrieved from
https://www.aauw.org/resources/research/the-stem-gap/.

Ward, Stephanie Francis. 2022. "Law School Achievement Gap by Gender for Faculty
and Deans Examined in New Paper," *ABA Journal*. Retrieved from https://www.
abajournal.com/web/article/paper-examines-law-school-achievement-gap-by-gen
der-for-faculty-deans.

"Women in Elective Office 2023." 2023. *Center for American Women and Politics*.
Retrieved from https://cawp.rutgers.edu/facts/current-numbers/women-elective-off
ice-2023.

"Women in the U.S. Congress 2022." 2022. *Center for American Women and Politics*.
Retrieved from https://cawp.rutgers.edu/facts/levels-office/congress/women-us-
congress-2022.

Yellen, Janet. 2020 The History of Women's Work and Wages and How It Has Created
Success for Us All," *Brookings Institute*. Retrieved from https://www.brookings.
edu/essay/the-history-of-womens-work-and-wages-and-how-it-has-created-succ
ess-for-us-all/.

Zaretsky, Staci. 2022. "Women Are Dominating When It Comes to Law School
Enrollment," *Above the Law*. Retrieved from https://abovethelaw.com/2022/07/
women-are-dominating-when-it-comes-to-law-school-enrollment/.

Q34: How Much More Likely Are Women to Experience Sexual Assault, Violence, and Online Harassment Than Men?

Answer: Women are much more likely to be targeted for sexual assault, violence, and online harassment than men. These traumas can haunt the average victim for the rest of her life. According to RAINN (Rape, Abuse, and Incest National Network, the largest anti-sexual violence organization in the United States), one out of six American women will be the victim of a rape or rape attempt in her lifetime. A 2002 federal study found that an estimated 91 percent of people who are raped or sexually assaulted are women, with men accounting for 99 percent of perpetrators of sexual assault and rape (US Department of Justice, 2002).

The Facts: An article titled "Women Feeling Unsafe Shouldn't Be Normal" begins with the following passage:

> Every girl knows the universal women's safety protocol. Don't walk alone at night. Put your keys between your knuckles in case you need a weapon. Always have pepper spray ready. Wear something bright. Don't wear anything too scandalous. Tell someone your whereabouts and even call someone if you do end up walking alone. And always be aware of your surroundings, even during the daytime. (Martin, 2021)

While many Americans believe that there has been a general increase in violence in recent years, some groups feel it more than others. A poll by Georgetown University found that "across the country, nearly half of women surveyed said they 'feel unsafe because they are a woman' frequently or sometimes in their daily life" (Klugman & Ortiz, 2021).

In addition, another survey found that only 46 percent of Black women in the United States report feeling safe walking alone in the area where they live. "Among all race and gender subgroups, Black women are the only group in which less than half say they feel safe walking alone in their neighborhood" (McCarthy & Lloyd, 2023).

It is not only while they are out walking that women can be specifically targeted. In a rising trend, cases of "women being raped in their rooms at top hotel chains are occurring because staff are allegedly handing over keys to sexual predators unchecked" (Martinez, 2023). The men allegedly broke into women's rooms after lying to staff in order to obtain keycards without proper identification.

While males also experience violence, women seem to be more frequent targets for violence, rape, and murder. One source cites statistics indicating that almost 52 percent of women in the United States reported experiencing physical violence at some point in their life. "This is higher than other developed countries" (Kliff, 2014). Along with one in five women being raped in their lifetime, some of which resulted in pregnancy, injuries that female assault victims can suffer include broken teeth, bullet wounds, head or spinal cord injury, and/ or being knocked unconscious. Kliff reports that many female assault victims do not receive medical care, while male victims are more likely to receive medical care than females.

Domestic violence by an intimate partner "is like no other crime. … It does not happen because someone is in the wrong place at the wrong time" (Snyder, 2019). Those types of assault take place in what is generally assumed to be the safe haven of the home, by an individual the victim presumably loves and trusts. Many are trapped in a cycle of violence that affects not only themselves, but also any children who are in the house. "America's broken legal system, combined with cultural beliefs about family, pressures women to stay in violent, dangerous marriages" (Snyder, 2019). Their victimization can go beyond assault to losing their life, as "nearly half of all murdered women are killed by romantic partners" (Snyder, 2019).

Another form of abuse affecting women more than men is sexual violence, defined as sexual activity when consent is not freely given. Such assaults are said to affect millions of people each year in the United States, although researchers often feel that the numbers underestimate the problem because many cases are unreported. "Survivors may be ashamed, embarrassed, or afraid to tell the police, friends, or family about the violence. Victims may also keep quiet because they have been threatened with further harm if they tell anyone, or do not think anyone will help them" ("Fast Facts: Preventing Sexual Violence," 2022). In addition, the abuse often starts early in the lives of girls, with almost half of female rape survivors reporting that they "were first raped as a minor (i.e., before age 18)" ("Fast Facts: Preventing Sexual Violence," 2022).

Males can also be affected by sexual violence. "About 3% of American men, or 1 in 33, have experienced an attempted or completed rape in their lifetime. One out of every 10 rape victims are male" ("Victims of Sexual Violence: Statistics," 2023), about half the rate of females.

The consequences of sexual violence can be both physical and mental. Bodily injuries, which can be chronic, can include bruising, gastrointestinal problems, genital damage, reproductive issues, sexual health problems, sexually transmitted infections, and unwanted pregnancy for women. Psychological problems often also occur, including post-traumatic stress disorder. Survivors of sexual violence can experience anxiety, depression, and suicidal thoughts. Many are likely to abuse alcohol, use drugs, smoke, and engage in risky sexual activity. Trauma from sexual violence can even have economic effects by impacting the survivor's employment because of diminished performance and having to take time off work, which could lead to job loss. "These issues disrupt earning power and have a long-term effect on the economic well-being of survivors and their families" ("Fast Facts: Preventing Sexual Violence," 2022).

While maliciousness in general has been constant in human history, there is a very recent development due to modern technology: online harassment. A Pew Research Center survey of American adults found that "41% of Americans have personally experienced some form of online harassment" (Vogels, 2021). The study found that gender plays a role in the type of online harassment people are likely to encounter. Men cite politics as being the trigger in their being targeted for venom, as opposed to women for whom the attacks are gender-related, being over three times "more likely than men to report having been sexually harassed online (16% vs. 5%)" (Vogels, 2021).

With social media being a relatively new form of communication, one that is used to a tremendous extent by young people, studies have found that "33% of women under 35 say they have been sexually harassed online" (Vogels, 2021), which is three times the rate reported by men. "Some 61% of women say online harassment is a major problem" (Vogels, 2021).

Sexual assault, violence, and online harassment continue to be a gender-based concern common to most women. "Women's safety, economic opportunities, and access to healthcare interact in important ways, especially for women who are disadvantaged on other fronts" (Klugman & Ortiz, 2021). Therefore, occurrences are not only traumatic in themselves, but also manifest themselves in negative ways across the spectrum of American society.

Further Reading

"Fact Sheet: Reauthorization of the Violence Against Women Act (VAWA)." 2022. *The White House*. Retrieved from https://www.whitehouse.gov/briefing-room/statements-releases/2022/03/16/fact-sheet-reauthorization-of-the-violence-against-women-act-vawa/.

"Fast Facts: Preventing Sexual Violence." 2022. *Centers for Disease Control and Prevention*. Retrieved from https://www.cdc.gov/violenceprevention/sexualviolence/fastfact.html.

Kliff, Sarah. 2014. "9 Facts about Violence Against Women Everyone Should Know," *Vox*. Retrieved from https://www.vox.com/2014/5/25/5748610/eight-facts-about-violence-against-women-everyone-should-know.

Klugman, Jeni & Ortiz, Elena. 2021. "Half of American Women Feel Unsafe Because They Are Women," *University of California at San Diego*. Retrieved from https://emerge.ucsd.edu/half-of-american-women-feel-unsafe-because-they-are-women/.

Martin, Olivia. 2021. "Women Feeling Unsafe Shouldn't Be Normal," *Baylor Lariat*. Retrieved from https://baylorlariat.com/2021/03/23/women-feeling-unsafe-shouldnt-be-normal/.

Martinez, Mary Ann. 2023. "Hotel Sexual Assaults on the Rise as Predators Given Access to Women's Rooms in Horrifying Trend," *New York Post*. Retrieved from https://nypost.com/2023/03/05/hilton-holiday-inn-allegedly-let-predators-into-womens-rooms/.

McCarthy, Justin & Lloyd, Camille. 2023. "Majority of U.S. Black Women Don't Feel Safe Walking Alone," *Gallup*. Retrieved from https://news.gallup.com/opinion/gallup/471236/majority-black-women-don-feel-safe-walking-alone.aspx.

Mikoley, Kate. 2021. *Cyber Mobs, Trolls, and Online Harassment*. New York: Cavendish Square Publishing.

Snyder, Rachel Louise. 2020. *No Visible Bruises: What We Don't Know about Domestic Violence Can Kill Us*. New York: Bloomsbury.

Snyder, Rachel Louise. 2019. "The Particular Cruelty of Domestic Violence," *The Atlantic*. Retrieved from https://www.theatlantic.com/family/archive/2019/05/no-visible-bruises-domestic-violence/588631/.

US Department of Justice. 2002. Violence against Women Report.

"Victims of Sexual Violence: Statistics." 2023. *Rape, Abuse & Incest National Network*. Retrieved from https://www.rainn.org/statistics/victims-sexual-violence.

Vogels, Emily. 2021. "The State of Online Harassment," *Pew Research Center*. Retrieved from https://www.pewresearch.org/internet/2021/01/13/the-state-of-online-harassment/.

7

Women's Equality and Abortion

On June 24, 2022, the Supreme Court issued a ruling in *Dobbs v. Jackson Women's Health Organization* that removed constitutional protections for access to abortion, a medical procedure to terminate a pregnancy. Through its 5–4 decision in the *Dobbs* case, the Court overturned the landmark *Roe v. Wade* decision of 1973, which had guaranteed federal safeguards for abortion rights on the grounds that reproductive rights were constitutionally protected. The *Dobbs* ruling removed those protections, turning the matter of abortion back to individual states to decide if it would be legal for the people of their jurisdiction.

In 1973, when the Supreme Court made its 7–2 decision granting abortion protection in *Roe v. Wade*, it came near the onset of what became known as the second wave of the women's equality movement. Prior to the *Roe* decision, abortion was legal in some but not all areas of the United States.

After the *Dobbs* decision overturned *Roe v. Wade*, many felt that a new sense of energy was launched among contemporary women's rights advocates with a goal of reinstating the federal protections provided by *Roe*. Protest signs appeared at women's rights demonstrations around the country, emblazoned with the words "We Won't Go Back" to the time before *Roe* legalized abortion. Coming a few months before the midterm elections of 2022, the Supreme Court's decision forced many candidates for office on the state, local, and national levels to choose and defend their stand on abortion. Endorsements by influential groups often hinged on that issue. Why? Because the *Dobbs* ruling meant that each state was responsible for its own laws on abortion. Mayors and governors and other state, county, and local lawmakers suddenly had a lot more power to shape abortion policies that would affect the lives of every person in the state.

When the 2022 elections were held several months after the Court overturned *Roe v. Wade*, there were a number of ballot measures addressing abortion in various states across America, the most on record for a single year.

A number of races between state, local, and national candidates were decided by extremely small margins, which some observers felt was symbolic of the virtually 50/50 political divide of the American public, in which abortion was a major source of conflict. Prior to the election, many media observers speculated that based on an upsurge in voter registration by women, the issue of abortion rights would be a significant factor in the outcome of a number of races, even in predominately "red" states. When the votes were counted, that prediction was proven correct.

Q35: How Important Was *Roe v. Wade* to the Women's Equality Movement?

Answer: The legal case known as *Roe v. Wade* was a landmark ruling in 1973 by the US Supreme Court. In the *Roe* decision, the Court ruled in favor of a woman's right to have the medical procedure known as an abortion to terminate a pregnancy, legalizing the practice in the United States. The *Roe* ruling became a touchstone issue in the women's equality movement. Since 1973, there has been a great deal of contention on all sides of the women's rights banner, continuing to the 2022 Supreme Court decision that overturned *Roe v. Wade*. Reinstating *Roe* became a goal of many women's rights advocates. For the women's equality movement, as well as in terms of the general political landscape of the nation, *Roe v. Wade* continued to be an issue, one of the most controversial and divisive in American history.

The Facts: *Roe v. Wade* had its roots in 1969 when a woman sought to terminate her pregnancy because she was unable to care for the child. However, she lived in Texas where abortion was illegal. Using the legal pseudonym "Jane Roe" to protect her identity, the woman's attorneys filed a lawsuit titled *Roe v. Wade* in their local district court in 1970. The suit named Dallas County's district attorney, Henry Wade, as defendant, alleging that abortion laws in Texas were unconstitutional. Henry Wade was no stranger to high-profile cases, having prosecuted the 1964 trial of Jack Ruby for killing alleged JFK assassin Lee Harvey Oswald.

When the three-judge panel in Texas ruled in "Jane Roe's" favor, the case was appealed to the US Supreme Court. In 1973, the Supreme Court issued a 7–2 decision on *Roe v. Wade*, holding that the 14th Amendment implies the right to privacy through its due process clause. This, the Court ruled, would protect a woman's personal decision whether or not to have an abortion without interference by the government.

After its enactment in 1973, *Roe v. Wade* became central to highly contentious debates about abortion rights and restrictions in the United States. It established a federally recognized right to abortion, superseding abortion laws that varied enormously from state to state. In fact, "in the absence of any legislation whatsoever on the subject of abortion in 1800, the legal status of the practice was governed by the traditional British common law as interpreted by local courts in the new American states" (Mohr, 1978, 3).

In colonial times, "laws prosecuted unwed mothers with fines, whipping, and public shaming. … [Terminating pregnancy] would avoid those penalties and protect the reputation of the woman" (Hull & Hoffer, 2021, 15). In the American colonies, "the community shared folk wisdom on how to procure an abortion. … Midwives sometimes doubled as abortionists" (Hull & Hoffer, 2021, 12).

Historians note the prevalence of pregnancies in early America among young female servants and mill workers, often impregnated by their employers. "Abortion, in short, was the last resort of a particular segment of the unmarried: seduced, abandoned, and helpless women, generally between the ages of sixteen and twenty-five" (Olasky, 2015).

By the mid-1800s, there was a brisk business in the termination of pregnancy by individuals such as a woman named Madame Restell who openly advertised providing abortion services for more than thirty years in cities including New York, Philadelphia, and Boston. Restell's clientele was "primarily married, native-born Protestant women of the upper and middle classes" (Reagan, 2022, 10).

As the 1800s wore on, there was an expansion of the American medical profession in which doctors, almost always male, became officially licensed. Some observers noted that the licensed physicians or "regulars" came up against the centuries-old tradition of midwives and other practitioners of female procedures, called "irregulars." With an increasing competition for patients in the latter part of the 1800s between male doctors and female midwives, the regulars became stronger, embarking "on their way to nearly complete control over American medicine" (Mohr, 1978, 239).

At the same time, some religious groups and social conservatives were gaining ground in their opposition to the concept of birth control, which was utilized as a means to curtail an unwanted pregnancy before it began. During the age of what was called the Social Purity movement in America during the late 1800s, most women found that obtaining information on how to avoid pregnancy was difficult to impossible. Under the Comstock Laws, an 1873 act of the US Congress, "contraceptives were banned as obscene, making it a federal offense to distribute birth control information" (Hendricks, 2021, 112).

By 1910, abortion was banned nationwide in America except in isolated cases, although sources indicate that women who were well-off financially could travel outside the United States to access medically licensed abortions that were legal elsewhere. "Women without means resorted to desperate—and often dangerous or deadly—measures" (Ravitz, 2016). Those measures included everything from drinking poison to inserting a knitting needle or wire coat hanger into their bodies.

To avoid the need for abortion, some women's rights advocates fought for decades to make family planning information available to American women. However, the Comstock Laws banning birth control–related materials were enforced until 1965. Some corporate entities marketed their merchandise as "feminine hygiene" products, which was often a euphemism for contraception. One that was widely advertised and popular in the 1930s was Lysol, a disinfectant used for cleaning toilets, which "was aggressively marketed to women as safe and gentle" (Eveleth, 2013). Lysol damaged women's internal organs and "hundreds of people died from Lysol exposure. ... As if that wasn't bad enough, Lysol isn't even an effective contraceptive" (Eveleth, 2013).

Before safe, effective birth control was available, each sexual act could mean pregnancy. Many women felt happy and fulfilled by motherhood, although for some, having little time to adjust to marriage plus having children close together was difficult. For unmarried women, there were few options. Along with being illegal, attempting to terminate a pregnancy was dangerous and expensive. Going to a home for unwed mothers frequently "brought shame to her and her family. Giving the baby up for adoption often left life-long emotional scars. And raising a child on her own was difficult at best" (Hendricks, 2021).

A social upheaval came in 1960, when the United States approved medication that could be used for birth control, later popularly abbreviated as "The Pill." However, it was not immediately available, in large measure due to opposition from religious and social conservatives. The US Supreme Court did not determine the right of married couples to use The Pill until 1965 in the case of *Griswold v. Connecticut.*

Some religious groups barred their members from using birth control pills or other contraception at any time. Regardless of religious considerations, doctors at the time usually required the husband's permission before prescribing The Pill for a woman, and there were some husbands who would not allow their wives to use it. Unmarried women did not receive full access to the birth control pill until 1972.

That was the landscape of the country when the *Roe v. Wade* decision was handed down by the Supreme Court in 1973. Women's rights groups applauded the ruling; social conservatives mourned. Maintaining a woman's right to choose an abortion via the *Roe* ruling became a rallying cry of women's rights advocates for decades, just as overturning it was a primary goal of its opponents.

With contradictory arguments about the costs and benefits of abortion, "activists on either side primarily discussed not what the Constitution allowed, but whether legal abortion was socially, culturally, and medically desirable or justified" (Ziegler, 2021, 3).

Three years after that March for Life, on June 24, 2022, the US Supreme Court did cite the Constitution by stating that nothing in the document provides the right to have an abortion.

When the 2022 ruling was issued, there was a sense of role reversal in the United States as *Roe v. Wade* was overturned by the Supreme Court via a new case called *Dobbs v. Jackson Women's Health Organization*. The named parties were Thomas E. Dobbs, an officer with the Mississippi State Department of Health, and the Jackson Women's Health Organization, which was Mississippi's only abortion clinic. In their decision on *Dobbs v. Jackson Women's Health Organization*, the Supreme Court reversed the constitutional right to abortion. With the coming of what came to be abbreviated as the *Dobbs* ruling, it was *Roe v. Wade* supporters who mourned while *Roe* opponents cheered.

Whatever their stance on the *Roe v. Wade* decision being overturned, many Americans might agree that "*Roe* sits on a fault line, a fissure between right and left, traditional and modern, running through our national politics" (Hull & Hoffer, 2021). Observers believe that the rift is unlikely to be healed any time soon. Just as some groups do their utmost to uphold the reversal of *Roe v. Wade*, the reinstatement of *Roe* to provide nationwide legal access to abortion remains the single greatest and most consequential cause for many in the women's equality movement.

Further Reading

Bluth, Rachel. 2022. "My Body, My Choice." *National Public Radio*, July 4. Retrieved from https://www.npr.org/sections/health-shots/2022/07/04/1109367458/my-body-my-choice-vaccines.

Eveleth, Rose. 2013. "Lysol's Vintage Ads Subtly Pushed Women to Use Its Disinfectant as Birth Control." *Smithsonian*, September 30. Retrieved from https://www.smithso

nianmag.com/smart-news/lysols-vintage-ads-subtly-pushed-women-to-use-its-disin fectant-as-birth-control-218734/.

Faux, Marian. 2001. *Roe v. Wade: The Untold Story of the Landmark Supreme Court Decision That Made Abortion Legal*. New York: Cooper Square Press.

Hendricks, Nancy. 2021. *Daily Lives of Women in Postwar America*. Santa Barbara, CA: Greenwood.

Hull, N. E. H. & Hoffer, Peter Charles. 2021. *Roe v. Wade: The Abortion Rights Controversy in American History*. Lawrence: University Press of Kansas.

March for Life. 2022. Retrieved from https://marchforlife.org/.

Mohr, James C. 1978. *Abortion in America: The Origins and Evolution of National Policy, 1800–1900*. New York: Oxford University Press.

Olasky, Marvin, 2015. "Did Colonial America have Abortions? Yes, but …" *World News Group*, January 17. Retrieved from https://wng.org/sift/did-colonial-america-have-abortions-yes-but-1617409251.

Ravitz, Jessica. 2016. "The Surprising History of Abortion in the United States." *CNN*, June 27. Retrieved from https://www.cnn.com/2016/06/23/health/abortion-history-in-united-states.

Reagan, Leslie J. 2022. *When Abortion Was a Crime: Women, Medicine, and Law in the United States, 1867–1973, with a New Preface*. Berkeley: University of California Press.

Ziegler, Mary. 2020. *Abortion and the Law in America*. New York: Cambridge University Press.

Q36: What Impact Did the Reversal of *Roe v. Wade* Have on the Women's Equality Movement?

Answer: When *Roe v. Wade* was overturned in 2022 by the US Supreme Court in the *Dobbs v. Jackson Women's Health Organization* decision, reactions among Americans were mixed. Social conservatives and various religious groups cheered the *Dobbs* decision that nullified *Roe*, which had been enacted in 1973 to legalize abortion in the United States. At the same time, many women's rights advocates mourned the *Dobbs* ruling and declared their determination to continue the fight for abortion rights at the local, state, and federal levels.

The Facts: The 1973 Supreme Court's *Roe v. Wade* decision that legalized abortion in the United States was overturned in 2022 by the Court's ruling on *Dobbs v. Jackson Women's Health Organization*. As many observers noted, the post-Dobbs landscape could make economic parity of genders a more difficult goal for the feminist movement to achieve, since "reproductive choice can help alleviate economic injustice" (Freedman, 2003).

When *Roe* was revoked, a number of states enforced a ban on abortion, with very limited exceptions. In some, the ban is being challenged in court but remains in effect. There are those with a near-total ban (Alabama, Arkansas, Idaho, Kentucky, Louisiana, Mississippi, Missouri, Oklahoma, South Dakota, Tennessee, Texas, West Virginia); those prohibiting abortion after a specific point in pregnancy (Arizona, Florida, Georgia); and those such as Indiana and Wyoming in which "a near-total ban has been blocked from enforcement while a legal challenge is pending in state court" (Nash & Guarnieri, 2023).

Defenders of abortion rights registered a number of important victories during the 2022 midterms—including the enshrinement of abortion rights in the constitutions of some "red states." However, abortion rights advocates have expressed concern about a national prohibition on abortion, suggesting that justices like Brett Cavanagh see "in the Constitution a basis for congressional authority to enact such a ban" (Schacter, 2022). Further, the 14th Amendment, which is the constitutional doctrine on which *Roe* was first approved and then later overturned, "also supports a host of other important rights, including access to birth control, a right to be intimate with the partner of your choice, and marriage equality" (Schacter, 2022). Civil rights and privacy activists are concerned that if the Supreme Court applies the same reasoning as it did in *Dobbs*, all these rights are threatened.

Although it is not the only feminist issue, there was a clear effect on many women's rights advocates by the reversal of *Roe v. Wade*. Along with matters such as financial equity, it is likely that the matter of access to abortion will continue to be of significance in the women's equality movement for the foreseeable future.

Further Reading

"Advancing Alternatives to Anti-Life Violence and Harm." n.d. *Americans United for Life*. Retrieved from https://aul.org/.

Andrews, Edmund. 2020. "Whose History? AI Uncovers Who Gets Attention in High School Textbooks." *Stanford University News*, November 17. Retrieved from https://hai.stanford.edu/news/whose-history-ai-uncovers-who-gets-attention-high-school-textbooks.

De Witte, Melissa. 2022. "Stanford Scholars Examine Gender Bias and Ways to Advance Equity across Society." *Stanford University News*, July 19. Retrieved from https://news.stanford.edu/2022/07/19/examining-obstacles-gender-equality/.

"Equal Pay Day: March 15, 2022." 2022. *United States Census Bureau*, March 15. Retrieved from https://www.census.gov/newsroom/stories/equal-pay-day.html.

Freedman, Estelle. 2003. *No Turning Back: The History of Feminism and the Future of Women*. New York: Ballantine Books.

Laughlin, Lynda & Wisniewski, Megan. 2021. "Unequally Essential: Women and Gender Pay Gap during COVID-19." *United States Census Bureau*, March 23. Retrieved from https://www.census.gov/library/stories/2021/03/unequally-essent ial-women-and-gender-pay-gap-during-covid-19.html.

Nash, Elizabeth & Guarnieri, Isabel. 2023. "Six Months Post-Roe, 24 US States Have Banned Abortion or Are Likely to Do So: A Roundup," *Guttmacher Institute*. Retrieved from https://www.guttmacher.org/2023/01/six-months-post-roe-24-us-sta tes-have-banned-abortion-or-are-likely-do-so-roundup.

"Our Issues." 2022. *National Organization for Women*. Retrieved from https://now.org/about/our-issues/.

Schacter, Jane. 2022. "A Constitutional Earthquake: Stanford's Jane Schacter on SCOTUS Decision to Overturn Roe v. Wade, Ending Constitutional Right to an Abortion." *Stanford University News*, June 24. Retrieved from https://law.stanford.edu/2022/06/24/a-constitutional-earthquake-stanfords-jane-schacter-on-scotus-decision-to-overturn-roe-v-wade-ending-constitutional-right-to-an-abortion.

Tracy, Abigail & Vanderhoof, Erin. 2022 "The Fight Ahead." *Vanity Fair*, November, 86–93.

"Women's Equality Day: August 26, 2022." 2022. *United States Census Bureau*, August 26. Retrieved from https://www.census.gov/newsroom/stories/womens-equal ity-day.html.

"Women's History Month: March 2021." 2021. *United States. Census Bureau, March 2*. Retrieved from https://www.census.gov/newsroom/facts-for-features/2021/wom ens-history-month.html.

"Women's Voices, Women's Votes, Women's Rights." 2022. *Clinton Foundation*. Retrieved from https://www.clintonfoundation.org/womensvoices/?emci=1e4db 3b4-8d71-ed11-819c-000d3a9eb474&emdi=0216a250-4372-ed11-819c-000d3a9eb 474&ceid=354383&utm_source=20221202womenvoices_tuneinreminder&utm_c ampaign=2022wv&utm_medium=email.

Q37: What Are the Potential Socioeconomic Implications of the 2022 *Dobbs* Decision?

Answer: When the Supreme Court issued its ruling on *Dobbs v. Jackson Women's Health Organization* in 2022, it handed abortion laws back to individual states. A number of states quickly acted to set in motion abortion-related legislation that would be applicable to their jurisdiction. Women's rights advocates claimed that these new restrictions on abortion would directly and negatively affect the lives of millions of American women across the nation.

Women's rights advocates who denounced the *Dobbs* Supreme Court ruling warn that lack of access to abortion "has significant ripple effects on the social and economic outcomes of women and their families" (Myers & Welch, 2021). They believe that these harmful effects on education, employment, and health are particularly acute within America's most socioeconomially disadvantaged homes and communities. They characterize the Supreme Court's *Dobbs* decision as not only a women's rights issue but also one of racial and socioeconomic inequality.

The Facts: Abortion laws have a significant impact on the health and socioeconomic well-being of women who are affected. After all, teens are the age group with the highest rate of unintended pregnancies, and "three-quarters of abortion patients in the United States are poor or low-income, and nearly half live below the U.S. federal poverty line" (Kobayashi & Thomas, 2022). There are also said to be deviations in employment rate, high school graduation rate, and college enrollment due to issues surrounding access or lack of access to abortion, which "are more pronounced among young Black women" (Kobayashi & Thomas, 2022).

In arguing against overturning *Roe v. Wade*, some pro-choice sources cited a study that found availability of abortion leading to "increases in post-high school professional training and ... around a 17% increase in annual income regardless of the woman's employment status" (Brooks & Zohar, 2022).

Pro-choice supporters who cited women's health issues stated that following the enactment of *Roe v. Wade*, "pregnancy-related death and hospitalization due to complications from unsafe abortions plummeted" (Cohen, 2009).

Pro-choice adherents cite a survey of those seeking abortion, which found that "49% are living below the poverty line, 59% already have children, and 55% are experiencing a disruptive life event such as losing a job, breaking up with a partner, or falling behind on rent" (Myers & Welch, 2021).

Further complicating matters is that in most discussions of the socioeconomic effects of abortion in America, the debate is often an "either/or" situation in which people are sorted into pro-life or pro-choice camps. The issue is often not that clear-cut. According to a 2022 study by the Pew Research Center, many Americans are open to some restrictions, with the opinion that abortion should be legal in some cases, illegal in others. The Pew study found that 61 percent of Americans felt that abortion should be legal in most cases. This broke into segments of 19 percent responding that it should be legal in all cases with no exceptions, 36 percent stating it should be legal in most cases, and 6 percent saying it should be legal in all cases but with some exceptions, which the researchers found generally pertained to the point in the pregnancy. Among the opposition, 37 percent said that abortion should be illegal in most cases, breaking down as 8 percent illegal in all cases, 27 percent illegal in most cases, and 2 percent illegal in all cases "but there should be some cases when abortion is legal" ("America's Abortion Quandary," 2022).

According to the Pew study, people's attitudes depend on situations such as the point in the pregnancy when the abortion takes place, if the pregnancy endangers the life of the mother, or if the baby would have severe health problems. Asking a specific question regarding rape, the Pew researchers found that 36 percent said abortion should be legal if the pregnancy results from rape, 37 percent opposed legal abortion even in that situation, and 27 percent said "it depends" ("America's Abortion Quandary," 2022).

Critics of the *Dobbs* ruling assert that the 2022 decision

> will not end abortions, it will simply shift where they are happening and for whom. ... [It] will relegate no-cost or lower cost reproductive services that are more commonly accessed and utilized by lower income women and women of color to those states that offer abortion care, and out of reach for those women without the means to access these services. (Gilbert, Sanchez, & Busette, 2022)

The theory of intersectionality becomes a part of the conversation when sources note that when low-income and/or nonwhite women are less able to access regular medical care, reproductive health can also become a form of racism and sexism. With "the lack of parental leave policies and adequate childcare, the U.S. will continue to cultivate the conditions for a permanent underclass of low-income families and families of color" (Gilbert, Sanchez, & Busette, 2022).

Further Reading

"America's Abortion Quandary." 2022. *Pew Research Center*. Retrieved from https://www.pewresearch.org/religion/2022/05/06/americas-abortion-quandary/.

Brooks, Nina & Zohar, Tom. 2022. *Out of Labor and Into the Labor Force? The Role of Abortion Access, Social Stigma, and Financial Constraints*. Retrieved from https://tomzohar.com/assets/writeups/brooks_zohar_abortion_access_israel.pdf.

Cohen, Susan A. 2009. "Facts and Consequences: Legality, Incidence and Safety of Abortion Worldwide." *Guttmacher Institute*. Retrieved from https://www.guttmacher.org/gpr/2009/11/facts-and-consequences-legality-incidence-and-safety-abortion-worldwide.

"Dobbs v. Jackson Women's Health Organization, 597 U.S. (2022)." 2022. *Justia U.S. Supreme Court*. Retrieved from https://supreme.justia.com/cases/federal/us/597/19-1392/.

Gilbert, Keon, Sanchez, Gabriel, & Busette, Camille. 2022. "Dobbs, Another Frontline for Health Equity." *Brookings Institution*. Retrieved from https://www.brookings.edu/blog/how-we-rise/2022/06/30/dobbs-another-frontline-for-health-equity/.

"The Impact of the Supreme Court's Dobbs Decision on Abortion Rights and Access Across the United States." 2022. *House Committee on Oversight and Reform*. Retrieved from https://oversight.house.gov/legislation/hearings/the-impact-of-the-supreme-court-s-dobbs-decision-on-abortion-rights-and-access.

Kobayashi, Alicja & Thomas, Madeline. 2022. "How will the Reversal of Roe v. Wade Affect American Women? *Economics Observatory*. Retrieved from https://www.economicsobservatory.com/how-will-the-reversal-of-roe-v-wade-affect-american-women.

Myers, Caitlin Knowles & Welch, Morgan. 2021. "What Can Economic Research Tell Us About the Effect of Abortion Access on Women's Lives?" *Brookings Institution*. Retrieved from https://www.brookings.edu/research/what-can-economic-research-tell-us-about-the-effect-of-abortion-access-on-womens-lives/.

Shimron, Yonat & Jenkins, Jack. 2022. "For the Religious Right, a Victory 50 Years in the Making." *Religion News*, June 24. Retrieved from https://religionnews.com/2022/06/24/for-the-religious-right-a-victory-50-years-in-the-making-dobbs-roe-overturned-falwell-ralph-reed/.

Sobolik, Chelsea Patterson. 2022. "Why We Should Celebrate the Dobbs Decision." *The Gospel Coalition*, June 24. Retrieved from https://www.thegospelcoalition.org/article/celebrate-dobbs/.

Q38: How Did the Reversal of *Roe v. Wade* Affect American Politics?

Answer: Reflecting the storm surrounding the reversal of *Roe v. Wade* by the Supreme Court's *Dobbs* decision, the midterm election season of 2022, which followed soon after the *Dobbs* ruling, saw six ballot measures—the most on record for a single year—addressing abortion in states across the nation. In addition, candidates for national, state, and local offices in the 2022 midterm elections found themselves asked to publicly support their positions on the controversial issue of abortion. Some political analysts believe that the issue was pivotal in deciding many close midterm elections.

The Facts: Because 2022 was a midterm election year, the Supreme Court's reversal of *Roe v. Wade* several months earlier manifested itself as a major issue for the voters of America. Apart from those who sought endorsements from either pro-choice or pro-life organizations, candidates for national, state, and local offices had to declare their view of abortion, even more so than in the past. While candidates had been asked their position on abortion in previous years, particularly in areas where there were large numbers of Catholic voters, the 2022 race was especially heated. In 1976, Republicans had adopted an antiabortion position in their party platform. Subsequently, "a more vocal Christian right started to rise, [and abortion became] not only political, but the most important political issue that there is" (Shivaram, 2022). With the reversal of *Roe v. Wade* earlier the same year, the issue was unavoidable for any candidate in the 2022 midterm elections.

In addition to individuals running for office, the 2022 midterm elections also saw six ballot measures in states across the country addressing abortion, the most on record pertaining to the matter of reproductive rights in a single year. Of the six, three were designed to uphold abortion rights, and three would limit them.

However, 2022 was not the first or only election year in which abortion was an issue. From 1970 to 2022, there have been forty-eight abortion-related ballot measures in the United States, about 85 percent of which were supported by pro-life groups. Voters approved 27 percent of the pro-life measures, rejecting 73 percent of those initiatives that were supported by pro-life groups. Of the forty-eight total abortion-related ballot measures considered during that time, seven had the support of organizations describing themselves as pro-choice. Of those initiatives, four were approved by voters (Ballotpedia, 2022).

After the Supreme Court made its decision supporting reproductive rights in *Roe v. Wade* in 1973, no abortion-related ballot measures appeared until 1978. That year, Oregon's Measure 7, which had been crafted to prohibit the use of public funds on abortions, was defeated.

The question of public funding for abortion came to the forefront in the 1980s, with voters being asked to decide on seven ballot measures during that decade to prohibit public funds being used for abortion. Of those, three were approved, and four were defeated. In Oregon, America's first measure requiring parental notification prior to an abortion was on the ballot in 1990; it was defeated. In 1998, the nation's second parental notification measure appeared in Colorado; it was approved. Ballot initiatives to prohibit abortion appeared in Arizona, Oregon, and Wyoming in the late 1990s; each was rejected by the voters in those states.

Nine abortion-related measures were taken to the voters in five states during the 2000s. In Florida, a parental notification measure was approved. The other eight initiatives, which included proposed laws to prohibit or limit abortions, were defeated in California, Colorado, Oregon, and South Dakota.

In the 2010s, initiatives regarding abortion-related amendments and interpretations of state constitutions became more common. In such states as Alabama, Tennessee, and West Virginia, voters approved amendments to provide that their state constitutions cannot be interpreted to establish a state constitutional right to abortion.

Throughout the decades, women's equality adherents often squared off against opponents on the other side of the abortion issue. While constitutional amendments, statutory interpretations, parental notification, public funding, and state's rights concerning whether to prohibit abortion were important matters, many women's rights advocates from 1973 onward felt that having *Roe v. Wade* in place as a federal ruling provided a safety net. That changed in 2022 with the Supreme Court's *Dobbs v. Jackson Women's Health Organization* decision overturning *Roe*.

About six weeks after the *Dobbs* ruling was passed down by the Supreme Court, voters in Kansas, a conservative "red state," went to the polls to vote on a proposal to amend the Kansas constitution to declare that nothing in it "creates a right to abortion or requires government funding of abortions, and to declare that the state legislature has the power to pass laws regarding abortion." Kansans firmly rejected the measure, which basically would have said there was no right to an abortion in the state.

Five states featured ballot measures addressing reproductive issues in the midterm election of 2022: California, Kentucky, Michigan, Montana, and Vermont.

Specifically, California's Proposition 1 sought to amend the state constitution to add the right to choose to have an abortion as well as to use contraceptives. It passed with 65 percent of the vote. In Kentucky, the ballot issue was whether to amend the state constitution to deny any constitutional protections for abortion. It was defeated by about a 52–48 margin.

Michigan's proposed amendment to its state constitution guaranteed the right to reproductive freedom, including abortion, contraception, and other birth control–related matters. It was approved with the support of 56 percent of voters.

Montana voters were asked to decide on a provision in state law that defines being alive at any stage of development as "legal personhood." It would require medical care to be provided to those born alive after an induced labor, cesarean section, attempted abortion, or other method. In addition, it proposed levying a $50,000 fine and/or twenty years in prison as the penalty for violating the law. The measure was narrowly defeated by about a 52–48 percent margin.

In Vermont, voters decided whether to amend Vermont's constitution to declare that a person's right to "reproductive autonomy is central to the liberty and dignity to determine one's own life." Passing with about 72 percent of the vote, reproductive rights became part of the Vermont Constitution.

Throughout the 2022 campaign season, pro-choice and pro-life groups poured funding, resources, and get-out-the-vote support for candidates based on their position on the abortion issue. This was particularly evident in races for the US Senate, which may be seen as a microcosm of the political effects of the Supreme Court's decision on *Roe v. Wade*.

The group known as NARAL (originally called the National Association for the Repeal of Abortion Laws, later National Abortion Rights Action League) released a list endorsing "Reproductive Freedom Champions and Leaders" in the senatorial race. Of the seventeen pro-choice candidates for the US Senate endorsed by NARAL, thirteen were elected.

The Susan B. Anthony Pro-Life America Candidate Fund released its list of endorsements in favor of right-to-life candidates in the race for the US Senate. Of the seventeen pro-life candidates endorsed by the Pro-Life America Candidate Fund, thirteen were elected.

A number of senatorial races in 2022 were won or lost by the slimmest of margins. An especially contentious development concerned the 2022 Senate race in Georgia. Herschel Walker, running against Rev. Raphael Warnock, stated that he opposed abortion in all situations, including rape and incest. Two women came forward to claim that Walker had impregnated them and that he had pressed each one into having an abortion. Walker denied both sets of allegations, and he kept the support of fellow "Republicans … [who were] willing to look past Walker's personal scandals" (Gibson, 2022). Election day tallies determined that Warnock had 49.4 percent of the vote and Walker had 48.5 percent. A run-off election had to be held the following month, when Walker (at 48.6 percent of the vote) lost his race against Warnock, who won with 51.4 percent.

According to an analysis of the 2022 midterm election by the Kaiser Family Foundation (KFF), a nonpartisan source for health policy research, the decision to overturn *Roe v. Wade* "motivated Democratic voters, first-time and younger voters, and women under age 50, both nationally and in key states" ("Analysis Reveals How Abortion Boosted Democratic Candidates in Tuesday's Midterm Election," 2022). KFF adds that the issue played a significant role in contributing to stronger-than-expected results for the Democrats, extending its control of the Senate.

Prior to 2022's election day, some observers had pondered whether the Supreme Court's decision on abortion would have an influence on the midterm vote, noting other issues competing for the attention of American voters such as immigration, inflation, the pandemic, student loans, and the invasion of Ukraine. "Just how important is the issue of abortion? Very," said political scientist Elaine Kamarck, director of the Center for Effective Public Management at the Brookings Institution. "The reason is that in politics, intensity matters. … Abortion and the broader questions it raises about reproductive health are central to the existence of 51.1% of the population in a way that no other issue in politics is or has ever been" (Kamarck, 2022).

Catherine Glenn Foster, president of the pro-life Americans United for Life (AUL), indicated that regardless of the outcome of the 2022 midterm elections, the group's "workload just tripled" (Tracy & Vanderhoof, 2022, 90), adding that her organization can be proud of how many abortion restrictions they have inspired. Through the use of what they call their Lincoln Proposal to protect life, they claim to "equip federal and state lawmakers to advance human rights across the spectrum. We advocate to the Supreme Court to restore justice to our nation" ("Americans United for Life," n.d.).

Fatima Goss Graves, president of the National Women's Law Center, stated that the Supreme Court's *Dobbs* ruling centered on the conservative majority's opinion that there is nothing in the US Constitution guaranteeing abortion. She said that the basis of their decision was "reliance on the norms of 1865, a time when women in this country were not allowed to vote, weren't allowed to own property, weren't allowed to even practice law—those were the norms that had to guide a decision in 2022" (Tracy & Vanderhoof, 2022, 89).

After *Roe* was reversed, some Supreme Court justices indicated that the high court could conceivably consider the constitutionality of other issues pertaining to reproductive rights such as contraception. In contemporary American politics, the "Court's decision to overturn a woman's right to an abortion may be, by far and away, the most powerful development" (Kamarck & Shapiro, 2022). That is unlikely to change in the foreseeable future, remaining a keystone on both sides of the women's equality movement.

Further Reading

"Americans United for Life." n.d. Retrieved from https://aul.org/.

"Analysis Reveals How Abortion Boosted Democratic Candidates in Tuesday's Midterm Election." 2022. *Kaiser Family Foundation*. Retrieved from https://www.kff.org/other/press-release/analysis-reveals-how-abortion-boosted-democratic-candidates-in-tuesdays-midterm-election/.

Bushard, Brian, 2022. "The Herschel Walker Scandals: Woman Claims He Attacked Her, Latest Story to Roil the Campaign." *Forbes*, December 1. Retrieved from https://www.forbes.com/sites/brianbushard/2022/12/01/the-herschel-walker-scandals-woman-claims-he-attacked-her-latest-story-to-roil-the-campaign/?sh=3f0fc13179dc.

Gibson, Brittany. 2022. "Georgia Senate Still Tied after New Walker Abortion Revelations." *Politico*, October 27. Retrieved from https://www.politico.com/news/2022/10/27/georgia-senate-tied-00063891.

"History of Abortion Ballot Measures." 2022. *Ballotpedia: The Encyclopedia of American Politics*. Retrieved from https://ballotpedia.org/History_of_abortion_ballot_measures#Timeline_of_abortion-related_ballot_measures.

Kamarck, Elaine. 2022. "The Abortion Issue in the 2022 Midterms—Unlike Any Other Issue." *Brookings Institution*, September 29. Retrieved from https://www.brookings.edu/blog/fixgov/2022/09/29/the-abortion-issue-in-the-2022-midterms-unlike-any-other-issue/.

Kamarck, Elaine & Shapiro, Celia. 2022. "Will Abortion Affect the Midterm Vote for Candidates?" *Brookings Institution*, September 15. Retrieved from https://www.brookings.edu/blog/fixgov/2022/09/15/will-abortion-affect-the-midterm-vote-for-candidates-lessons-from-the-ban-gay-marriage-ballot-initiatives/.

Kansans For Life. 2022. Retrieved from https://kfl.org/.

Shivaram, Deepa. 2022. "Abortion Wasn't Always the Politically Charged Issue it is Today," *NPR*. Retrieved from https://www.npr.org/2022/05/04/1096719971/abortion-wasn-t-always-the-politically-charged-issue-it-is-today.

Tracy, Abigail & Vanderhoof, Erin. 2022 "The Fight Ahead," *Vanity Fair*, November, 86–93.

"2022 Abortion-Related Ballot Measures." n.d. Ballotpedia. Retrieved from https://ballotpedia.org/2022_abortion-related_ballot_measures.

"2022 Endorsed Candidates." 2022. *Susan B. Anthony Pro-Life America*. Retrieved from https://sbaprolife.org/election-hq.

"We're Proud to Endorse These Reproductive Freedom Champions and Leaders." 2022. *NARAL Pro-Choice America*. Retrieved from https://www.prochoiceamerica.org/elections/endorsements-2/.

Index

Wiggin, Kate Douglas 55
Willard, Frances 26, 27, 33–4
Williams, Michelle 148
Wolf, Naomi 107–8
Woman's Christian Temperance Union
    (WCTU) 26–7, 33, 34
Women's Joint Congressional Committee
    (WJCC) 42
Women's Liberation movement 2, 49, 151

Women's March (2004) (*see* March for
    Women's Lives)
Women's March (2017) 91, 111, 114,
    126
Woodhull, Victoria 16, 59, 62
Woodward, Charlotte 13–14

Yellen, Janet 168
#YesAllWomen (movement) 113

About the Author

Nancy Hendricks holds a doctorate in education and has written several books for ABC-CLIO, including *Ruth Bader Ginsburg: A Life in American History* (2020).